THE LICHFIELD BOOK OF DAYS

NEIL COLEY

Dedicated to all Lichfeldians - past, present and future.

First published 2014

The History Press
The Mill, Brimscombe Port
Stroud, Gloucestershire, GL5 2QG
www.thehistorypress.co.uk

© Neil Coley, 2014

The right of Neil Coley to be identified as the Author
of this work has been asserted in accordance with the
Copyright, Designs and Patents Act 1988.

British Library Cataloguing in Publication Data.
A catalogue record for this book is available from the British Library.

ISBN 978 0 7524 9948 2

Typesetting and origination by The History Press
Printed in India

– January 1st –

1830: On this New Year's Day, a stagecoach called *The Telegraph* left Leeds at 6 a.m. bound for Birmingham, via Lichfield. Three miles from Ashbourne, at Swinscoe Hill, the driver was thrown off and the panicked horses headed downhill at top speed. At the bottom of the hill the coach hit the wall of a public house, smashing one of its wheels, before carrying on until it was broken to pieces against a toll house. The guard and two passengers had managed to jump out, but a passenger who remained in the coach was seriously injured. The *Staffordshire Advertiser*, reporting on the accident, said, 'The guard and the coachman, it is feared, were far from sober, as they had called at many inns on the road to drink in commemoration of the day.' A group of passengers who were waiting to board the coach at Lichfield's George Inn eventually heard of the accident and had to wait for the following day to travel. *The Telegraph* was one of the first coaches to go at 20mph. Other stagecoaches had similarly exotic names: *The Rapid*, *The Quicksilver* and *The Tartar*. (Clayton, Howard, *Coaching City*, Dragon Books, 1970)

~ January 2nd ~

1925: On this day, the *Lichfield Mercury* reported the wedding of Mary Taylor of Abingdon Villas, Cherry Orchard, and Frank Halfpenny of Golden Hill, Staffordshire, which took place at Lichfield's Wesleyan church in Tamworth Street. The bride wore a dress of ivory satin and lace, with a tulle veil and orange-blossom wreath, and carried a bouquet of lilies and white heather. Her two sisters, Kathleen and Joyce Taylor, were bridesmaids. The ceremony was conducted by the Rev. Stirzaker and the hymns 'O Perfect Love' and 'In All My Vast Concerns with Thee' were sung, with the married couple leaving the church to Mendelssohn's 'Wedding March', played by the organist Mr R. Earle. A reception was held in the Wesleyan schoolroom attached to the church and the bride and bridegroom later left for a honeymoon in London. The couple were given many presents, including a cheque from the bride's father, household linen from the bride's mother and a willow-pattern dinner service from the groom's mother. The bride gave her new husband a solid silver cigarette case and he gave her a fur coat. Mary and Frank Halfpenny were later both to serve on Lichfield City Council. (*Lichfield Mercury*)

~ January 3rd ~

1879: On this day, the death was announced of James Robinson of Chasetown, near Lichfield, a veteran of the Battle of Waterloo in 1815. Robinson had been a private in the Coldstream Guards and on that fateful day had been one of the defenders of Hougoumont – a fortified farmhouse in the centre of the battlefield where the fight was long and fierce and many died. Robinson himself was hit by a bullet which entered his left eye and lodged in his jaw. Left for dead among the piles of bodies, it wasn't until the next morning that someone noticed him moving and he was taken to the surgeon. The operation, in the days before anaesthetics and antibiotics, was deemed too risky and so the musket ball remained with him until his death. Robinson was known to remark that, apart from the loss of his eye, the only inconvenience that resulted from his injury was 'a perpetual noise in his head as of a watermill'. He was, apparently, in all respects a model soldier – his proud boast being that he 'never had a black mark against his name'. He died, well into his 80s, as a result of 'taking his last cold'. (*Lichfield Mercury*)

– January 4th –

1942: On this day, the prime minister's wife, Mrs Clementine Churchill, was in Lichfield. She first visited the Young Women's Christian Association (YWCA) building in Wade Street, where she expressed her appreciation of the organisation and her pleasure at the warm welcome she had received there. Mrs Churchill was informed that the patrons of the YWCA included members of the different services, such as the Wrens, as well as nurses and land girls. Mrs Hodson, who greeted Mrs Churchill, said that the organisation also made a special effort to cater for the 'convey girls' (who transported planes from one place to another), as she felt that there ought to be a place where they could go for warm drinks and food, especially in the winter. Mrs Churchill, having met some of the volunteers at the YWCA, then visited the YWCA services at Whittington Barracks, where she received an 'enthusiastic welcome' and dined with Mrs Hester Smith, the 'leader in charge'. The women of the married quarters at the barracks presented Mrs Churchill with a sum of money for the Aid to Russia Fund, which she ran. (*Lichfield Mercury*, January 9th 1942)

– JANUARY 5TH –

1993: On this day, Lichfield magistrate John Wilson, who had recently retired from the bench after twenty-five years' service, called for more people from a wider social background, including the unemployed, to be made Justices of the Peace. Wilson believed that too many magistrates were drawn from a 'middle-class, middle-income, middle-age' background. 'I see no reason,' he added, 'why there shouldn't be a few unemployed people on the bench in the future as they represent such a high proportion of the population nowadays.' Mr Wilson, an ex-mayor of the city, admitted that he had decided to retire because he believed that he was 'out of touch with young people and the complex social problems often revealed in court cases these days. There is a desperate need for more younger men and women to become magistrates.' Commenting on his twenty-five years on the bench, Mr Wilson said he had noticed that transport-related crimes and burglaries had increased, but there had been a big drop in drink-driving offences. (*Lichfield Mercury*, January 7th 1993)

~ January 6th ~

1865: On this day, the *Lichfield Advertiser* was published by F.W. Meacham at the price of 1 (old) penny. Meacham published the paper, which replaced the defunct *Lichfield Mercury* (which would be revived in 1877), as well as providing many other services for the folk of the city from his shop in the Market Square. He described himself as a printer, bookseller, stationer and bookbinder, as well as a newspaper agent. He sold cheap stationery – notepaper cost 6*d* (3p) for five quires and envelopes cost 6*d* per hundred. He printed such documents as pamphlets, circulars, handbills and funeral cards and also provided albums for the popular *cartes de visite*, as early photographs were known. Also for sale were the new stereoscopic pictures of Lichfield Cathedral and other local sights, and foreign postage stamps for collectors. Meacham's shop also sold books – among the ones he advertised were Bible stories, cookery books (including *Mrs Beeton's Book of Household Management*), Tennyson's poems and boys' annuals. The new paper's first edition did not contain much news, but it did have many adverts for local shops and businesses and a whole page of railway timetables. (*Lichfield Advertiser*, first edition)

− JANUARY 7TH −

2008: On this day, Lichfield was awarded Fairtrade City status. The Fairtrade movement started in the UK in the 1970s, at the time The Body Shop began and the Traidcraft company was set up, both of which were endeavouring to ensure that Third World producers had better and more equal trading conditions for their produce. In 2000 the Lancashire town of Garstang became the first community in the world to be designated as a Fairtrade town and many other towns and cities across Britain followed suit. In Lichfield the campaign to achieve Fairtrade status was started by a small group of activists in 2005. They persuaded Lichfield City Council to pass a resolution that all of their council meetings, and all events run by the council, would only use fairly traded products. Soon many organisations in the city − churches, schools, voluntary groups and small and large businesses − were represented on a steering group, whose aim was to raise awareness and produce promotional materials. By 2008 the campaign had achieved its aim and in an official ceremony in March, broadcaster George Alagiah OBE presented the Fairtrade Foundation's certificate to the Mayor of Lichfield, Councillor Mark Warfield, in an official ceremony. (Bardsley, Warren R., *Fair City*, Church in the Market Place Publications, 2008)

~ January 8th ~

1904: On this day, shocking details emerged about the cruelty shown by a Lichfield couple towards their son. At their trial, John and Sarah Langley, bakers at a shop in Tamworth Street, were charged with neglecting their 6-year-old son Arthur, who was a child from John Langley's previous marriage. Arthur, who was described as small for his age and 'not as bright as other children', had been seen picking up refuse in the street and eating it. When he was examined by Dr Rowland, medical officer of the Lichfield workhouse, he was found to be emaciated, showing signs of consumption (T.B.), with bruises on his legs and a partially paralysed arm. Further investigations revealed that neighbours had seen the boy chained up in his backyard in all weathers, with inadequate clothing and having to eat from the pigswill bucket. The parents were found guilty by the jury, but the judge said that he was reluctant to send them to prison as they had another six small children. So instead they were fined £25 and warned about their future behaviour. A crowd, unhappy at the verdict, formed outside the court and later windows at the Langley's shop were broken. (*Lichfield Mercury*, January 15th 1904)

~ January 9th ~

1961: On this day, workmen, demolishing some old brick buildings to the rear of shops in Bird Street, were surprised to discover a 'secret room'. The circular room was decorated with illustrations made with shells and pebbles, one of which depicted Lichfield Cathedral. A wooden door led from the room, down some stairs and into a small, walled garden to the rear of the school clinic in Sandford Street. The room, which had been forgotten about for many years, was in fact referred to in a book by former city librarian, the late J.W. Jackson. In his book *Historical Incidents In and Around Lichfield*, published in the 1930s, he wrote about how the room had housed French prisoners during the Napoleonic Wars and how the pictures were created to relieve some of the boredom they doubtless experienced. Seventy-four such prisoners were kept in Lichfield from 1797 on their parole of honour. These included General Marquet, three other officers who lived in Heath Cottage in St John Street and de Giborne, who lived in Cherry Orchard in a residence that was later called Frenchman's Cottage. Another prisoner, Cato, settled in Lichfield and one of his descendants later ran the Three Crowns pub. (*Lichfield Mercury*, January 13th 1961)

~ January 10th ~

1893: On this day, the coming of age of Mr W.W. Worthington
of Maple Hayes Hall was marked with a grand fancy-dress ball.
The guests, on their arrival to celebrate Mr Worthington's 21st
birthday, found the carriage driveway from the lodge to the hall
itself brightly illuminated with fairy lights. The drawing room of
the hall was filled with an array of flowers and in the dining room
a portrait of Mr Worthington painted by the Hon. J. Collier
was displayed. Birthday presents were laid out in the Oriental
Room and included a silver salver and an illuminated address
in album form from the tenants and tradesmen of Lichfield.
The ball, which was attended by many of the local 'elite', started
at 9.45 p.m. and continued 'with great enthusiasm' until 5 a.m.
Dances included polkas, lancers and 'valses'. Many of the
costumes, not only of the ladies but the men too, were 'varied and
many were beautiful'. Costumes included a French peasant girl,
a Neapolitan fishermen, Sir Francis Drake, Britannia and Marie
Antoinette 'in a prison dress'. There were also two Mary, Queen
of Scots and several magpies and matadors. (*Lichfield Mercury*,
January 13th 1893)

— January 11th —

1933: On this day, Dr Hogarth, past president of the British Medical Association and senior surgeon at Nottingham General Hospital, made a speech in Lichfield about the health of the population. According to Hogarth, 'cheerfulness' was one of the ingredients of health, whereas 'fear' was the 'arch-enemy of mankind' and a 'potent contributor to disease'. People in Britain, he believed, regarded the medicine bottle as a 'fetish' and doctors often prescribed pointless medicine just to ensure that patients did not lose faith in their abilities as doctors. However, he did notice a number of good developments in recent times – people had generally stopped spitting in the street, a habit that spread diseases, and he was also pleased that cigarettes had largely replaced the short clay pipe and twist tobacco. Active life was important too, according to Dr Hogarth, as was proper food, although he thought that the meals that 'came to the British table' did not compare favourably with those of other nations. Dr Hogarth finished his speech by saying that 'a child born today has an expectation of twenty years more than his grandfather and those born fifty years hence will certainly be the heirs of a longer span'. (*Lichfield Mercury*, January 13th 1933)

~ January 12th ~

1902: On this day, an outbreak of smallpox in Lichfield's workhouse caused a panic across the city. The workhouse master discovered that a tramp named Frederick Hemmings, who had been admitted two days before, was suffering from the disease and was quickly moved to the 'infectious hospital'. As a result the 'tramp wards' were closed for a week and everyone who had come into contact with the man, both inmates and officials, were given smallpox vaccinations. One resident of the workhouse, Thomas Bevan, refused to be vaccinated and was locked in a room by himself after he had hit one of the officials over the head with a stick and pulled out a knife. More vaccine had been sent for when it was discovered that the sick man's shirt had been sent to the laundry in the female section of the workhouse and that the women who worked there needed to be vaccinated too. The Lichfield Board of Guardians, the body in charge of the workhouse, was told that vaccination would defeat the disease and that recently the king had been vaccinated to set an example to others. Hemmings recovered from the disease. (*Lichfield Mercury*, January 31st 1902)

— January 13th —

1928: On this day, Lichfield City Council voted to re-erect Lichfield's clock tower after it had been demolished to make way for the new Friary Road, which was needed to relieve traffic congestion in the city. Built in 1863, the tower had been erected on the site of the Crucifix Conduit – the medieval water supply to the city – at the junction of Bore Street and St John Street. There was considerable controversy about whether the tower should be saved – the *Lichfield Mercury* published a poll of its readers which showed that 66 per cent thought that rate-payers' money should not be spent on its reconstruction. Mr E.W. Wiseman, the leader of the opposition on the council, was against the site chosen for the rebuilt clock tower – on an island at the back of the bowling green. He said that 'they might as well rebuild it in Timbuctoo, as the only people who would benefit from its new location would be those on the bowling green, while passing motorists might be able to synchronise their watches'. But in April, local benefactor Sir Richard Cooper offered to pay for the road and the transfer of the clock tower to its present position. (*Lichfield Mercury*, January 20th 1928)

− January 14th −

1856: On this day, a meeting at the George Hotel declared Richard Greene bankrupt and confirmed the collapse of his bank, Lichfield Bank, in Market Street. The bank had shut its doors on December 31st 1855, much to the dismay of its many customers such as Lichfield Cathedral, the Conduit Lands Trust, the Staffordshire Yeomanry and most of the city's gentry and tradesmen. In the days when banks could print their own bank notes, as long as they were backed by larger banks, the Lichfield Bank was thrown into disarray when the London firm of Smith, Payne & Smith withdrew their credit facilities. The bankruptcy meeting discovered that one of the bank's long-serving employees − 73-year-old William Lawton − had, over the years, embezzled the bank to the tune of over £7,000, a massive sum in 1856. Richard Greene, his wife and five children were forced to sell their home, Stowe House, which was sold for £4,860. Their possessions were also sold off and at the age of 56 Greene became a social outcast after being one of the most respected citizens in Lichfield. (Clayton, Howard, *Cathedral City*, Abbotsford Publishing, 1981)

— January 15th —

1926: On this day, in its editorial, the *Lichfield Mercury* commented how spelling and punctuation in schools was 'nearly always overlooked'. The paper opined that 'Children are taught art, science and music, but the most useful subjects, writing, spelling and dictation, take quite a secondary place'. The editorial went on to put forward the view that of the children leaving school at the age of 15 to seek their fortunes – 'perhaps as teachers, clerks, servants etc.' – only a small number would use their knowledge of science, chemistry or drawing, but all of them 'will require writing, arithmetic and geography', adding that 'before free education became available to all children they learned fewer subjects and they had a better grasp of them', but since then, in its opinion, 'too many subjects are taught in schools. How depressing it is to see a clerk look in a dictionary to check a spelling or to receive a letter from a friend and find words spelt wrongly.' The paper's editorial concluded by saying that a 'great improvement in spelling and punctuation would occur if more time was devoted to them in the public and private schools of Britain'. (*Lichfield Mercury*)

~ January 16th ~

1941: On this day, a Polish airman was fined for assault and causing damage at a city fish and chip shop. Wiltold Szpaczynski, who was serving with the Royal Air Force, was found guilty of drunkenly assaulting Blanche Annie Mullarky of Tamworth Street on New Year's Eve 1940, and also causing damage to a door and a vinegar bottle. When asked to plead the man said, through an interpreter, that he could not remember committing the assault. Szpaczynski had bought some chips but seemed to believe that the change he had been given was wrong and that he had been cheated. After an argument he was asked to leave the shop, but he refused and threw the chips and a bottle of vinegar at Mr Mullarky. Mrs Mullarky tried to persuade him to go but he proceeded to grab her arm, causing some 'very bad' bruises, and kick her – at which point she hit him with a rolling pin and the police were called, but not before he had pulled a door off its hinges. Szpaczynski was fined a total of £1 15*s* (£1.75). (*Lichfield Mercury*, January 17th 1941)

— January 17th —

1831: By this day, it was decided that Madame Tussaud's and Son's waxwork exhibition would remain for an extra week in Lichfield. The organisers had had many requests for the exhibition to stay longer, due to 'the unfavourable weather which has prevented families from the country from paying a visit'. The waxworks exhibition, which was situated in Lichfield's Theatre Royal in Bore Street, was described by the *Lichfield Mercury* as 'a splendid novelty'. Admittance cost 1*s* (5p) for adults and 6*d* (3p) for children under 8 years old and the exhibition was open each evening from 6.30 p.m. until 10 p.m. The Quadrille Band played a variety of music for visitors to enjoy and, presumably because of the poor weather, the organisers assured potential visitors that 'a good fire will be kept'. The figures in the exhibition that excited the most interest from the public were those of the infamous murderers Burke and Hare, whose trial in Edinburgh three years before had shocked the nation. Their likenesses, it was pointed out, were modelled from the men's actual faces. (*Lichfield Mercury*, January 21st 1831)

— January 18th —

1921: On this day, the deputy mayor appeared before the Lichfield Court, appealing against a decision to fine him for not having a dog licence. Councillor Henry George Hall, a former mayor of the city and a magistrate, had been issued with a fine of 15*s* (75p) after police had discovered that he had not taken out a licence for his dog. Telling the police he had left his licence in his butcher's shop in Conduit Street, he took out a licence later that day. As a result the police had reported the matter to the Taxation Committee of the County Council who contacted Councillor Hall and issued the fixed penalty. The County Council had agreed that although the failure to take out the licence was 'an oversight' they could not treat him any differently to anyone else who found themselves in a similar position. The appeal was allowed by the Recorder of the Lichfield Court and the penalty was reduced to one of 5*s* (25p). Dog licences were first introduced in England and Wales as a result of the Customs and Inland Revenue Act of 1869 and were abolished by Parliament in 1987. (*Lichfield Mercury*, January 21st 1921)

~ JANUARY 19TH ~

1818: On this day, 'a Grand Exhibition of Illusions (and) Ventriloquism' took place at the Theatre Royal, Lichfield. The show, which also included 'Mechanical Games' and 'Philosophical Recreations', was performed by Mr Charles, who said that he had 'the honour to acquaint the [City's] Nobility and inhabitants' with the wonders of his show and that 'every exertion has been made to render the evening's entertainment pleasant and the theatre comfortable to all visitors'. Tickets for the show, which started at 7 p.m., cost 3*s* (15p) for a box, 2*s* (10p) for the pit and 1*s* (5p) for the gallery and could be obtained at the Mercury Office in Market Street. The theatre, it was stated, was heated by 'a newly invented process'. Another attraction available to Lichfield folk in the same week was a 'Ball and Supper' held at the George Hotel in honour of the queen's birthday. According to the *Mercury* the ball attracted a 'most brilliant assemblage of rank and fashion' and was attended by 'most of the noble and respectable families in the neighbourhood'. The ball started at 9 p.m., with dancing from 10 p.m. (*Lichfield Mercury*, January 23rd 1818)

~ January 20th ~

1968: On this day, Miss Noele Gordon, television personality and star of the long-running soap opera *Crossroads*, opened Lichfield's newest central heating centre – Whiteheat in Tamworth Street. Before the official opening ceremony took place local children were allowed into the shop to collect signed photographs of the television celebrity. In her opening speech Miss Gordon said it was her first visit to Lichfield since she had been the presenter of the ATV programme *Lunch Box*. She went on to wish the shop a very prosperous future. She was thanked by Mr W.D. Dulson, the regional manager of the National Coal Board (NCB), and Mr Tony White, a managing director of Whiteheat. Miss Gordon was presented with a bouquet of flowers by 7-year-old Susan Tasker, the daughter of the shop's sales manager, Mr Peter Tasker. At the opening there were forty guests representing the NCB, the gas board, merchants and manufacturers. At a time when many householders were installing central heating for the first time, the Whiteheat showroom was the first of its shops in the Midlands. (*Lichfield Mercury*, January 26th 1968)

~ JANUARY 21ST ~

1988: On this day, Lichfield was hit by arctic conditions as heavy snow fell across the district late on in the day, leaving terrible conditions for commuters to deal with. Traffic queues soon formed between Lichfield and the surrounding villages, with abandoned cars adding to the problems. In Burntwood, police turned back drivers headed for Lichfield because of blocked roads. Fourteen snow ploughs based in Lichfield worked through the night to try and keep roads clear and Lichfield firefighters, called to a house fire in Burntwood, had to move abandoned cars off the road before they could get through. In some places electric cables were brought down by falling trees, leaving Elford, Shenstone and parts of Rugeley without power. Telephones were also affected in some parts after snow got into underground ducts. AA patrols were kept busy as the organisation received over 3,000 calls from stranded motorists and those seeking information about road conditions. Rail travellers faced delays on the Birmingham to Redditch line when falling trees blocked the tracks at Four Oaks. (*Lichfield Mercury*, January 29th 1988)

– JANUARY 22ND –

1930: On this day, an inquest was held into the death of a Burntwood woman, 21-year-old Jennie Ross of Blue Ball Row, Chase Road. Her body had been found in a canal in nearby Brownhills and the verdict was 'death by her own hand'. The coroner severely reprimanded her lover – Albert Victor Champ, aged 26 or 27, of Vincent Parade, Balsall Heath, Birmingham – who had deserted the woman on at least two occasions, the latest being just before the couple's proposed wedding day. Prior to her disappearance, Jennie Ross had told her father that she was going to drown herself as she, and the rest of her family, believed that she 'was in a certain condition' and was planning to marry Champ 'to save her honour'; however, the post-mortem later found that the she was not pregnant. The police found that Champ was in Birmingham when the death took place but they considered him 'morally responsible' for what had occurred. The Coroner said that he had acted 'most disgracefully to this girl in twice deserting her' and concluded by telling Champ that he would not be granted any expenses for his trip from Birmingham. (*Lichfield Mercury*, January 24th 1930)

— JANUARY 23RD —

1936: On this day, the Mayor of Lichfield, Councillor C.H. Averill, read an announcement outside the Guildhall proclaiming the new king, Edward VIII. The proclamation, made at midday, was greeted by a large crowd which had turned out 'right loyally' despite the bitterly cold weather. Before the announcement the flags on the council buildings had been flying at half-mast to mark the death of the former King George V, who had died at the age of 70 at Sandringham on the 22nd. After the announcement a fanfare was sounded by a detachment from the North Staffordshire Regiment and the flags were raised to full-mast. The mayor finished with the words 'God Save the King' and the National Anthem was sung. Plans were made on this day for the city's marking of George V's funeral on January 29th when all Lichfield's schools would close and most social events would be postponed. Edward VIII would abdicate in December 1936 due to his relationship to Mrs Simpson who, as a divorcee, was considered unsuitable by the government. (*Lichfield Mercury*, January 24th 1936)

~ January 24th ~

1969: On this day, Edward Heath, leader of the Conservative Party, visited Lichfield, where he spoke to a packed audience of invited Conservative supporters at the Guildhall. A large crowd gathered outside the historic building for the arrival of Mr Heath, greeting him with cheers. At the meeting the Tory leader said that during the last two years the Conservative Party had experienced a period of political success unequalled by any other, capturing a 'mass' of local government seats, adding: 'people are moving to our cause.' Mr Heath promised that once in government the Conservatives would change the tax system and get rid of waste, as well as reforming the trade unions and reappraising social services so that people were 'encouraged to stand on their own feet'. He also promised farmers would be given a chance to expand and everyone would be urged to save. Mr Heath later met the Bishop of Lichfield, the mayor, the sheriff and the town clerk. In the June 1970 General Election, Edward Heath became prime minister when the Tories beat the Labour Party of Harold Wilson. (*Lichfield Mercury*, January 31st 1969)

– January 25th –

1950: On this day, Ernest Hiskins of Lichfield began the 1,956-mile journey from Glasgow to Monaco as he took part in the Monte Carlo Rally. Mr Hiskins, owner of Midland Auto Electric Co. of Trent Valley Trading Estate, used a 1,265cc Hillman Minx in the rally. The car, the latest model, had an 11hp water-cooled engine, a top speed of 80mph and was fitted with a number of innovative gadgets designed by Mr Hiskins. These included an auxiliary fuel tank, a heater, window washers, map-reading lamps, a thermos-flask holder and special lights under the bonnet to allow work on the engine in darkness. Ernest Hiskins was well known in Britain and on the Continent as a motor car racing enthusiast. During the 1948 International Alpine Rally he made national headlines when his Sunbeam car fell 70ft into a ravine, miraculously escaping uninjured. Hiskins, along with his co-driver Mr A. Gee from Whittington, finished thirteenth in their class at the end of the Monte Carlo Rally and vowed to take part in the race again in the future. (*Lichfield Mercury*, January 27th 1950)

− January 26th −

1900: On this day, men of the Staffordshire Yeomanry left Lichfield to serve in the Boer War in South Africa. Before they departed the soldiers paraded on Friary Field watched by a large crowd. The Rev. James Gillart, the company chaplain, addressed the men saying: 'You are going out to do your duty for your country and your God … and you will remember that the path of duty is the path to glory.' A service at the cathedral followed the parade − the troops processing through the 'gaily decorated' streets lined with people cheering and waving flags. At the cathedral the men were addressed by the Bishop of Lichfield, who told them: 'It is better to die for Queen and country than to live at ease at home.' A banquet was given in honour of the yeomanry at the Guildhall where sole, turkey, goose, sirloin, pheasant, plum pudding, fruit tarts, stewed fruit and mince pies were served. One hundred and twenty-one men of all ranks left from Lichfield City station at 2 a.m. bound for Liverpool, where they then caught a troopship headed for South Africa. Each soldier was given 1lb of tobacco as he boarded the ship. (*Lichfield Mercury*, February 2nd 1900)

- January 27th -

1992: On this day, Lichfield's Friary School celebrated its centenary. It was named after the Franciscan friary that once stood on the site and which had been dissolved in 1538 during the Reformation. The girls' school had been housed in Yeomanry House in St John St. since its foundation in 1892, but in 1921 Sir Richard Cooper presented the friary estate and buildings to the City of Lichfield and the school moved onto the site. The school was extended in 1926 and Lichfield Girls' High School became the Friary School. The new school's crest displayed the eagle of Mercia, the cross and chevrons of the City of Lichfield and three doves to represent the connection with the Greyfriars. In 1971 the school became a mixed comprehensive and in 1973 a new site was opened – Friary Grange – in the north of the city. The transition was overseen by Miss K.C.M. Gent, who had been headmistress since 1945 and who retired with the coming of the new school. In 1987 the school left the old friary building completely and today the Public Library and Records Office is housed there. (Bird, Jean, *Hyacinths and Haricot Beans*, The Lichfield Press, 1995)

- January 28th -

1916: On this day, the *Lichfield Mercury* reported on the most serious measles epidemic to hit the city in fifty years. The epidemic had caused all of Lichfield's schools to be closed for two weeks and hospitals were being used to isolate infected people in an attempt to halt the spread of the disease, the *Mercury* noting that: 'It is quite impossible to isolate cases in the houses of the working classes and to prevent the inter communication between inhabitants of infected houses.' The Medical Officer for the area and the local nursing staff found it impossible to keep up with the number of cases being reported to the authorities – two schools alone reported thirty-four cases in one day. Altogether there were more than 350 measles cases identified in the city and, in the entire district, some sixteen deaths were attributed to the disease, mainly as a result of people subsequently developing bronchitis or pneumonia. The Medical Officer admitted that 'the disease had made such enormous progress, in all quarters, it is practically useless to try and stop it'. (*Lichfield Mercury*)

— January 29th —

1940: On this day, wartime blackout measures were said to blame for the deaths of two railway employees killed near Lichfield City station. Thirty-six-year-old Horace Downes of 56 Chesterfield Terrace and 55-year-old Charles Taylor, a lodger at 22 Stowe Street, were killed while working on points 100yd from the station platform on the Birmingham side. In the dark they failed to notice the approach of the 4.54 a.m. train from Monument Lane and it hit both men, causing severe injuries and instantaneous death. Mr Downes was well known in the city and 'was a popular member of the Lichfield Company of the Territorial Army for thirteen years'. People were asked to take greater care and take no chances and 'look out in the blackout'. They were also urged not to step off kerbs without looking both ways and to use torches remembering to shine them on to the ground so as not to dazzle motorists. During the previous December over 1,200 people in Britain had died as a result of blacked-out streets and motor vehicles. (*Lichfield Mercury*, February 2nd 1940)

~ January 30th ~

1935: On this day, a dinner was held at the Malt Shovel in Market Square for the drivers and proprietors of motor coaches, or charabancs as they were commonly known. Seventy-two people from all over the Midlands were there for the dinner, which had been organised by the inn's landlord Mr Wilkinson. Lichfield benefited greatly from charabancs bringing day-trippers to Lichfield, particularly in the summer months, and this contribution to the city's tourist trade was acknowledged by the presence of a number of local aldermen and councillors. The City of Lichfield was toasted by Councillor Davies who, in a speech, extolled the virtues of Lichfield as a place for tourists to visit, with its cathedral, the Johnson birthplace, the Garden of Remembrance and, 'of course', the Bower celebrations on every Whit Monday. The only problem that existed with Lichfield, according to Councillor Collins, who also made a speech, was with the Market Square – the place where charabancs unloaded and picked up, and where the cobble stone surface sometimes 'caused problems for ladies wearing high heeled shoes'. (*Lichfield Mercury*, February 1st 1935)

~ JANUARY 31ST ~

1879: On this day, the *Lichfield Mercury* reflected on the harsh winter the city had been suffering. It blamed the Gulf Stream for the poor weather and said that it had 'taken a severe cold from some cause or other more or less connected to the North Pole'. The paper went on to say that it would have to look further and further back in history to find its parallel' and 1818 was discussed as 'the nearest prototype', although the winter weather was even compared to that of 1684–85 – 'the great frost'. The cold winter was taking a toll on birds, with robins and sparrows being found dead in the streets of Lichfield, victims of starvation due to them being unable to get at 'their customary food source'. The newspaper reported, however, that there were many 'kindly-hearted people' who had been feeding the birds throughout the winter and had, in doing so, attracted many unusual birds into their gardens. 'Titmice, blackbirds, thrushes and even fieldfares had been rendered bold by the greatness of their need,' reported the *Mercury*, which said that the weather throughout Europe had been even worse, causing migrating birds such as Brent geese to be spotted in some places. (*Lichfield Mercury*)

~ FEBRUARY 1ST ~

1901: On this day, the *Lichfield Mercury* reported on the death of Queen Victoria and gave details of the funeral arrangements that had been made. The paper, whose columns were bordered in black, also informed its readers of the way in which the queen was going to be remembered in Lichfield, with a memorial service at the cathedral and a special meeting of the city council where a 'vote of condolence would be passed'. According to the *Mercury* of February 8th, when a special supplement was produced, the day of Victoria's funeral was one of 'reverend, deep and profound homage' in Lichfield for a monarch who 'had been loved by all classes of her sorrowing subjects'. The bells of the cathedral tolled as did those of all the churches in the city. Shops did not open, public houses closed and the blinds and curtains in people's homes remained drawn. In the *Mercury* a large drawing of the queen, who had reigned since 1837, was printed, as were the portraits of the new king and his wife – Edward VII and Queen Alexandra. (*Lichfield Mercury*)

~ February 2nd ~

1939: On this day, Lichfield's Lido cinema began showing the latest Hollywood blockbuster: *The Adventures of Robin Hood*. In an advertisement, the film was described by the Lido's management as 'History's greatest adventure – Lichfield's greatest event'. The movie, which had a 'U' certificate and starred Errol Flynn, would be shown for six days and was promoted as being 'photographed throughout in natural Technicolor', with the advert going on to say that Flynn was 'handsome, young and adventurous – the perfect Robin Hood'. The film also starred Olivia de Havilland as Maid Marion and Basil Rathbone as Sir Guy of Gisbourne. The event gave an opportunity for other Lichfield traders to get in on the act. In an advert for the Robin Hood pub in St John Street, for example, it was described as 'Lichfield's most modern licensed premises' and suggested that filmgoers might want to call in after seeing the film. Garratt's bakery claimed that its 'Nottingham Earls' cakes containing 'a light sponge mixture and fruit and nuts' were 'reminiscent of the days of Robin Hood'. *The Adventures of Robin Hood* was very successful in the city, with 'phenomenal crowds' attending all showings of the film. (*Lichfield Mercury*, January 27th 1939, February 3rd 1939)

~ February 3rd ~

1915: On this day, a report was published examining the record of Lichfield's Truant School during the previous year. The school, founded in 1893 and situated in Beacon Street, was an institution to which boys from all over the Midlands could be sent. Of the seventy-two boys admitted to the school during 1914, thirty-three were there for non-compliance of an attendance order, twenty-three were found wandering and the rest were found to be not under the proper control of parents or had been found guilty of a punishable offence. During the previous year eighty-three boys had been sent home under licence and given another chance to attend ordinary school. It was found that once they had been given this second chance over 97 per cent went on to attend school regularly. Of the twenty boys at the Truant School who were 14 and of leaving age, most had been found jobs, including eight sent to army or navy training; three to farms; two to cotton mills; and two to coal mines. Many of the old boys of the school had written letters to the school's governor thanking him for the way they had been treated. (*Lichfield Mercury*, February 5th 1915)

~ February 4th ~

1936: On this day, Frenchman Marcel Robert Richard, aged 41, died in mysterious circumstances while passing through Lichfield. Richard had entered Boots chemist in Bore Street complaining that he had been poisoned and after receiving some medication and given milk to drink he was taken to Victoria Hospital where, a few hours later, he died. A post-mortem was carried out and some of his internal organs were sent to the county pathologist for examination. Richard was a district manager at the Michelin Tyre Company in Stoke-on-Trent and had lived in Britain for fifteen years. His landlady, who had made him some veal sandwiches earlier that day, later said that Richard had often complained about his digestion and always carried magnesia powder and calcium tablets. An inquest held at the Victoria Hospital found that there was no evidence for the man having been poisoned and the cause of death was an arterial aneurism. Dr Menton, the county bacteriologist, said that this was an unusual condition for one so relatively young and that the condition was inoperable. The coroner's verdict was death from natural causes and Richard's body was taken back to France for burial. (*Lichfield Mercury*, February 7th 1936)

⌐ February 5th ⌐

1952: On this day, Milley's Hospital in Beacon Street, Lichfield, was given Grade II listed building status. Founded in 1424 as a place of residence for fifteen poor women, the building was endowed between 1502 and 1504 by Dr Thomas Milley, a canon of the cathedral. Each woman received 5*s* (25p) each quarter and by 1821 the almswomen received £1 per quarter and 5*s* each week. Since 1893 it has been run by the Charities Commission and in 1906–07 a much needed modernisation programme was carried out; alterations to the building meant that only eight residents could be housed, but their accommodation was much more comfortable than before. Between 1985 and 1987 the building was again restored and modernised, with the number of available flats increased from eight to ten, along with the addition of a common room. The general appearance of the red-brick, two-storey building has not changed much since 1907. A plaque over the entrance commemorates Thomas Milley's re-founding of the Hospital. (Greenslade, M.W. (ed), *A History of Lichfield*, Staffordshire Libraries, Arts and Archives, 1994)

— FEBRUARY 6TH —

1970: On this day, the *Lichfield Mercury* announced three 'decisive steps' it had taken to propel the paper 'into the seventies' and make it 'one of the best weekly newspapers in the country'. The 'latest computer equipment' had been installed at a cost of 'several thousand pounds', which would 'ensure speedier production and greater clarity of text'. It had introduced the *Chase Mercury*, a 'paper within a paper – the first time anywhere this had been done' – especially designed for all those in the rapidly growing area of Burntwood, Chasetown, Chase Terrace, Hammerwich and Boney Hay who needed 'a paper of their own'. The readers of the *Rugeley Mercury* would also have their own front page each week, something the new computers made possible. The new equipment, which had been installed in the paper's Bird Street premises, was supplied by a firm that had produced computer technology for the United States space programme – Fairchild Graphic Equipment (UK) Ltd., whose giant American parent company was based in New York. The paper was actually printed in Tamworth where the introduction of the web-offset printing system had greatly improved the appearance of the paper and enabled twenty-four broadsheet pages to be produced each week. (*Lichfield Mercury*)

~ FEBRUARY 7TH ~

1890: On this day, the *Lichfield Mercury* carried its usual array of advertisements. These included the announcement of a sale at Shakeshaft and Playfer's, two clothes stores in Market Street and Dam Street where shoppers could find 'great reductions in all departments'. W. Walker's grocery shop at 5 Bird Street advertised a number of its goods including muscatels, sultanas, raisins and citron peels, as well as tinned meats and fruit and a 'good selection' of Huntley and Palmer's biscuits. China, Assam and Ceylon teas were on sale for 1*s* 4*d*, 1*s* 8*d* and 2*s* per pound (6p, 7p and 10p). J. Salloway's in Bore Street were offering the latest in clocks and watches 'perfect for time, beauty and workmanship', as well as 'artistic jewellery' and medals for cyclists, cricketers and 'all other athletic sports'. Popular products advertised in the *Mercury* included Pears soap, Cockle's Antibilious pills, artificial teeth ('with painless dentistry'), Dr Brown's Chlorodyne ('effective treatment for colds, coughs, asthma and epilepsy') and Tamworth Pig Powder ('no person who keeps pigs should be without this compound'). (*Lichfield Mercury*)

– February 8th –

1946: On this day, the first two post-war council houses to be built in Lichfield were completed and were formally opened by the mayor – Councillor Frank Williams. The council had been proud to announce that it was one of the first housing authorities in the country to build permanent houses as opposed to the pre-fabricated bungalows, fifty of which had already been constructed in Weston Road as well as many more throughout Britain. The houses, in Ponesfield, were designed by city engineer Leslie Straw and built by the Lichfield firm J.R. Deacon Limited. They were semi-detached homes with entrance hall, living room, kitchen, three bedrooms, bathroom, lavatory and outhouse. They had a 'two-room grate' which gave an open fire in the living room and cooking facilities in the kitchen. Back gardens 'were of a good size' and the front gardens were grassed and had no fences, 'to give an effect of spaciousness'. Thirty-four more houses were planned for Ponesfield, with each one costing £1,100 to build. Rents had yet to be decided. (*Lichfield Mercury*, February 11th 1946)

– February 9th –

1749: On this day, famous manufacturer and industrialist Matthew Boulton married his distant cousin, Mary Robinson, at St Mary's church in Lichfield. Mary was the daughter of Luke Robinson, a wealthy mercer who had a farm at Whittington, 3 miles from Lichfield. The couple lived in Lichfield for a short time before moving to Birmingham where Boulton helped run his father's business of making small metal objects such as buttons and buckles (known as toys in the eighteenth century). Boulton was born in 1728 after his father had moved from his home town of Lichfield to Birmingham in order to make his fortune. After his father's death Boulton expanded the business and built a factory and house in the Soho area of Birmingham. It was Boulton's partnership with James Watt and the installation of steam engines at mines and other businesses throughout Britain and the world that made Boulton and Watt's reputation, increasing the pace at which the industrialisation of Britain took place. Boulton, along with Watt, was a key member of The Lunar Society, which met each month at Soho House or in Lichfield at the home of Erasmus Darwin. (Uglow, Jenny, *The Lunar Men*, Faber and Faber, 2002)

~ February 10th ~

1950: On this day, the *Lichfield Mercury* reported on a visit that had been made to the city by Prime Minister Clement Attlee, during which he spoke at the Guildhall in favour of the Labour candidate Captain Julian Snow in the forthcoming General Election. It was not Mr Attlee's first time to Lichfield, as he had visited the city on several occasions during the war when his son was a pupil at Belmont School, which had been temporarily transferred to Lichfield from Brighton for safety reasons. The prime minister, who was received with 'loud applause' from the packed meeting, spoke about the election and how Labour hoped 'to be granted an extension to their power to enable the work that they had started to continue'. He also told the audience about some of the achievements of the government, including the establishment of the Welfare State, the Education Act and the nationalisation of mining and other industries. There was a minor disturbance during the meeting when a member of the audience accused Attlee of being a 'communist sympathiser'. Julian Snow won in the Lichfield constituency and Labour won the General Election, but with a much-reduced majority. (*Lichfield Mercury*)

– February 11th –

1977: On this day, Lichfield Council was criticised by one of its councillors for having an 'abysmal attitude' towards promoting the city to tourists. The *Lichfield Mercury* joined the criticism in its editorial saying: 'how long can Lichfield attract tourists without cash to promote itself.' Criticism began when a recently published *Heart of England* visitors' brochure was found to have no mention of Lichfield at all. Councillor Bill Kerr called for the setting up of a tourist sub-committee which could 'promote various aspects of the city and could ensure funds are available for promotional activities'. A former president of the city's Chamber of Trade thought that the main drawback was the lack of hotel accommodation in Lichfield: 'Tourists take a glimpse at the Cathedral, a photo of Johnson's Birthplace and a look at the statue of Boswell and are off to somewhere else to spend the night.' The council was also being pressed to set up a new Tourist Information Centre next to the Johnson's Birthplace Museum, to replace the Dam Street office which was dealing with increased inquiries – over 8,000 in 1976. (*Lichfield Mercury*, February 11th 1977)

— February 12th —

1918: On this day, during work to widen the Lichfield to Tamworth road at Freeford, builders unearthed the remains of some sixty skeletons. Experts found that the skeletons were in a good state of preservation, that they had been buried without coffins and that the items found with the bodies suggested that the burials had been Christian ones. From the teeth, which in some cases were perfect, the ages of the bodies were ascertained – the youngest found being about 18 or 19 years old. At first it was thought that the bodies were those of Civil War soldiers, buried after the sieges of Lichfield; however, it was later discovered that they were the remains of those who had sought sanctuary at the Leper Hospital of St Leonards in the Middle Ages. The Leper Hospital at Freeford was in existence by the thirteenth century when several grants were made to it by the king. It stood near to Freeford Manor, about 1 mile from St Michael's church, under whose auspices it operated. No buildings now remain on the site. (*Lichfield Mercury*, February 15th 1918)

~ February 13th ~

1879: On this evening, the first performance of the pantomime *Robinson Crusoe* took place at St James's Hall in Bore Street. Described as a 'pantomime-burlesque' and presented by 'Miss Sarah Thorne's Company' it began a short run in Lichfield after being staged for seven weeks at the Theatre Royal in Cheltenham. The *Lichfield Mercury* was fulsome in its praise of the production, which it said was 'excellently told' and was full of songs and choruses of a 'most attractive character'. The acting was described as 'capital' and the singing of Miss Soulby, playing the part of 'pretty' Jenny Crusoe, was singled out for special praise. Mademoiselle Rosa was 'a most excellent dancer – possibly the best ever seen in Lichfield', according to the *Mercury.* The scenery was 'good and appropriate', the 'transformation scene [was of] a brilliant character' and the costumes were described as 'characteristic'. The *Mercury* concluded that 'on the whole, Lichfield has never had such a good pantomime and there is little doubt that Miss Thorne's venture will meet with the measure of success it so thoroughly deserves'. Admission prices for the pantomime cost 2*s* (10p) for the balcony and 1*s* (5p) for the stalls. (*Lichfield Mercury*, February 14th 1879)

~ February 14th ~

1958: On this day, the opening of the Windmill pub took place. Situated on the corner of Wheel Lane and Grange Lane, it was the first new pub to be built in Lichfield since the Second World War. It opened to the public at 6 p.m., but before that an opening ceremony had taken place attended by the mayor and representatives of the brewery and the builders. The Windmill was described by owners Atkinson's Brewery as having all that was best in a modern pub building and would be a great 'asset' to the people of the area. The pub was equipped with 'tastefully decorated' lounge, bar and smoke rooms and featured a 'temperature controlled' cellar to 'ensure that all drinks were served at the correct temperature whatever the season'. The pub also featured an upstairs assembly room which could seat ninety and could be booked for private parties and functions. This room had an outside veranda 'from which could be seen an excellent view of the surrounding countryside'. The Windmill closed down in 2010 and at the time of writing was scheduled for demolition and is to be replaced by a care home. (*Lichfield Mercury*, February 14th 1958)

~ February 15th ~

1895: On this day, the fortnightly meeting of Lichfield's Board of Guardians, the body that was in charge of the workhouse, took place. The workhouse master, Mr Williams, reported that there were 101 women, 47 men and 35 children who were inmates there. The Lichfield Union Workhouse had also provided relief for 264 vagrants, both men and women, during the previous quarter-year, as opposed to 328 in the corresponding period the previous year. In the Lichfield district as a whole, 406 individuals had been provided with relief in the previous six weeks – 70 were able-bodied, 239 were not able-bodied and 154 were children. Mr Williams also reported that there had been a concert performed for the inmates by Mr Harrison, with which they were 'very pleased' and 'they hoped that it would not be the last'. The meeting heard that the government had urged all parish workhouses to find work for the unemployed, if possible, but the Board of Governors expressed concern that this would cause unfair competition with those doing paid work for local firms. Mr Gordon criticised the government for allowing 'uncontrolled immigration' into Britain, which had been 'flooding the labour market'. (*Lichfield Mercury*, November 22nd 1895)

─ February 16th ─

1940: On this day, the *Lichfield Mercury* reported that over £109 had been raised from the public to enable cigarettes to be sent to 'local lads' serving in France with the British Expeditionary Force. The fund, set up by the *Mercury* itself, attracted donations from people all over Lichfield District and was a popular way of showing support for the troops fighting against Nazi Germany. The paper received a number of messages from soldiers who had already been sent cartoons of 120 cigarettes. Gunner Rock wrote: 'I received the cigarettes with more joy than if someone had given me a seven course meal.'

Sergeant Cullen wrote to the *Mercury* to say that he had already received three parcels of cigarettes and wanted to 'convey my thanks to the readers of your most excellent paper'. He added that 'to my knowledge the *Mercury* is the only paper to have organised such a fund and this, I am sure, reflects great credit to you and the citizens of Lichfield'. A serving soldier's wife, Mrs C.S. Yates, wrote about the gift of cigarettes to her husband: 'I'm sure it helps to cheer the boys to know they are in the thoughts of so many people from their hometown.' (*Lichfield Mercury*)

— FEBRUARY 17TH —

1941: This day saw the beginning of War Weapons Week in Lichfield. The week began with the mayor opening the Campaign Centre at 8 Market Street, which had been loaned for the week by Hepworth's. The aim of the campaign week was to raise £50,000, enough to buy ten Spitfires. During the week many events had been planned including an exhibition of official war photographs; a parade through the principal streets of Lichfield by the Army, Air Force, the Home Guard and Civil Defence contingents; public meetings at the Guildhall; and special speakers before each evening performance at the Regal cinema. Advertisements were placed in the *Lichfield Mercury*, such as: 'Citizens of this loyal City – our aim is £50,000 – Play your Part!' Local businesses also urged Lichfield folk to invest in war bonds and the Post Office Savings Bank in order to raise much needed funds for the war effort. Savings were seen as an essential factor in Britain's eventual victory – something in which everyone could participate. In the end a grand total of £129,891 was raised by the people of Lichfield and the surrounding district, including Burntwood, Chase Terrace and Chasetown. (*Lichfield Mercury*, February 21st 1941)

— February 18th —

1921: On this day, a public meeting was held at Lichfield's Guildhall, organised by the Lichfield Branch of the National Council of Women, designed to explain the duties of women on juries. The mayor, who attended the meeting, said that women would not find the job of sitting on a jury 'a bed of roses, [as] crime and sordid phases of life had not been subjects to which women, as a whole, had devoted much attention'. In some quarters the inclusion of women on British juries had been strongly condemned and even ridiculed, but the general feeling at the meeting was that women now had on opportunity 'to take their proper place in every sphere of life'. Councillor Mrs Merry, in an address to the meeting entitled 'Women jurors: the duties and opportunities', urged women to 'render valuable service to the Country by taking jury service as seriously as possible'. Women were first given the right to sit on juries in 1920 – the first were six women who were sworn in as jurors at Bristol Quarter Sessions in July of that year. (*Lichfield Mercury*, February 25th 1921)

~ February 19th ~

1717: On this day, the famous actor David Garrick was born. His family moved from Hereford to Lichfield soon after his birth and lived in Beacon Street, opposite the west gate of the cathedral. Garrick first attended the local, free grammar school and later enrolled in Samuel Johnson's school at Edial, just outside the city, the two becoming close friends. In March 1737, when Johnson's school closed, the two men set out for London; both men were virtually penniless and they hoped to seek their fortunes in the capital. They were to become 'the greatest man of the theatre and the greatest man of letters of their day'. Following a spell as a wine merchant, Garrick became an actor and a playwright and soon attracted attention for his innovative acting style, which was realistic, relaxed and naturalistic – a departure from the stylised acting that had been the norm before. He rose to become the most influential and well-known figure on the London stage. At his death in 1779, Garrick was the first actor to be given the honour of being buried in Poet's Corner in Westminster Abbey. (McIntyre, Ian, *Garrick*, Allen Lane, 1999)

~ February 20th ~

1781: On this day, William Dyott of Freeford Hall, Lichfield, decided to start a diary which he would keep until 1845. Dyott was from a very old and illustrious Lichfield family (his ancestor Dumb Dyott was famous for killing Lord Brooke during the first siege of Lichfield during the Civil War) and was born in 1761 as the second son of Richard Dyott. He and his elder brother were two of the first people to be inoculated against smallpox. He joined the army and served in Ireland, the West Indies, Egypt and Spain during the Napoleonic Wars, rising to the rank of Lieutenant General. His diary also recounts personal tragedies in his life such as the death of his father in 1787 and his night-time burial at St Mary's church, in accordance with family tradition. Dyott also documents his strange relationship with his wife, who first became an invalid and then eloped with a man called Dunne – an Act of Parliament in those days was needed to settle the couple's divorce. Dyott retired from the military and became a gentleman farmer on his estate. He died in 1847. (Jeffery, R. (ed.), *Dyott's Diary*, Archibald Constable & Co. Ltd, 1907)

~ February 21st ~

1891: On this day, the unusual funeral of Colonel Richard Dyott (the son of William Dyott) took place at St Mary's church in Lichfield. Dyott, a former Lichfield MP, was the last in the line of a family that had been greatly influential in the city. The Dyotts of Freeford Hall had also had a long and curious habit of only being buried at night-time; no one is quite sure why this tradition came about, but it may go back to the time of Cromwell's Commonwealth when certain elaborate church services were frowned upon and needed to be kept as secret as possible. Crowds lined the route as the torch-lit funeral procession wound its way through the streets of Lichfield. A thick fog had descended on the city that evening and must have made the sight an eerie one. The procession arrived at the church at 10 p.m. and such was the press of people outside that tempers flared and the crowd 'got out of control'. It was some time before order was restored. According to the Dyott family tradition no hymns were sung during the short service, nor were any flowers or wreaths displayed. (*Lichfield Mercury*, February 27th 1891)

— February 22nd —

1856: On this day, the official opening of the work to clear out Lichfield's two pools took place. A platform was erected at the western end of Stowe Pool on which a number of civic dignitaries and the engineers Messrs McLean and Stileman stood to perform the opening ceremony. Unfortunately the platform gave way under the weight of people and it was fortunate that no one was seriously hurt. Over the years the pools had silted up and there were some who, like Richard Chawner, Chairman of the South Staffordshire Water Company, wanted Minster Pool filled in completely, saying that it was 'undesirable to have a body of water in the middle of the City where people might throw dead dogs and other unpleasant objects'. Luckily, however, Lichfield people had protested against Chawner's idea and the pools were cleared out rather than filled in. In Minster Pool various historical artefacts were found including many cannonballs and mortar shells, which had been used during the Civil War sieges. The dredged up mud from the pools was donated to local farmers to put on their land and water levels in the two pools was increased. (Clayton, Howard, *Cathedral City*, Abbotsford Publishing, 1981)

― February 23rd ―

1951: On this day, adverts in the *Lichfield Mercury* illustrated the range of entertainments available to local people during the week. The Regal cinema was showing a film called *Caged*, starring Eleanor Parker and Agnes Moorhead, whereas the Garrick Theatre was presenting a play called *A Lady Mislaid*, a comedy by Kenneth Horne which starred Lionel Jeffries. Live theatre was also available at the Guildhall, where Lichfield Amateur Operatic Society were putting on Gilbert and Sullivan's *The Gondoliers*, and at Chase Terrace Secondary Modern School, where the Chase Amateur Dramatic Society were presenting a comedy by Edith McCraken entitled *Quiet Weekend*. Locals who wanted to dance had a number of choices including a Grand Gala Dance at the Guildhall, with dancing from 8 p.m. to 11.45 p.m. to Johnny Neenan's Quintet, or a Young Farmers' Dance at the Red Lion, Longden Green, with dancing until 1 a.m. Another advert was promoting HMV televisions, which perhaps pointed the way for future entertainment in the home. The advert informed readers 'Now was the time to buy your television', with a 10in table receiver costing 48 guineas (£50.40) which was 'the ideal size for the average home'. (*Lichfield Mercury*)

~ FEBRUARY 24TH ~

1956: On this day, the *Lichfield Mercury* gave its verdict on the television transmitter that had been built near Lichfield to broadcast the new commercial TV channel. The 500ft-high Independent Television Authority (ITA) transmitter had been built at Common Barn Farm at Hints, 5 miles from the centre of Lichfield. It brought the second TV channel to the Midlands and for the first time the BBC's monopoly of the television airwaves was challenged. The *Mercury* reported that the picture quality from the new transmitter was very good even though it would not be broadcasting on full power for two months. There had been, the paper noted with some surprise, instances of good reception 100 miles away. Commenting on seeing advertisements on TV for the first time the *Mercury* said 'it had come as a bit of a shock particularly when they break into a programme or between rounds of a boxing tournament'. Programmes on the new channel in the first week included *Playhouse*, *The Adventures of Noddy*, a filmed report of a cup-tie between Birmingham and West Bromwich, *I Love Lucy*, *Sunday Night at the London Palladium* and *The Adventures of Robin Hood*. (*Lichfield Mercury*)

~ February 25th ~

1913: On this day, the annual meeting of the Ladies Association for the Care of Friendless Girls was held at the Bishop's Palace. The annual report of the association stated that during the previous year, fifty-three girls had been in care at its home in Beacon Street, twenty-two of them being described as 'fallen' (a euphemism used at the time to describe young women who had become pregnant out of wedlock, or who had worked as prostitutes). During the year, eight of the girls had been sent off to become servants, thirty-two had been sent to other homes, six had been returned to their families and one girl had been transferred to Lichfield's workhouse. The report added that most of the girls at the home went on to have 'purer and better lives' as a result of their stay, but the refuge was in jeopardy due to financial problems, with a shortfall of £9 in the previous year. The report also went on to make the point that 'there may be a lack of funds but there is never a lack of girls to be helped'. (*Lichfield Mercury*, February 28th 1913)

~ February 26th ~

1954: On this day, following the queen's coronation of the previous year when many people had acquired television sets for the first time, the *Lichfield Mercury* published a weekly guide advising viewers what they should watch. According to the newspaper, highlights of the following week included a documentary about an exhibition of plates belonging to the Royal family at the Victoria and Albert Museum; the programme was presented by a young David Attenborough. A programme of brass band music from the Free Trade Hall in Manchester was also recommended. It was entitled 'Men of Brass' and included music by Wagner, Bizet and Kenneth Guest. A play set in Russia in 1801 and a number of programmes from Wales to celebrate St David's Day, including an amateur football match presented by Kenneth Wolstenholme, were also selected as highlights by the paper. A show called *Variety Parade* starring Max Wall, Bob Monkhouse and the Tiller Girls was a popular choice for Sunday evening and a children's programme called *Adolphus* was all about an old cart horse that was being replaced on a farm by a tractor. (*Lichfield Mercury*)

~ February 27th ~

1934: On this day, a radio broadcast was made from Lichfield Cathedral for the first time. The programme, entitled Choir and Cloister, took the form of 'microphone impressions' of the building and was one of a series of programmes that were broadcast from a number of cathedrals by the Midland Regional Station. The programme was heard between 9 p.m. and 9.45 p.m., its narrator was Walter Pitchfork and the cathedral choir performed the hymn *All People That On Earth Do Dwell*, along with a number of other pieces. 'Various apparatus' were installed in the cathedral for the broadcast, with microphones being placed in the treasury from where the narrator spoke and this was linked to the main equipment in the sacristy. The General Post Office (GPO) set up a cable from the cathedral, across Minster Pool, to its building in Bird Street and from there the broadcast was relayed to the GPO in Birmingham and on to to the Midland Regional Studios. The broadcast, it was hoped, would be the first of many from the cathedral, the next one being an organ recital in March. (*Lichfield Mercury*, February 30th 1934)

- February 28th -

1925: On this day, the tragic death of a 4-year-old girl took place at Wall, a village 1 mile from Lichfield. Joan Rollason of Watling Street stood in front of the fire warming her hands when her pinafore caught fire. She ran into the street with her clothes ablaze, where several people covered her with an overall and an overcoat to put out the flames. Her burns were 'dressed with oil' and she was taken to Victoria Nursing Home. Her sister Winnie, aged 17, was in the process of running an errand when the accident took place and later told the inquest that she had been intending to clean the floor, and various items around the hearth had been removed, including the fire guard. The 4-year-old was treated at the hospital by Dr Shaw, who said that it was impossible to do anything about the burns, which were 'very extensive over the front of her body'. She died an hour after being admitted from shock caused by her burns. The verdict of the deputy coroner was one of accidental death. The child was buried in Wall churchyard. (*Lichfield Mercury*, March 6th 1925)

~ February 29th ~

1924: On this day, the *Lichfield Mercury* published a letter from John Williams of Detroit, USA, in which he expressed the pleasure he got from receiving the *Mercury*, which he had specially delivered to him. He also highlighted a number of differences he had noted between his hometown and Lichfield. There was, for example, much less advertising of shops and businesses in the *Mercury* than in typical American newspapers, where much more space was given over to the promotion of commercial enterprises. He also expressed surprise that Lichfield had no city-wide electric lighting, unlike Detroit, which had 'splendid lighting' all around the city. It was in the area of crime, however, that Mr Williams had noticed the biggest difference. In Detroit, Mr Williams noted, there were six to twelve robberies or 'hold-ups' every day and one murder every three days. A total of 7,063 road accidents had taken place in Detroit during the previous year, with 284 people killed as a result. All Lichfield had, he said, 'were a few drunks, a few quarrels and a few motorists who fail to obey the law'. (*Lichfield Mercury*)

— MARCH 1ST —

1643: It was on this day that Robert Greville, Lord Brooke, arrived on the outskirts of Lichfield with a Parliamentary force and prepared to besiege Lichfield Cathedral, which was a Royalist stronghold. He, along with 1,200 men, marched unopposed into the city on the following day and set up a demi-culverin cannon in Dam Street, which attempted to blast a hole in the south gate. Brooke, keen to see what damage had been inflicted on the gate and nearby walls, stepped out into the street and, almost immediately, was hit in his left eye by a shot fired from the roof of the cathedral; he died instantly. The bullet had been fired by a man called John Dyott – who was nicknamed 'Dumb' Dyott on account of his inability to hear or speak. The Royalists hailed the shot as miraculous and certain proof that God was on their side, as Brooke was killed on St Chad's Day. Their jubilation was short-lived, however, for on Sunday March 5th the king's men in the cathedral surrendered. A plaque now marks the spot in Dam Street where Brooke died. (Clayton, Howard, *Loyal and Ancient City*, Abbotsford Publishing, 1987)

— MARCH 2ND —

672: On this day, St Chad, the patron saint of Lichfield, died. Chad had been sent to help establish and spread Christianity to the lands of Mercia. He built a house in Stowe, a short walk from the site of the present cathedral, and baptised people at a well which still bears his name and which lies next to St Chad's church. When the Gothic cathedral was built a shrine was constructed, where the remains of St Chad were kept in an ornate box, and pilgrims who soon came to the shrine were also shown the skull of St Chad. At the Reformation, when many such shrines were destroyed and statues defaced, the bones of St Chad disappeared; it was rumoured that the remains were given to the Dudley family in 1538 for safekeeping. Some bones eventually found their way to Birmingham and were placed in the city's Catholic cathedral when it was built in 1841. The bones were examined in 1995 and, although five of them were shown to have come from the time of Chad, it was also discovered that they belonged to at least two individuals. (*St Chad and the Lichfield Gospels*, published by Lichfield Cathedral)

~ March 3rd ~

1893: On this day, the *Lichfield Mercury* printed a letter from George Edalji apologising for being the author of anonymous, offensive letters and withdrawing certain charges against a sergeant of the police. The trouble was, as the *Mercury* acknowledged a week later in its edition of March 10th, this letter was a fake and was not actually sent by Edalji. The *Mercury* went on to add that it hoped the author of the offending letter 'may soon be discovered and punished as they richly deserve to be'. Edalji was an Anglo-Indian solicitor, the son of Rev. Shapurji Edalji – vicar of St Mark's church in Great Wyrley, who was wrongly accused and convicted of maliciously wounding a pony and other animals and also of sending out libellous and offensive letters. The case, which had obvious racist overtones, became world famous when the writer Sir Arthur Conan-Doyle, creator of Sherlock Holmes, successfully defended him. It was not until thirty years later that the true perpetrator of the crimes was discovered. The whole story is told in Gordon Weaver's 2006 book *Conan – Doyle and the Parson's Son* and also in Julian Barnes' 2005 novel, *Arthur and George*. (*Lichfield Mercury*)

- March 4th -

1932: On this day, John Cheshire, a miner from Chorley, near Lichfield, died. His death occurred at Number Three Pit at the Cannock Chase Colliery Company where he was engaged in moving empty coal wagons from the sidings to the pit – he would move four at a time using a horse to pull them. While performing this task he had, apparently, got his foot wedged in the tracks and a number of wagons had rolled over him. He was taken to Hammerwich Hospital where he was treated by Dr William Fraser, who said that Mr Cheshire was alive when he arrived at the hospital but died of his injuries soon afterwards. The doctor stated that the deceased man had suffered serious injuries to his legs and groin and that his death was due to shock. The inquest, held at Hammerwich Hospital a few days later, heard from his widow Rosa Mary Cheshire, who said that her husband was perfectly healthy and had never been attended to by a doctor. The inquest returned a verdict of accidental death having found that no equipment had malfunctioned at the site of the accident and no one had been to blame. *(Lichfield Mercury,* March 11th 1932)

— MARCH 5TH —

1737: On this day, Samuel Johnson and David Garrick arrived in London. Johnson was hoping to have a play that he had recently written called *Irene* presented on the stage. Garrick, who had been a pupil at Johnson's short-lived school at Edial, was also hoping to find fame and fortune in London. They travelled with one horse using the 'ride and tie' method, where one of the men would ride the horse ahead for a while as the other walked. The one with the horse would then tether it to a tree and walk ahead, leaving the second traveller to get to the horse, ride it past the first man for a while and then, in turn, tie it to a tree for the process to continue. They followed the main route from Lichfield to London along Watling Street (now the A5) and passed through Coleshill, Coventry, Dunchurch, Daventry, Towcester, Stony Stratford, Dunstable, St Albans and High Barnet. Tragic news awaited both men in London: Garrick discovered that his father had died while they were on the road and Johnson found out that his brother Nathaniel had died at the age of 25. (Martin, Peter, *Samuel Johnson: A Biography*, Phoenix, 2008)

~ MARCH 6TH ~

1978: On this day, Kenneth Williams, television and radio personality and star of the *Carry On* films, visited Lichfield. He was invited to the city by an old friend, businessman Michael Whittaker, who was a former cathedral choirboy. Williams was always an admirer of Lichfield's most famous son, Dr Johnson, and so leapt at the chance to pay a visit to the city of his birth. He found the Johnson Birthplace Museum 'very worthwhile', adding, 'The House has so much atmosphere and there are so many things there connected with Dr Johnson and his life that any devotee of his could not fail to be delighted.' After lunch at the George Hotel, Williams visited the cathedral before leaving the city in order to return to London for a recording session of the popular radio programme *Just a Minute*. His latest film, *The Hound of the Baskervilles*, in which he starred with Peter Cook and Dudley Moore, was going to be released soon afterwards and he was also due to begin shooting on his next and, as it turned out, last *Carry On* film – *Carry On Emmanuelle* – later in the year. (*Lichfield Mercury*, March 10th 1978)

– March 7th –

1895: On this day, the last ever race at Lichfield Racecourse on Whittington Heath took place. The Lichfield race meeting, one of the oldest in the country, had taken place every year since 1702 and for much of that time was the city's biggest social event of the year. Three days of horse racing every spring for steeple chasing and autumn for flat racing had traditionally been accompanied by other activities such as running races and cock fighting. At the height of its popularity the race meeting would attract crowds of thousands from all over the Midlands and a large grandstand was erected to cater for them. The races declined somewhat in the nineteenth century, largely due to the demise of the stagecoach routes, of which Lichfield was an important centre. The building of Whittington Barracks on the land, which was owned by the War Office, meant that the races could no longer take place, despite many protests and petitions made to the prime minister of the time, Lord Rosebery. The racecourse's grandstand can still be seen today as the clubhouse of Whittington Golf Club. (*Lichfield Mercury*)

~ MARCH 8TH ~

1907: On this day, the *Lichfield Mercury* published a feature which speculated on what Lichfield would be like a hundred years into the future. The article took the form of an imaginary tour around the streets of the city in 2007, looking at the changes that would have taken place by that far-off 'future date'; indeed, a few of the guesses were quite accurate. The writer predicts a city lit by electric lights which contains a shopping precinct and where people use decimal currency. However, other predictions were wide of the mark: the David Garrick Theatre, 'a magnificent structure', dominated Market Square (now called Johnson Square); the pavement was made up of tessellated tiles of many colours and everywhere is 'scrupulously clean'; the *Lichfield Mercury* was published daily; express trains took twenty minutes to get to London and uniformed guides were provided for all visitors to the city. In the year 2007, according to the article, the Swan and George Hotels had been rebuilt and Sandford Street had become 'a magnificent thoroughfare'. Perhaps the most remarkable prediction, however, involved Lichfield City Football Club, which would, according to the article, be playing in the top-tier of the football league having won the FA Cup for the previous seven years. (*Lichfield Mercury*)

~ March 9th ~

1927: On this day, a meeting was held in Bishop's Place to discuss the humane slaughtering of animals. The meeting was organised by the RSPCA and was addressed by Miss Wedgewood, secretary of the RSPCA in North Staffordshire, who told those attending the meeting there was a huge need for reform in the slaughtering industry. She added that although many of those working in slaughterhouses were experienced and expert in their business, many others were not and the methods often used to dispatch animals were too inefficient. The pole axe was frequently used to kill animals, but it often took two or more blows with it before an animal was brought down. She urged slaughtermen to use modern, mechanical killing devices which were almost 100 per cent efficient in dispatching animals quickly. Mr Collinge, who represented the National Federation of Meat Traders, also spoke at the meeting. He told the audience that it was important for the quality of the meat that animals were killed carefully and with the minimum of cruelty. The meeting passed a resolution urging Lichfield City Council to ensure that all animals slaughtered in the city were treated humanely and stunned before being killed. (*Lichfield Mercury*, March 11th 1927)

~ March 10th ~

1905: On this day, at Lichfield Petty Sessions Edward Clarke, alias 'Nobby', was brought before the Mayor of Lichfield charged with allowing his dog to be at large without a muzzle or collar bearing his owner's name. Clarke was also charged with using indecent language and with assaulting a police officer, PC Bennett. He had been in his back yard in George Lane late at night, swearing loudly, when he was overheard by the policeman, who turned his lamp on him. Clarke then threw some bricks, one of which hit the PC on the leg. He was found guilty and fined a total of £1 17s 6d (£1.88), but as he could not pay the fine he was sent to prison for one month with hard labour. In the same week a man was found with his throat cut in the lavatory of the London to Glasgow express train when it stopped at Lichfield Trent Valley station. The man, William Howes, a butler, survived and was later charged and fined with attempting to commit suicide – suicide and attempted suicide being treated as criminal offences in England and Wales until 1961. (*Lichfield Mercury*, March 17th 1905)

~ March 11th ~

1938: On this day, with the fear of war uppermost in people's minds, 'the eyes of Europe' were on the city of Lichfield when the 'most effective street-lighting and air-raid control system known to modern science' was tested. Four hundred experts from all over the country, as well as Home Office officials, were present for the test, which involved a complete blackout of street lighting and the sounding of air-raid sirens. Householders were asked to co-operate by darkening their windows or putting out their lights completely during the blackout period. Lights in the city were turned out at 11.19 p.m. after a siren had been heard warning people to get off the streets. After ten minutes an 'all clear' siren was sounded. A second test was conducted half an hour later and the street lights were restored to normal at midnight. The test, the first of its kind anywhere in Britain, was proclaimed a success, although an RAF plane, which had been due to fly over Lichfield in order to try to 'find the city', was unable to take off because of weather conditions. (*Lichfield Mercury*, March 11th 1938)

~ MARCH 12TH ~

1943: On this day, the *Lichfield Mercury* reported on the 'shocking case' of a Lichfield house used as a brothel which had been frequented by American soldiers. The trial of the owner of the Wade Street house – a 37-year-old widow – as well as two other women aged 20 and 25 was presided over by Councillor H.G. Hall, who said that the case would produce evidence of 'an unpleasant character' and that 'any female who elected to leave the court should do so'; no women left the courtroom. The court heard that the woman lived in the house along with six children aged between 1 and 10. When the police raided the house, accompanied by American military policemen, they found all six children sleeping in one room 'in very dirty conditions' while one of the women was in bed with an American soldier in another bedroom. Two other American soldiers and another woman 'wearing no shoes or stockings' were found 'waiting' downstairs. The children were taken into care by the RSPCC, the owner of the brothel was jailed for three months with hard labour and the other women were fined. (*Lichfield Mercury*)

‒ March 13th ‒

1964: On this day, it was reported that the manager of Lichfield's Regal cinema, Brian Thompson, had been awarded a certificate of honorary life membership of the Kinematograph Weekly Company of Showmen. The award was very prestigious, as the magazine was the official journal of the cinema industry. It was presented to Mr Thompson at the Albany Hotel in Birmingham at a special ceremony attended by prominent members of the film trade. Presenting the award was the actor Stanley Baker, the star of the film *Zulu*, which had recently been released. In the film Baker played Lieutenant Chard, the commander of a small group of soldiers who defended Rorke's Drift against thousands of Zulu warriors. The certificate, given to Mr Thompson for 'recognition of his service and contribution towards the maintenance of a consistently high standard of showmanship', was added to his impressive collection of industry awards. He was already preparing for the arrival of *Zulu* at the Regal and had arranged for the Regimental Museum to put on a display of weapons of the time in the cinema's foyer. (*Lichfield Mercury*)

~ March 14th ~

1947: A man accused of stabbing a Lichfield woman was charged with her attempted murder after he had been arrested in Leeds. Denis Wood, aged 19, a soldier formerly stationed at Whittington Barracks, was charged with attempting to murder Bridget Mary Russell as she walked home along Stowe Street on her way back to her lodgings in Gaia Lane after visiting her sister-in-law. Wood, who had never met Miss Russell before, stabbed her in the back with a knife and when she turned around to look at her attacker he slashed her across the face. Altogether Miss Russell received over twenty-five injuries and was lucky to survive. After the attack Wood fled in the direction of St Chad's church and was later arrested in Leeds after attacking and robbing another woman, Miss Elizabeth Donaghie. Miss Russell worked as a bank clerk at the Lichfield Branch of the National Provincial Bank and was the sister of Colonel Russell, who, at the time, was serving with the armed forces in Palestine. (*Lichfield Mercury*, March 21st 1947)

– MARCH 15TH –

1770: On this day, a performance of George Farquhar's comedy *The Recruiting Officer* took place in Lichfield, most probably at the city's Guildhall. The play was written while Farquhar was staying at the George Hotel in Bird Street. Farquhar, who later set his best-known play – *The Beaux Stratagem* – in Lichfield, was born in Ireland in 1677 and was just 30 years old when he died. Sarah Siddons, the famous eighteenth-century actress, performed in Lichfield on many occasions and it was due to her urging that a theatre was built in Bore Street in 1790 – a theatre that lasted until 1870 when it was replaced by St James's Hall. To mark the opening of Lichfield's new Garrick Theatre complex in 2003, Farquhar's *The Recruiting Officer* was chosen as the first production. The play, which starred Corin Redgrave as Captain Brazen, caused a great deal of controversy when it was performed, due to the inclusion of an epilogue written by poet Tony Harrison which referred to contemporary conflicts in Iraq and Afghanistan and was critical of the then-prime minister Tony Blair. (Clayton, Howard and Simmons, Kathleen, *Lichfield in Old Photographs*, Sutton Publishing, 1994)

– March 16th –

1906: On this day, a report on the health of the people of Lichfield was issued by the medical officer of the city, Mr G.W. Homan. The report stated that the population of Lichfield was 7,902 and that the total number of births registered during the previous year had been 229 (119 females and 110 males), giving a birth-rate per 1,000 people of 28.6 – the highest rate for ten years. The total number of deaths reported in 1905 had been 122, an average of 15.2 per 1,000 people, with twenty of the deaths occurring at the workhouse. Thirty cases of infectious disease had been diagnosed in 1905, including chicken pox and scarlet fever, but only two people had been admitted to the Isolation Hospital. The entire district had been free of all dangerous diseases in the previous year. The housing situation in Lichfield had improved and the extension of the sewerage system in the city had been working well. Annual inspections of lodging houses, slaughterhouses, cowsheds, milk shops and bake houses had been made by the sanitary inspector, who had found that considerable improvements had been made and that such establishments were generally cleanly and satisfactorily kept. (*Lichfield Mercury*)

~ March 17th ~

1949: By this day, the new David Garrick repertory theatre was starting to attract big audiences. The Bore Street theatre had been converted from the Lido cinema and its first stage production was *Rebecca* by Daphne du Maurier. The auditorium had been completely redesigned by the building's new owners, Mr and Mrs Cowlishaw, with all 591 seats refurbished and the floors recarpeted. A cocktail bar had been added in the main foyer and an orchestra pit accommodating twelve musicians had been installed. The proscenium arch opening had been enlarged and the stage roof altered in order to permit large-scale scenery changes. The main aim of the theatre, according to the owners, was to present 'high class repertory productions and to become one of the best companies in the country'. The theatre stood where the Wilkinson's store is now located and was, originally, St James's Hall, a venue built in 1872 for concerts and lectures until it was converted into Lichfield's first cinema. The first theatre on the site, the Theatre Royal, had been built in 1790 and was demolished to make way for St James's Hall. (*Lichfield Mercury*, March 18th 1949)

~ MARCH 18TH ~

1910: On this day, Lichfield was visited by the explorer Captain Robert Falcon Scott, who, at the time, was raising funds for his attempt to reach the South Pole. Scott gave a lecture at the city's Guildhall where he spoke about his forthcoming Antarctic expedition. The lecture was attended by 'a large and fashionable audience' including the Bishop of Lichfield and proceeds raised on the evening were given to the expedition fund. Scott's lecture was illustrated by 'limelight views' (picture slides) of the Antarctic region and included scenes of icebergs, pack ice, glaciers and seals. Scott explained that the expedition would involve a total of fifty-five people for two years and would cost over £40,000. The *Mercury*'s wish that 'the first person to the Pole would be an Englishman' would not come true, however. Scott and four others died from the cold while returning, disappointed, from the Pole in March 1912, having been beaten to their objective by the Norwegian explorer Roald Amundsen. (*Lichfield Mercury*)

~ MARCH 19TH ~

1886: On this day, the *Lichfield Mercury* reported on a spate of drunkenness in the city. Michael Smith, a labourer of no fixed abode, was brought before the court charged with being drunk and disorderly in Sandford Street. PC Hutchins said that he had been sent for at around 11 p.m. by the owner of a lodging house, who had found Smith drunk and causing a 'great disturbance'. The lodging housekeeper had asked Smith to leave but he had refused and so the constable arrested him. On the way to the police station Smith used threatening language and his conduct during the rest of the night was 'very bad', with Smith shouting, swearing and threatening police officers. In court the prisoner 'appeared not to have recovered from his previous day's libations' and was very 'excitable', accusing police of kicking and 'ill-using' him. Magistrates sentenced Smith to one month's imprisonment with hard labour and he was taken to the cells still struggling and swearing. Also in court for drunkenness was regular offender Sarah Thacker of Stowe Street. She was given fourteen days' in gaol with hard labour; it was her thirtieth such conviction. (*Lichfield Mercury*)

~ March 20th ~

1915: On this day, the Secretary of State for War, Field Marshall Lord Kitchener, visited Whittington Barracks. Kitchener arrived at Lichfield's Trent Valley station on a special train and then drove to the barracks by motor car. The visit was supposed to be a secret one, but somehow the news had leaked out. The Secretary of State was greeted by thousands of people on Whittington Heath, keen to catch a glimpse of the man who was in charge of the armed forces during the First Word War, which had been raging since August 1914. At the barracks Kitchener reviewed the lines of soldiers on the parade ground before being driven back to the city station. On the way he passed 'a number of conveyances bringing wounded soldiers from the station to the barracks hospital'. In 1915 Kitchener was one of the most famous people in the country, his face appearing on recruitment posters alongside the slogan 'Britain Wants You'. He died in 1916 when the warship he was travelling on was sunk by a German mine. (*Lichfield Mercury*, March 26th 1915)

- March 21st -

1812: This day saw the death of Rev. William Robinson, Prebendary of Lichfield Cathedral. His death in his 30s from tuberculosis set in train a series of tragic events for his family. His wife, Ellen-Jane Robinson, was left to bring up two young girls on her own and while on a trip to Bath her oldest daughter (also called Ellen-Jane) died from burns after her nightdress burst into flames when she got too near to the fire in the hearth. The following year her youngest daughter, Marianne, contracted tuberculosis and also died. Consumed with the grief of losing her entire family in two years, Mrs Robinson commissioned Sir Francis Chantrey to design a memorial for her daughters. Chantrey, the most famous sculptor of his day, exhibited the statue at the Royal Academy where it caused a sensation before it was placed in the south choir of Lichfield Cathedral in 1817, where it can be seen today. The memorial, entitled 'The Sleeping Children', is made from white marble and depicts the two girls as they lie asleep in each other's arms. Marianne holds a small bunch of snowdrops in her hand. (Clayton, Howard, *Cathedral City*, Abbotsford Publishing, 1981)

— March 22nd —

1776: On this day, Samuel Johnson, along with his close friend and future biographer James Boswell, visited Lichfield. They stayed at the Three Crowns Inn, next door to the building where Johnson had been born, and had a 'comfortable little supper' and lots of Lichfield ale. Boswell found the two-bedded room in which they stayed only 'tolerable', but Johnson was adamant that they lodged at the inn, as he liked the innkeeper Mr Wilkins. While in Lichfield, Johnson introduced Boswell to his family and friends including Lucy Porter, his step-daughter; Peter Garrick, the brother of David, the famous actor; Dr Seward and his daughter Anna at Bishop's Palace; and Mrs Gastrel at Stowe Hill. The two men also visited the various sights of Lichfield, notably Richard Greene's museum in Market Street, the cathedral and the Guildhall to see a play called *Theodosius*. While in the city Boswell was served Staffordshire oatcakes for breakfast, describing them as 'not hard like in Scotland, but soft like a Yorkshire cake'. Boswell recorded that the people of Lichfield were 'the most sober, decent people in England'. (Boswell, James, *The Life of Samuel Johnson*, George Dearborn, 1833)

~ March 23rd ~

1918: This day marked the end of Lichfield's Aeroplane Bank Week, which was an appeal by Lady Charnwood on behalf of the government to raise money to supply extra planes for the war effort. At the start of the appeal, the people of Lichfield had pledged to raise a total of £25,000 for the purchase of ten aircraft by buying war bonds and War Savings Certificates. The *Lichfield Mercury* explained that 'the great and speedy expansion of the air service is one of the most potent factors in the attainment of victory'. The week's appeal had been opened by the mayor and Lady Charnwood, who had appealed especially to the women of the city. Speeches were made in Market Square, where a large crowd had gathered to see one of the 'fighting planes' that was being displayed there. A temporary bank was also set up where people could purchase the bonds and certificates and within two hours of the launch of the appeal £20,000 had been raised. By the end of the week's campaign over £90,000 had been collected. (*Lichfield Mercury*, March 29th 1918)

~ MARCH 24TH ~

1933: On this day, the *Lichfield Mercury* published a report about the People's Theatre, which stood opposite the Guildhall in Bore Street. A venue that put on variety shows, the short-lived People's Theatre was the closest thing Lichfield had to a traditional music hall, but it had to compete with the city's two cinemas. Entertainment provided in this particular week 'reached a very high standard' and included David Clark and Partner, 'easily one of the finest musical acts ever seen here', who played a wide variety of instruments including violins, cellos, banjos and mandolins. Also appearing was a comedian, Dan E. Marsh, 'there is never a dull moment when he occupies the boards'. Altogether the theatre provided entertainment from ten 'clever' artists and the *Mercury* advised its readers to visit the theatre 'to see this excellent show'. 'With such an array of talent,' the *Mercury* proclaimed, 'there is now no need to leave the city in search of entertainment.' Shows at the People's Theatre were put on each night at 7.45 p.m. and twice on Saturday; seats cost 6*d* (3p) and 1*s* (5p). (*Lichfield Mercury*)

~ March 25th ~

1705: On this day, Colonel Luke Lillingston raised a regiment of volunteers that later became the 38th Regiment of Foot and eventually the South Staffordshire Regiment. The event took place at the Kings Head, a former coaching inn in Bird Street, Lichfield, and which today has a plaque on its outside wall in commemoration. The regiment went on to see distinguished service over the years, including the Peninsular Campaign during the Napoleonic War, the Crimean War and the First and Second World Wars. The South Staffordshire Regiment amalgamated with the North Staffordshire Regiment in 1959 to form the Staffordshire Regiment, and a further reorganisation took place in 2007 when the Staffordshire name was lost completely and the Mercian Regiment was formed. The City of Lichfield has long been connected with the military. Whittington Barracks was built in 1880 and became the home of the Staffords in their various incarnations. Another pub in Lichfield, The Earl of Lichfield in Conduit Street, is nicknamed The Drum due to a tradition which holds that in the 1830s a recruiting sergeant would stand outside the pub literally drumming up recruits. (Vale, W.V., *A History of the Staffordshire Regiment*, Gale & Polden Ltd, 1969)

— MARCH 26TH —

1949: This day was the last of a week-long exhibition of local products held at the Guildhall entitled 'Lichfield Can Make It'. At a time when British industry was trying to get back on its feet after the long years of war, the organisers were endeavouring to develop the city's own industry. Factories were springing up on the new Trent Valley Trading Estate and also in the area around Shenstone, and although many locals were already being employed there were still plenty of vacancies to be filled, with many firms interested in attracting more labour to Lichfield. The exhibition was opened by Lord Lucas, Lord-in-Waiting to the king, and many well-known local firms, some twenty-four in total, had set up displays. These included Bridgemans and Son, the nationally famous builders and church restoration experts; Garratt's Bakeries, long established in the city; W.J. Mercers and Sons, saddlers and harness makers; Tuke and Bell; and J.R. Deacon Limited. The exhibition also included a special arts and crafts section that had been organised by Mrs Flint, Head of the Lichfield School of Art. (*Lichfield Mercury*, March 25th 1949)

~ MARCH 27TH ~

1908: On this day, a meeting took place in Lichfield to protest against government plans to reduce the number of pubs in the city. The Liberal government's Licensing Bill would have had the effect of reducing the number of public house licences by a third, as well as reducing Sunday opening hours and banning women from working in pubs. Pressure from the influential Temperance movement and a landslide victory by the Liberal Party in 1906, many of whose members were worried about the level of drunkenness in Britain, had led to the introduction of the Bill. In Lichfield the number of pubs would have been reduced from about sixty to just sixteen and local politicians, as well as licensees, many of whom would lose their livelihoods, were strongly opposed to the measure. The Lichfield meeting ended with the singing of the National Anthem accompanied by the Chasetown Brass Band. The Bill was eventually defeated in the House of Lords in November 1908. (*Lichfield Mercury*, April 3rd 1908)

— MARCH 28TH —

1975: On this day, the weekly 'discotheque' at the Civic Hall was cancelled following a spate of vandalism and misbehaviour at the recently opened venue – the latest incidents involved damage to toilet fittings and a brawl. Councillor John Shaw, chairman of the council's leisure committee, which ran the hall, said: 'We will not tolerate this kind of behaviour.' At the previous week's disco, water pipes were ripped off a wall, a hand basin in the gents' toilet was pulled from the wall, a hand basin was badly cracked in the ladies' toilet and cisterns were damaged in toilets reserved for disabled people, putting them out of action. A spokesman said 'it could be some weeks before we are able to repair them because of a shortage of supplies'. Police were called to the hall when a fight broke out between 'two factions of youths' and as a result councillors were considering closing the bar at future discos and only allowing soft drinks to be sold. Councillor Shaw said 'young people are always talking about having nothing to do and then commence to not only cause a nuisance, but do serious damage to the Hall'. (*Lichfield Mercury*, March 28th 1975)

— MARCH 29TH —

1984: On this day, Lichfield businessmen claimed that rate-payers' money would be squandered if a new toilet block was built in the Market Square only for the benefit of market stallholders. Lichfield's Chamber of Trade and Commerce (LCTC), which represented local business interests, believed that people should not have to pay for a facility which they could not themselves use, but also agreed that there was a huge need for more public toilets in the city centre. Members wanted the city and the District Councils to get together to provide toilets for the public in the Market Square or in the shopping precinct, but stressed that they would have to be open to the public and not only for market traders, who would be supplied with their own keys. Plans to build the 'restricted toilets' had been given the go-ahead by the City Council and £50,000 had been earmarked for the project. Vice President of the LCTC, James Thomas, called the plan 'preposterous when there is a desperate need for public toilets, particularly in the south of the City'. (*Lichfield Mercury*, March 30th 1984)

— March 30th —

1752: On this day, Francis Barber became Samuel Johnson's servant. Barber was born into slavery in Jamaica in about 1742 and was brought to Britain at the age of 8 by Richard Bathurst, a plantation owner. Bathurst sent Barber to Johnson in order to be his valet. Johnson, who was engaged in his mammoth task of writing his dictionary, soon grew very fond of the boy, who apart from a period at sea serving in the navy, was to stay with Johnson for the rest of the writer's life. Barber was left a large sum of money by Johnson in his will and, with his wife Betsy, moved to Lichfield. They lived in a house in Stowe Street and Barber spent his time fishing and growing potatoes. However, he managed to squander the money he had been left by Johnson and so opened a small school in Burntwood to make ends meet. He died in Stafford infirmary in 1801 following an operation. Betsy died in 1816 and is buried in St Chad's church. Many of Barber's descendents live in Staffordshire to this day. (*The Life of Francis Barber*, The Samuel Johnson Birthplace Museum, 2007)

— MARCH 31ST —

1856: On this day, Mary Anne Evans, better known as the novelist George Eliot, paid a visit to Lichfield and stayed in the Swan Hotel in Bird Street in order to break her train journey from North Wales to Dorset. This was her third visit to the city. She had first stayed in the Swan with her parents when she was 5 years old and she visited again at the age of 20 when she and her father were on their way to Derbyshire. Another Eliot connection with Lichfield was Samuel Evans, her uncle, who she based her character Seth on in her novel *Adam Bede* and who, in 1860, carved the Bishop's throne in Lichfield Cathedral. George Eliot was born in Nuneaton in 1819 and was the author of seven novels. She used a male pen name in order that her work would be taken seriously because, at the time, women writers were often perceived as only writing inconsequential romances. Another reason for adopting a man's name was in order to avoid scandal, as she lived with another woman's husband for twenty years. (Clayton, Howard and Simmons, Kathleen, *The Lilly-White Swann: History of the Swan Hotel Lichfield*, Abbotsford Publishing, 1996)

– April 1st –

1912: On this day, Lichfield's Central School was officially opened. A site in Frog Lane (now occupied by the police station) had been purchased from Basil Levett by the newly formed Local Education Authority in 1909 and the building constructed there was designed by F.T. Beck of Wolverhampton. The new school had eight classrooms to house 410 children (including 140 infants) and an entrance hall with cloakrooms, each with two washbasins supplied with cold water. Toilets were situated in a shed placed at the rear of the playground. The Central School was a boys' school until 1921 when girls were admitted. The first headmaster was Mr B.D. Pinder, whose 'office' consisted of a desk on a raised platform near a cloakroom. The early years were difficult, with two world wars and a serious measles epidemic disrupting children's education, but generally the school was a successful one and many ex-pupils in Lichfield have fond memories of it. The school closed in 1964 when pupils and resources were transferred to the newly built Netherstowe Comprehensive School in the north of the city. (Williams, Margaret, *Central School*, Maney Press, 1991)

– April 2nd –

1965: On this day, the *Lichfield Mercury* reported on the oldest living veteran serviceman in Lichfield, 89-year-old Fred Smith. Smith, who lived with his wife Florence in Curborough Road, had an eventful life. Born in Dublin, he joined the navy at the age of 18 and quickly saw action fighting pirates in the Persian Gulf. In 1906 he was shipwrecked when his vessel HMS *Montagu* sank off Lundy Island, after which he had a picture of the ill-fated ship tattooed on his chest. He left the navy in 1908 and did a number of jobs including playing piano in a music hall. At the start of the First World War he joined the South Wales Borderers and won the Military Medal after saving three other soldiers who were trapped by machine-gun fire. He left the army in 1918 and for a time worked as a miner in South Wales, a 'navvy' and a gardener before rejoining the forces and serving in Ireland where, at one time, he was captured by the IRA but managed to escape. In Lichfield, Fred Smith was still able, occasionally, to pop into the Anglesey Arms for a pint of mild. (*Lichfield Mercury*)

— APRIL 3RD —

1936: On this day, the *Lichfield Mercury* reported on the busy week that had been experienced by the manager of Lichfield's Regal cinema. The manager, Mr J.W. Burns, had been awarded a special and prestigious award for 'exploitation and showmanship' for the way in which he had promoted the film *One Night of Love*, and had thus been the first cinema manager to gain the award two years running. In the same week Mr Burns was also able to meet two famous British film stars – Jack Hulbert and Cicely Courtneidge – who had been dining at the George Hotel on their way to Liverpool to see the Grand National. Mr Burns conducted an interview with the pair, 'assuming the role of *Mercury* reporter' for the occasion. The stars were so impressed with the reception they had received in the city that they decided to visit Lichfield again on the way back to London. Coincidentally, another film star, Tom Walls, also called in at the George and was again greeted by Mr Burns, who managed to obtain his autographed photo, which, along with those of the other two stars, were hung in the foyer of the Regal. (*Lichfield Mercury*)

~ APRIL 4TH ~

1833: On this day, advertisements in the *Lichfield Mercury* provide an interesting insight into the sorts of medicine and other 'remedies' people in the city were prepared to buy. J. Edwards, for example, sold a range of 'Dr Congreve's medicines' from his druggist's shop in Market Street. These included 'Congreve's Petroleum Pills: justly celebrated' as a 'specific remedy in all nervous complaints' and which were, it was said, capable of curing 'chronic indigestion, spasms of the stomach and bowels, female complaints' and many other ailments. 'Congreve's Saline Apeilent Powders' were sold as a purgative cure for various 'inflammatory disorders including rheumatism and gout'. J. Edwards' shop also sold for 1*s* (5p) a bottle 'Bott's Cloth Powder' for taking grease spots out of silks and woollens 'without discharging the colour'. W. Playfer's hairdresser shop in Breadmarket Street sold 'Hendrie's tooth powder and aromatic tincture for the teeth, which cost 2*s* 9*d* (18p) per box and was used 'for beautifying the teeth'. The aromatic tincture was 'excellent for washing and refreshing the mouth and alleviating and removing the rheumatic pains which are often mistaken for toothache'. It cost 4*s* 6*d* (23p) per bottle. (*Lichfield Mercury*)

~ April 5th ~

1809: On this day, George Augustus Selwyn, the great missionary Bishop of Lichfield, was born in Hampstead in London. Educated at Eton and Cambridge (he rowed in the first ever University Boat Race in 1829), Selwyn became the first Bishop of New Zealand in 1841, where he was responsible for the organisation of the Anglican Church. He learned the Maori language while on the long sea voyage to New Zealand and astounded the locals when he preached sermons in the language of the indigenous people there. In six years he visited the whole of New Zealand as well as the many Pacific islands, which were also part of his diocese. Returning to England he was appointed Bishop of Lichfield in 1867 and was the first bishop to live in the Bishop's Palace for many years, improving and extending it. Among his many accomplishments as bishop, Selwyn initiated the first diocesan conference where laity were represented. He died in office in 1878 and is buried in the grounds of Lichfield Cathedral. Selwyn College Cambridge and Selwyn College Otago, New Zealand, were named in his honour. (*Lichfield Mercury*, April 23rd 1909 – the centenary of his birth)

‒ APRIL 6TH ‒

1995: On this day, the *Lichfield Mercury* reported on plans made by Lichfield District Council (LDC) to install twenty CCTV cameras in city streets and car parks, with a grant of £93,000 that they had been awarded by the government to help finance the security cameras. The whole scheme was expected to cost £300,000, with the remaining funds coming partly from local businesses and partly from LDC coffers. Lichfield was one of few places to receive the grant and was allocated the second highest amount in the West Midlands. Arnold Ward, leader of the LDC, said, 'This is marvellous news. I have no doubt CCTV will reduce crime tremendously on the streets of Lichfield. It will make ordinary people feel safe on a Friday and Saturday night.' The news of the extra money came at the same time that the St Martin's Property Corporation – the company that was in the process of redeveloping the old Baker's Lane shopping precinct – was planning to put sixteen CCTV cameras in the new Three Spires shopping centre. (*Lichfield Mercury*)

~ April 7th ~

1903: On this day, Lord Roberts, the Commander in Chief of the British Army, visited Lichfield. Roberts, nicknamed 'Bobs' (1832–1914), was a national hero after his leadership in the Second Afghan War and in the recent Boer War. He was still remembered for leading a British army across 300 miles of rough Afghanistani terrain to relieve the city of Kandahar in 1880. He arrived at Lichfield's Trent Valley station and was greeted there by a large crowd. After being entertained by Colonel Swinfen-Broun at Swinfen Hall, he visited the Soldiers' Home at Whittington Barracks. The Soldiers' Home was once the grandstand of Lichfield racecourse until 1895 when the races ceased. (Today the building is the clubhouse of Whittington Golf Course.) Roberts inspected troops of the North Staffordshire Regiment on the parade ground of the barracks and at 2 p.m. arrived in the city's Market Square where a huge crowd, including many of the city's schoolchildren, had gathered to greet him. After some speeches the mayor called for three cheers for 'Bobs' Roberts. (*Lichfield Mercury*, April 10th 1903)

~ April 8th ~

1643: On this day, Prince Rupert arrived in Lichfield in order to recapture the Cathedral Close for the Royalists. He decided to begin this second siege of the cathedral by placing his artillery on a piece of high ground to the north of the fortified walls (to this day the hill is still called Prince Rupert's Mound) and rained cannonballs onto the defenders. He also ordered tunnels to be built under the north-west wall, a feat performed by fifty Staffordshire miners. On April 20th five barrels of gunpowder were placed in the tunnel and ignited. The blast was huge and left a breach in the wall 'wide enough for six men to enter abreast'. The following day the Parliamentarians surrendered and the cathedral and its close were back in Royalist hands. The king's forces were to hold Lichfield for the next three years; Charles I himself spent a night in the Bishop's Palace after the battle of Naseby in 1645. In 1646 Parliament recaptured the cathedral after bombarding it from gun emplacements in Gaia Lane, Dam Street and the back of the George Hotel, the result of which caused the central spire to collapse. (Upton, Chris, *A History of Lichfield*, Phillimore, 2001)

~ April 9th ~

1761: On this day, Erasmus Darwin, Lichfield physician, writer, scientist and founder member of The Lunar Society, became a Fellow of the Royal Society. This allowed him to conduct anatomical dissections in his house in Beacon Street, as the following advert from Aris' *Birmingham Gazette* published on October 3rd shows:

> The body of the malefactor ordered to be executed at Lichfield on Monday the 25th inst. Will be afterwards conveyed to the house of Dr. Darwin, who will begin a Course of Anatomical Lectures, at four o'clock on Tuesday evening and continue them every day as long as the body can be preserved and shall be favoured with the company of any who profess Medicine or Surgery, or who the love of science may induce.

The execution of criminals was a rarity in Lichfield in the eighteenth century but when they did occur Darwin was obviously ready to take advantage. The Murder Act of 1752 had made it legal for the bodies of hanged murderers to be medically dissected, which acted as a further deterrent to murder and also meant there was a supply of bodies for teaching hospitals and for scientists like Darwin. (Uglow, Jenny, *The Lunar Men*, Faber and Faber, 2002)

— APRIL 10TH —

1347: On this day, Edward III and his court were in Lichfield to celebrate the English victory over the French at the Battle of Crécy by holding a jousting tournament during the day and feasting during the evening. In fact, the celebrations lasted for a week as each day the king, accompanied by his knights and ladies, rode from the West Gate of Cathedral Close, over the drawbridge and into the area now known as Beacon Park. There, the lists where the armoured participants of the joust performed were set up, along with an elaborate pavilion and a grandstand for the king and his guests. A large crowd watched the jousting and was also treated to a melee where eleven of the king's knights battled with eleven led by Sir Humphrey Stanley. The Prince of Wales (The Black Prince) was one of the members of the king's side, who were displaying the king's colours of blue and white. Soon afterwards Edward III, who was always interested in the concept of chivalry, inaugurated the Order of the Garter. (*The Times of Lichfield*, The Guild of the St Mary's Centre, 1982)

~ April 11th ~

1612: On this day, Edward Wightman was taken to Lichfield's Market Square to be burnt alive as a heretic. He was a Puritan who publically rejected many Christian doctrines and who declared himself to be a mouthpiece for God. At the final moment he recanted; however, two weeks later, after he had 'blasphemed more audaciously than before', he was taken back to the stake and this time there was no reprieve. (Upton, Chris, *A History of Lichfield*, Phillimore, 2001)

—

1838: It was on this day that the last mail coach ran from Lichfield to London; it was the end of an era. For fifty years Lichfield had been an important stop on the vital coaching routes linking London with Liverpool and Birmingham with Sheffield. But by this year England's biggest towns were linked by railways which bypassed Lichfield. Many of the inns in the city had relied on the custom brought by the regular stagecoach traffic and jobs were also lost in the blacksmith, leather and stabling trades. For the next decade Lichfield remained a backwater and it was only when the city got its own railway station in 1847 that the economy of the area recovered. (Clayton, Howard, *Coaching City*, Dragon Books, 1970)

— April 12th —

1986: On this day, the first broadcast of an episode of the HTV programme *Robin of Sherwood*, set in medieval Lichfield, took place. The episode, entitled Herne's Son (part two), saw Robin Hood (Jason Connery) search for his friend Will Scarlet (Ray Winstone). Scarlet, also known as Scathlock, had been staying at his brother's inn, which 'serves the best ale in Lichfield', and Robin, along with Little John and Friar Tuck, travelled there to persuade him to rejoin the band of outlaws back in Sherwood Forest. Scarlet was reluctant to do so and he and Robin ended up having a fist fight in the street. Meanwhile, the villainous Sir Guy of Gisburne had followed the outlaws to Lichfield in the hope of capturing Robin. He tried to enlist the help of Ambrose, Sheriff of Lichfield, who was only interested in drinking and angering Gisburne by mispronouncing his name. Sheriff Ambrose, when asked to hurry by Sir Guy, replies 'that's not how we do things in Lichfield'. Lichfield was represented by the ale house and the street outside, which appeared to be the market place. (*Robin of Sherwood*, Series 3, Network DVD)

~ April 13th ~

1948: On this day, Lichfield's Lido Cinema showed the film it described in its adverts as 'the most discussed film of today'. *The Birth of a Baby* was shown three times a day at 4 p.m., 6 p.m. and 8 p.m. and only 'patrons of 18 years of age and over' were admitted. Commenting on the film, the *Lichfield Mercury* said that it was 'dignified and delicately produced'. The *Mercury's* reporter informed readers that he had seen the film, along with Lichfield Magistrates, who had decided that the film could be seen by the public. The reporter went on to say that any patron of the Lido expecting 'an entertaining show of a sensual nature' would be disappointed, as the subject had been treated 'reverently, modestly and discreetly'. *The Birth of a Baby* was sponsored by the National Baby Council and was designed to encourage more women to attend ante-natal clinics and to 'bring home to men the duty of greater consideration for their wives during pregnancy.' The *Mercury's* reporter recommended that all 'intelligent and broad-minded' adults should see the film. (*Lichfield Mercury*, April 9th 1948)

~ April 14th ~

1943: On this day, Colonel H.P. Hunter, chief constable of Staffordshire, spoke about the recent outcry there had been about the 'moral danger of young girls running wild in the streets of Lichfield'. Speaking to the council in the Guildhall, Colonel Hunter referred to the recent debate that had taken place when councillors raised concerns about the behaviour of girls and members of the armed forces in the city. Councillors and members of the public, he said, had called for more police officers, including women, to patrol the streets, but this, in his view, was unlikely to happen. The chief constable said that the police force would decrease in the immediate future and, in any case, police officers had limited powers and could only take action if a crime was committed, or about to be committed. Police authorities, he said, 'could not be expected to cater for moral salvage'. Colonel Hunter concluded by saying that 'considering the inadequate resources for entertainment in the City the conduct of the people, on the whole, is good and compares well with other towns'. (*Lichfield Mercury*, April 16th 1943)

~ April 15th ~

1755: On this day, Lichfield's most famous son, Samuel Johnson, published the book for which he is most remembered: *A Dictionary of the English Language.* There had been English dictionaries before Johnson's – some twenty in the previous 150 years – but his dictionary, published in two volumes and containing over 42,000 'carefully constructed' entries, was more comprehensive and authoritative than any previous one. The dictionary took almost nine years to compile and in it Johnson attempted to define the parameters of his native language, doing so with 'a steely wit and remarkable clarity of thought'. For example, he defined lexicographer as: 'A writer of dictionaries; a harmless drudge that busies himself in tracing the original and detailing the significance of words.' The book was not an instant best-seller; its cost of £4 10s (£4.50) represented a considerable amount of money in the eighteenth century and was beyond the reach of most people (by his death in 1784, 6,000 copies had been sold). However, Johnson's masterwork has influenced every English dictionary since produced in the English-speaking world. (Hitchings, Henry, *Dr Johnson's Dictionary*, John Murray Publishers, 2005)

— APRIL 16TH —

1830: On this day, the *Lichfield Mercury* announced that Miss Foote, the famous actress, would be appearing for one night only on stage at the Theatre Royal, Lichfield. Foote, who had regularly appeared at Covent Garden and other London theatres, was appearing in a play called *The Wonder! A Woman Keeps a Secret*, a romantic drama in which she would sing a new song entitled 'The Love Letter'. On the same bill she would also star in a farce called *The Little Jockey* in which she would play the part of Arinette, the little jockey of the title, and would also sing three songs. Foote was one of the most famous actresses of the time and was described as 'fascinating and popular' and 'expressive' and as having an 'abundance of light brown hair'. She was particularly well known for playing Shakespearean heroines such as Juliet and Miranda in *The Tempest* and for her singing and the playing of the harp, guitar and piano. Born around 1797 she retired from acting in 1831 when she married Charles Stanhope, the 4th Earl of Harrington, becoming Maria Stanhope, Countess of Harrington. She died in 1867. (*Lichfield Mercury*)

~ APRIL 17TH ~

1994: On this day, two of the biggest names in snooker entertained a packed Lichfield Civic Hall as they took part in the first Tippers' Snooker Classic. Alex 'Hurricane' Higgins took on John Virgo on a night that also included a demonstration of trick shots and a challenge frame between Higgins and local amateur champion John Hoggarth. Hoggarth had beaten sixty-three others to have the opportunity to play the former world champion and, against all expectations, managed to win 64 to 52 and earn himself a silver trophy. In the main match of the evening Higgins 'brimmed with nervous energy, strutting around the table and banging balls home with deadly accuracy as he chain-smoked and downed cans of his favourite tipple – Guinness'. Virgo was 'stately' and a 'real entertainer' and now ranked only sixty-fourth in the world had begun to make a name for himself as a television star on the popular BBC show *The Big Break*. A number of local businesses had sponsored the various frames in the contest between the two, which produced 'some superbly entertaining snooker', with Virgo eventually winning by four frames to three. (*Lichfield Mercury*, April 21st 1994)

~ April 18th ~

1929: On this day, four people died of gunshots in the village of Shenstone, near Lichfield. At 7 a.m. the postman discovered the body of 34-year-old Henry Sim, a stockman of Pringlefied Cottages, on the roadside outside his home. Lying beside his body was a shotgun. The police were contacted and they found the bodies of Sim's wife Elsie, aged 35, and the couple's 9-year-old son Cyril, both lying in their beds dead from gunshots. The *Mercury* report spared no gruesome detail as it described the walls of both rooms 'bespattered with blood and brains'. The police also discovered the body of Sim's next-door-neighbour Henry James Woodman, aged 35, who had been shot through the back of the head. Sim and Woodman worked together at Shenstone Hall Farm and Sim believed that the other man was 'trying to do him out of a job' and the two had argued on many occasions. Sim left a note before killing Woodman, his wife, son and himself which read: 'I am sorry to do this but I can't die and leave Elsie and Cyril to suffer.' An inquest found that the tragedy was 'caused by insanity'. (*Lichfield Mercury*, April 19th 1929)

~ APRIL 19TH ~

2001: On this day, the *Lichfield Mercury* reported on a major fundraising campaign designed to safeguard the Lichfield and Hatherton canal restoration project. To help with the appeal, David Suchet, television's Hercule Poirot and noted canal enthusiast, spoke to a capacity audience at the Civic Hall. He talked about the urgent need to raise money before the M6 Toll motorway, which was in the process of being constructed, 'slices across the canal's path'. The cash was needed quickly to build a culvert which would take the canal under the route of the motorway because if the work had been delayed until after the road had been built it would have cost ten times as much. David Suchet said he had been excited by the restoration work carried out on the canal during the previous ten years when sections of the canal had been excavated, locks restored and a lift-bridge installed. 'We must not lose our canals,' said the actor, 'they are a national treasure.' The Lichfield and Hatherton canal opened in 1757, but was abandoned in the 1950s when much of it was filled in. (*Lichfield Mercury*)

~ APRIL 20TH ~

1892: This day saw the official opening of Lichfield Methodist Church in Tamworth Street, which had been designed in the Gothic ornamental style and built by E. Williams of Tamworth. The foundation stones had been laid in August 1891 by the Mayor of Lichfield (Councillor S. Haynes) and the stone-laying ceremony had been followed by a public tea in the Guildhall, the tickets for which cost 6*d* each. When the church building was having some repairs done in 2004, a time-capsule, which had been buried under one of the foundation stones, was discovered. Inside the tightly sealed Victorian bottle were found a number of local newspapers dated August 7th 1891, a penny, halfpenny and farthing dated 1891, a drawing of the building then under construction and a Preaching Plan for the Tamworth and Lichfield Circuit showing times of services and preachers for the year in question. The church and its hall, which had been renovated and developed in the 1990s and 2000s, is today the scene of many community activities including children's holiday clubs, organisations for various age groups, pastoral visitors and a coffee shop. (*Lichfield Methodist Church 1892–1992 Centenary History*; *The Story of Lichfield Methodist Church*, both booklets published by Lichfield Methodist Church)

~ April 21st ~

1910: On this day, a man calling himself Samuel Eccleston was found dead in a police cell, apparently having committed suicide. The man, who had said he was aged 50, was a tailor from Wales and had been arrested the previous day after obtaining food and lodging at Shaw's Refreshment Rooms in Bird Street, Lichfield, and then presenting the owner with a cheque which turned out to be worthless. He was arrested, taken to the police station and placed in a cell. On checking the cell at 10.45 a.m. the following morning, Detective Constable Eley found Eccleston lying face down in a pool of blood having apparently cut his own throat – DC Eley said that his head was almost severed from his body. Eley went on to say that the incident was extremely strange, as the man had eaten a hearty breakfast at 8.45 a.m. and 'seemed quite cheerful at the time'. The coroner's inquest, held at the Britannia Inn in Stowe Street, returned a verdict of suicide. (*Lichfield Mercury*, November 29th 1910)

~ APRIL 22ND ~

1890: This day saw the death of Charles Simpson, 'one of Lichfield's legendary characters'. Simpson, who was born in 1800, succeeded his father and grandfather as Lichfield's town clerk and city coroner in 1825. In 1880 the local authority had tried to retire him but he had refused to go. When he was eventually dismissed from his post he took with him the City Seal and refused to hand it back, thus making it impossible for the City Corporation to carry out its official business until a new seal could be made. An obituary published in the *Lichfield Mercury* pronounced him to be 'the greatest personality in the contemporary life of the nineteenth century in the City of Lichfield'. In the 1874 General Election he stood for the Liberal Party in the Lichfield constituency, but was defeated by the Tory candidate, Colonel Dyott. Simpson's funeral of April 26th 1890 was attended by many dignitaries and local people, with some city centre businesses closing for the day as a mark of respect. He was buried in St Michael's churchyard and was survived by four of his ten children. (*Lichfield Mercury*, May 2nd 1890; Clayton, Howard, *Cathedral City*, Abbotsford Publishing, 1981)

– April 23rd –

1910: This day saw an aeroplane land in the Lichfield area and a great crowd gathered to see what for many of them would have been their first sight of a flying machine. The Farman plane, flown by Claude Grahame-White, was taking part in the Manchester to London air race when a faulty inlet valve forced it to land in a farmer's field. The pilot, while waiting for his plane to be fixed, drove into Lichfield and had lunch at the George Hotel before returning to attempt a take-off. The farmer wasted no time in charging people admission to see Grahame-White try to take off, which, as it turned out, proved impossible due to 'heavy rain and boisterous winds'. Eventually the flimsy aircraft was 'completely capsized by a strong gust of wind' and was subsequently dismantled, put on lorries and taken to Trent Valley Station where it was put on a flatbed truck, attached to a train and sent back to London. The London to Manchester air race was one of the first of its kind and the *Daily Mail* offered a £10,000 prize for the first to complete the journey. (*Lichfield Mercury*, April 29th 1910)

~ APRIL 24TH ~

1896: On this day, the Lichfield Amateur Operatic Society started, forerunner of the present-day society. The first production was *Sherwood's Queen*, a musical based on the Robin Hood stories, performed at St James's Hall in Bore Street. The lead female role of Maid Marian was played by Miss Edith Welling, who 'captivated the audiences with her charming performance and delightful voice'. The production played to full houses, the best seats costing 3*s* 6*d* (18p), and the show was 'pronounced a resounding success'. The society became particularly well known for its annual presentations of Gilbert and Sullivan comic operas. In 1912, however, disaster struck when St James's Hall was transformed into a cinema and the society, left without a venue, was forced to close down. It was revived in 1920 as the Lichfield Music Society but this organisation was also suspended at the outbreak of war in 1939. However, in 1943 the society was re-established, partly as an attempt to provide entertainment for the public and raise morale in Lichfield. Its first production was *Merrie England* and since then the society has thrived up to the present day. (Clayton, Howard and Simmons, Kathleen, *Fifty Years On Stage*, Abbotsford Publishing, 1992)

~ April 25th ~

1941: This day saw the opening of Lichfield's Civic Cafe, the city's response to the government's wartime Ministry of Food's call for local authorities to provide feeding centres which served a daily hot meal for all men, women and children. It was hoped that such centres would help eliminate waste of time, food and fuel and would provide a welcome change from the privations of food rationing, thus boosting people's morale. The cafe was based at the Methodist hall in Tamworth Street and served hot meals every day between 12 noon and 2 p.m. Meals consisted of meat and two vegetables and a pudding for 8*d* (3p), with tea, coffee and soup costing extra. The Mayor of Lichfield, Councillor C.H. Averill, opened the cafe and thanked the Methodist church for providing the hall and furniture rent free. After the opening ceremony the civic party were served with soup, roast beef, Yorkshire pudding, potatoes and carrots, and boiled jam pudding and coffee, all for 10*d* (4p). In its first year the Civic Cafe would go on to serve a staggering 79,190 meals to the Lichfield public. (*Lichfield Mercury*, May 2nd 1941)

~ April 26th ~

1912: On this day, the *Lichfield Mercury* reported on the memorial services that had been held in the district to mark the loss of life that had taken place in the *Titanic* disaster a few days earlier. At Lichfield Cathedral prayers were said for the victims and the congregation sang the hymn 'For Those in Peril on the Sea'. At St Mary's church special prayers from the burial service were read and the preacher informed the congregation that out of 2,300 souls on board *Titanic* only 700 were saved and that the words of the captain, 'Be British', showed how bravely a man could die. At St Michael's church the rector stated that the sinking of the ship was 'without parallel in the annals of the shipping world' and that even such 'a great ship built almost regardless of cost' could do nothing against the 'irresistible forces of nature'. Services 'with appropriate hymns' were also held at St Chad's, the Congregational church, the Wesleyan church in Tamworth Street, as well as the churches at Armitage, Brownhills, Gentleshaw, Shenstone and Wall, where 'touching references were made to the maritime disaster'. (*Lichfield Mercury*)

~ April 27th ~

1756: On this day, legal documents show that Elizabeth Aston of Stowe House gave a sum of money to nearby St Chad's church for the construction of a set of pews for herself, her tenants and servants. Stowe House had been built by Miss Aston, along with two other properties on Stowe Hill, which gave wonderful views over Stowe Pool to the cathedral. Elizabeth and her sister Jane Gastrel were paid regular visits by Samuel Johnson, who loved to walk from the city to the small hamlet of Stowe about fifteen minutes away to spend time with the two ladies. The imposing building of Stowe House has been the home of a number of notable Lichfield residents: Thomas Day and Richard Edgeworth, members of Darwin's Lunar Society, both rented the house, and the prominent Lichfield banker Richard Greene also lived there with his family. However, in 1856 Greene was declared bankrupt and the house and his property were sold by auction. In the twentieth century the house was owned by the Birmingham Regional Hospital Board and was used as a training centre. The present owners, ILM, are unfortunately not keen on members of the public visiting the splendid house. (Lichfield Records Office, document D15/11/14/90-96)

1643: On this day, King Charles I sent a letter to his nephew Prince Rupert, who was the commander of the Royalist army involved in the siege of Lichfield's Cathedral Close during the English Civil War. Rupert had recaptured the cathedral on April 21st when the Parliamentary forces, which had originally captured the Close in the previous month, surrendered. In the letter the king thanked Rupert for his 'constant and faithful service' in the war, but asked him not to use any cruelty towards the people of Lichfield. Charles expressed his wish that soon 'a divine opportunity' would arise that would end the fighting which was 'the universal distraction of our Kingdom'. Rupert was urged by the king to show the people of Lichfield mercy and 'show them a king tender of the welfare of his subjects'. He also asked him, when dealing with the prisoners, to guard against the 'spilling or shedding of innocent blood' and to allow those who wished to leave the city to be able to do so with 'bagge and baggage' provided they do not offer any 'violence against the said town of Lichfield'. (*Lichfield Mercury*, July 24th 1908)

APRIL 29TH

1865: On this day, a meeting organised by the Emancipation Society was held in St James's Hall in Lichfield for the purpose of 'expressing detestation' at the assassination of Abraham Lincoln, which had recently taken place in the United States. The murder of the American president had 'filled Europe, as well as America, with horror'. The hall in Bore Street was 'crowded in every part' and was also 'draped in black'; American flags were hung in the upper gallery and a 'scutcheon emblazoned with the letter L' hung beneath. The stewards that showed the audience to their seats were 'hung with funeral ribbons' and many of 'the assembly' wore black crêpe hatbands and 'other insignia of mourning'. The meeting was attended by a number of MPs, who were also members of the Emancipation Society which had been formed to oppose the continuance of slavery. One of the speakers at the Lichfield meeting, W.E Foster MP, said that Lincoln had understood that God had wanted 'the offence of slavery to end and that if any good should come of this foul crime it would be to seal the speedy and irrevocable doom of slavery'. (*Lichfield Advertiser*, May 5th 1865)

~ April 30th ~

1963: On this day, Lichfield's MP Julian Snow spoke out in the House of Commons against the government's plan for the nation's railways. The plan, based on a report by Dr Richard Beeching, saw the closure of many stations and hundreds of miles of railway lines. Mr Snow criticised the Beeching Plan, declaring that 'the country can survive only if we have a properly integrated transport system'. He went on to say that the plan would have a great impact on the West Midlands, a region where the population was rapidly expanding, and would lead to thousands of train passengers having to use the roads instead. The only thing to do with the Beeching Plan was, he said, 'to take it away and cut its throat'. However, the Beeching Report was implemented by the government and did, indeed, have a great impact. Over 2,000 stations and 5,000 miles of line were closed and to this day Beeching's name is associated with the wholesale closure of railways. (*Lichfield Mercury*, May 3rd 1963)

1994: This day saw the first performance of the *Lichfield Mysteries*. The idea of performing a cycle of medieval plays was initially suggested at the beginning of the 1990s and it quickly grew into a community project involving hundreds of people and local organisations, such as schools, drama groups, societies and churches. The play cycle is performed every three years, free of charge, over the May Bank Holiday weekend at various outdoor venues across Lichfield, including the historic Market Square. The finale takes place in Lichfield Cathedral with the spectacular presentation of Doomsday. The plays, which involve twenty-seven biblical stories each produced by a different local group, were first put together by Dr Robert Leach. The scripts include 'fragments of Lichfield's medieval plays as well as some from other cycles'. Over 600 people take part and the plays are witnessed by thousands of spectators. The tradition of mystery plays goes back to the Middle Ages 'when each play was adopted by one of the Guilds of merchants who would vie with each other to produce the best performance'. (www.lichfieldmysteries. co.uk/history.pl)

– MAY 2ND –

1919: On this day, the *Lichfield Mercury* reported the tragic death of the son of Lord and Lady Charnwood of Stowe House. The Hon. Christopher Benson, aged 8, was riding his horse in Curborough with his sister Antonia when, on turning into the entrance to a meadow belonging to the farm of John Heathcote, his horse suddenly bolted, throwing the boy onto his head. Antonia carried her unconscious brother to the farmhouse where he was looked after by the farmer's wife, while she galloped off to find a doctor. The boy later died at the farm, as it was considered too dangerous to move him, and his mother, Lady Charnwood, was with him at the end. Christopher had just completed his first term at Lichfield High School and 'had brain power far above the average'. He was the great-grandson of the Right Hon. A.J. Mundella, Minister for Education in the Government of Gladstone and MP for Sheffield for many years. An inquest held later at Stowe House found that the cause of death was severe concussion and brain haemorrhage caused by the fall; a verdict of accidental death was reached. (*Lichfield Mercury*)

~ MAY 3RD ~

1991: By this day, the Lichfield–Redditch Cross City Railway electrification project was well under way. The work would cost £64.5 million and would include the installation of masts and wiring, new signalling and eighteen new trains. The new class 323 trains, which would run on the route, would, British Rail believed, cut journey times and provide a cleaner and more reliable service for passengers. The main contractor for the project was Pirelli Construction and the work consisted of not only erecting the overhead masts but also, in some places along the 33-mile line, the lowering of track to provide clearance for the overhead wires beneath twenty-five bridges. All of the work was done at night and on Sundays, with workers completing long shifts and a total of seventy-two hours each week. The work went ahead in all weathers, stopping only for deep snow and high winds, which made ladder work dangerous. Safety standards were very high, with passing trains and 25,000-volt cables being only two of the hazards involved in the work. (*Lichfield Mercury*, May 3rd 1991)

~ MAY 4TH ~

1979: On this day, John Heddle, the Conservative Party candidate, was elected as MP for the Constituency of Lichfield and Tamworth in the General Election. He gained 41,454 votes, as opposed to Labour's sitting MPs Bruce Grocott's 33,006 and Liberal Philip Rule's 7,408. In the national election the Conservatives achieved victory over James Callaghan's Labour Party, with a majority of forty-three seats, and, as a result, Margaret Thatcher became Britain's first female prime minister. In 1983 the constituency, now called Mid-Staffordshire, was again won by Heddle, who increased his majority as part of the Conservative landslide of that year. He held the seat again in 1987. In December 1989 Heddle was found dead in his car near a chalk pit close to Canterbury, having committed suicide. It was revealed that he had suffered from depression for a number of years and his businesses had gone into debt. On March 22nd 1990 a by-election took place and Labour's Sylvia Heal won the seat, with Conservative candidate Charles Prior in second place. (*Lichfield Mercury*)

~ MAY 5TH ~

1854: On this day, shops closed and flags flew at half-mast, as the funeral of Henry William Paget took place in Lichfield. Paget, the 1st Marquess of Anglesey and Earl of Uxbridge, had been the Duke of Wellington's second-in-command at the Battle of Waterloo in 1815, where he was badly wounded and lost his right leg, causing him to be known thereafter as 'One-leg Paget'. The funeral carriage was transported by train to Lichfield's Trent Valley station and from there the hearse, pulled by six black horses decorated in black ostrich feathers, processed through the streets of Lichfield to the George Hotel. There, the coffin was displayed on a catafalque and, during the evening, many local people filed past to pay their respects. The next day the coffin was taken to the cathedral, led by a military band that played the 'Funeral March' along streets lined with troops. Following a solemn service the coffin was placed in the Paget family vault in the cathedral. Paget's amputated right leg, which had been buried at Waterloo beneath a monument, was later disinterred and became a tourist attraction in Brussels. (Clayton, Howard, *Cathedral City*, Abbotsford Publishing, 1981)

~ MAY 6TH ~

1977: On this day, the plan to build a massive housing and industrial development in the Boley Park area of Lichfield was given the final go-ahead. The 'mini-town' scheme was to be phased in over ten years and, it was hoped, would eventually provide homes for 6,000 people and create 1,500 jobs, particularly in the depressed building trade. A consortium formed by two building firms – Wetenhall Cooper from Lichfield and Ash Homes of Sutton Coldfield – were to begin work on the first 200 houses, the first-phase of the project, which would take eighteen months to complete. A spokesman for the consortium said, 'We are hoping to get a good mix with some homes around the £28,000 mark and others as low as about £13,000 to £14,000.' Development was limited to 200 houses per year so as 'to give the new population time to settle in'. Local councillors, Church leaders and Lichfield's MP, Bruce Grocott, all sought assurances that roads, shops, schools, parks and health facilities would keep pace with the new housing. (*Lichfield Mercury*, May 6th 1977)

~ MAY 7TH ~

1880: On this day, the *Lichfield Mercury* carried a report of a performance given by Dr Gough, the 'noted conjuror', at the George Hotel in Lichfield. Dr Gough presented a 'dark seance' in one of the sitting rooms of the hotel to a number of Lichfield's leading residents in a private performance which was designed to illustrate how spiritualists used various tricks to convince people that they were in touch with the spirit world. One of the illusions Dr Gough performed was to make a number of tambourines appear to float in the air and some bells begin to ring of their own accord. In another trick, Dr Gough was able to speedily don an overcoat in complete darkness while tightly bound to a chair by ropes. He was then able to release himself from his bonds 'almost instantly' at the end of a performance the *Mercury* described as 'wonderful and extraordinary'. Dr Gough went on to appear in public performances at the Corn Exchange every evening in the following week. *(Lichfield Mercury)*

~ MAY 8TH ~

1840: On this day, Lichfield Union Workhouse opened on land opposite St Michael's church. Inmates would rise at 5.45 a.m. and work from 7 a.m. until 12 noon, when they would have a break of one hour before starting work again at 1 p.m. and continuing until 6 p.m. Bedtime was at 8 p.m. Work for men consisted of picking oakum and stone-breaking, while the women were employed in cleaning or sewing. All inmates wore a uniform of grey cloth. The workhouse diet was generally created from the cheapest ingredients: breakfast and supper was usually gruel (a watery porridge) and lunch usually consisted of cheap cuts of meat and potatoes. Toilet and washing facilities were extremely spartan for both sexes. From the 1870s hospital wards were added to the site and gradually the main purpose of the building began to change. By the outbreak of the Second World War there were over 200 patients being cared for and in 1948 the workhouse officially became St Michael's Hospital. Today, the Victorian workhouse, now a listed building, houses mental health services and adjoins the Samuel Johnson Community Hospital, which was opened in 2007. (Hutchinson, Mary, Coot, Ingrid and Sadowski, Anna, *This Won't Hurt: A History of the Hospitals of Lichfield*, The Lichfield Hospitals History Group, 2010)

– MAY 9TH –

1791: On this day, in a letter to his friend George Gray, Erasmus Darwin – writer, scientist and inventor – gave details of a speaking machine he had built some years earlier. He had become interested in how words were formed by sound and had had discussions with the American politician and scientist Benjamin Franklin about the possibility of making a machine that could talk. Darwin, in his book *The Temple of Nature*, described how he had made the machine. He built a head containing a wooden mouth with lips of leather and a valve at the back to represent nostrils, which could be opened or closed by fingers. A silk ribbon was stretched between two pieces of wood, which, when blown on, created a sound like the human voice. The machine could produce the sounds of p, b, m and a and managed to 'deceive all who heard it unseen' when it pronounced words like mama, papa, map and pam. Darwin never finished the machine, but he did imagine that one day similar machines would be able to sing or recite the Lord's Prayer. (Uglow, Jenny, *The Lunar Men*, Faber and Faber, 2002)

— MAY 10TH —

1905: On this day, Richard Wilson, a signalman working for the London and North Western Railway Company at Lichfield's Trent Valley station, was killed when he was hit by an express train. Wilson was 52 years old and had been employed as a signalman for twenty-six years. According to witnesses he had been oiling a set of points and failed to notice the express train approaching. Despite a number of people on the platform 90yd away who shouted at him to move out of the way, Wilson, who had hearing problems, only turned at the very last second – too late for him to jump out of the path of the train. The unfortunate man was found lying on the track and managed 'one or two gasps and then expired'. The body was later identified by the dead man's wife, Jane, and an inquest held later at the Trent Valley Inn pronounced a verdict of accidental death. Deputy Coroner Mr S.W. Morgan said that the deafness from which Wilson suffered was a contributory factor to his death. (*Lichfield Mercury*, May 19th 1905)

- May 11th -

1945: On this day, the *Lichfield Mercury* reported on the week of celebrations in Lichfield that had followed the announcement of victory in Europe and the defeat of Germany in the Second World War. The VE celebrations started with a proclamation made by the mayor, Councillor T. Moseley, to a large crowd in the Market Square, with the buildings around it soon to be decorated with flags and bunting. Pubs remained open until 11 p.m., a 'Victory Ball' was held in the Guildhall, a bonfire blazed in the recreation grounds and the cathedral was lit up 'by electricity'. It was considered important to give the children of Lichfield a special treat, so parties were held for them at various locations around the city, including Ponesfields, where about 235 children were present, and at the Railway Tavern, where the entertainment was provided by American Slim Malway. Military bands were popular during the week with both the South Staffordshire Regimental band and the band of the US 10th Reinforcement Depot, which was based at Whittington Barracks, parading around the streets of the city. (*Lichfield Mercury*)

– MAY 12TH –

1937: On this day, the people of Lichfield celebrated the coronation of King George VI and, in the words of the *Lichfield Mercury*, 'there was not the slightest doubt as to their loyalty and patriotism'. The day started with the firing of signal rockets and the ringing out of church and cathedral bells. The Lichfield City Military Band played the National Anthem in various parts of the city and the schoolchildren of the city were assembled in the Market Square to 'salute' the mayor and councillors as they made their way in procession to the cathedral for a special coronation service. The children were later treated to a free film show at the Regal cinema, where Mickey Mouse cartoons soon 'had the youngsters in roars of laughter'. Ex-servicemen were given lunch at the Bridge Tavern in St John Street, there was a public luncheon held at the George Inn and an 'old folks' tea at Minster Hall in Dam Street, where entertainment was provided by 'Jimmy Walters and his Merry Uns'. During the afternoon, sports events were held in the recreation grounds and in the evening an open-air concert took place and most public buildings were illuminated. (*Lichfield Mercury*, May 14th 1937)

~ MAY 13TH ~

1865: On this day, an inquest was held into the death of a private in the Number 2 Company of the Staffordshire Militia Regiment which had been training in Lichfield. The dead man, 32-year-old James Richards, had got drunk in Lichfield and decided to walk to Wolverhampton. He got a lift in a horse and cart, but at Pipe Hill 'something occurred' which resulted in a woman, Mrs Wright, being thrown from the cart and Richards being found unconscious. He was taken to the Three Tuns Inn (now Panache Indian restaurant) where he woke up and demanded some ale and to fight 'the best man in the house'. The landlord, Mr Biddle, refused to let him in the inn. The next morning Mr Biddle found Private Richards lying on the ground near the stables. He was taken inside and given some brandy and covered in blankets before being tended by the regimental surgeon, Mr Hichens, who happened to be passing. Richards, however, died soon afterwards and the inquest, held at the Three Tuns, found that he had died 'in a natural way after being intoxicated and remaining outside for the whole night'. (*Lichfield Advertiser*, May 13th 1865)

~ May 14th ~

1926: On this day, the *Lichfield Mercury* reported on the end of the General Strike and how Lichfield had been affected by the nationwide stoppage. Ordinary life in Lichfield, reported the paper, as with everywhere else in the country, had been 'seriously disturbed' by the strike. Railway and bus services had been non-existent, although road traffic was heavier than normal. A number of employees at R. Bridgeman and Sons, a building and restoration firm, had gone on strike, but most had stayed at work, and 25 per cent of workers at builders J.R. Deacon had also gone on strike. Food supplies in Lichfield and district had been described as satisfactory during the strike, A.H. Perrins had been appointed food controller for the city. Coal rationing was in force and permits to enable people to collect a week's worth of coal had been available at the Guildhall. The colliery villages of Chasetown and Chase Terrace were described as 'quiet and peaceful' – collieries had been at a complete standstill but, for the most part, older miners had occupied themselves with gardening, while the younger men had played football, cricket or bowls. *(Lichfield Mercury)*

– MAY 15TH –

1990: On this day, Staffordshire education chiefs issued a statement banning beef products from county school lunch menus, due to the fears about BSE, or 'mad cow' disease. Councillor Roger Wright, Chair of Staffordshire Education Committee, said, 'To avoid any possibility of risk to our children, the authority has decided to take beef sausage, beefburgers and minced beef dishes off the school menus. Sliced beef will stay and more fish, cheese, pork and chicken dishes are available.' Local butchers had reported no drop off in beef sales, although some expressed concern that the constant media coverage of the BSE scare could lead to local shoppers refusing to buy beef products in the future. The assistant manager at Walter Smith's in Market Street, Nigel Higham, said, 'We have not found any difficulties selling beef at all, but in a few weeks people might start to think about the risks more.' Local farmers also expressed some concern. Tony Ridgeway of Winterton's cattle auction centre was certain that the issue had been blown out of proportion by the media and 'there was nothing to suggest that there was anything wrong with British beef'. (*Lichfield Mercury*, May 18th 1990)

− MAY 16TH −

2001: This day marked the official opening of the National Memorial Arboretum on a site near the village of Alrewas, 5 miles from Lichfield. The idea to have a living memorial to the servicemen and women was conceived in 1988 and backed by Lichfield District Council and the British Legion. Tree planting started on the 150-acre site in 1997 and the area now contains 50,000 trees, with more being planted each year. It is dominated by the impressive Armed Services Memorial where, on the curved walls, the names of all the Service and Merchant Navy personnel killed on active service since the end of the Second World War are written. A poignant tableau of statues entitled 'The Pity of War' depicts a wounded soldier being carried away by his colleagues while an anxious mother and child look on. Other memorials on the site include one dedicated to the Royal National Lifeboat Institute and a section of the infamous Burma Railway, on which many allied soldiers lost their lives. (Childs, David, *Growing Remembrance: The Story of the National Memorial Arboretum*, Pen & Sword Military, 2008)

~ MAY 17TH ~

1957: On this day, the *Lichfield Mercury* reported on the burgeoning career of 'Lichfield Lad' Greville Starkey, who was in the process of making his name in the horse-racing world. The son of Mr and Mrs Starkey of 79 Weston Road, Greville's most outstanding success so far came when he 'cleverly' rode the favourite, Orinthia, at Kempton Park in the Great Jubilee Handicap. Earlier that week he had ridden the winner of the Duke of York stakes, Hiseod. Greville's father said that from an early age his son's ambition was to become a jockey and even before he left school he used to work at the stables of R. Hollinshead at Upper Longdon every weekend. When he left school he obtained an apprenticeship with another well-known trainer, Mr Thompson Jones, and to date had ridden eighteen winners for the stable. His father was proud to have the trophy that was presented to Greville by the legendary jockey Sir Gordon Richards. Greville went on to become one of the country's top jockeys. In a career that lasted thirty-three years, he won 1,989 races on the flat, including the Derby in 1978 on the horse Shirley Heights. (*Lichfield Mercury*)

– MAY 18TH –

1900: This day saw great rejoicing in the streets of Lichfield as the news was announced of the relief of Mafeking, a town in South Africa, during the Boer War where a British force of about 2,000 under the command of Colonel Baden-Powell had been besieged by the Boers for 217 days. Powell's use of a cadet force of boys aged 12 to 15 to carry messages led, after the war, to the establishment of the Scouting movement. The rescue, or relief, took place on May 17th and was carried out by a British army commanded by Lord Roberts. As soon as the news was announced in Lichfield at about 10 p.m., despite the lateness of the hour, church bells rang and people marched in the streets waving flags, banging drums and singing patriotic songs such as 'The Soldiers of the Queen' and 'Rule Britannia'. During the next day an official procession led by a military band took place and Lichfield folk decorated their homes and businesses with flags, red, white and blue bunting and portraits of Baden-Powell and Roberts, the heroes of the hour. (*Lichfield Mercury*, May 25th 1900)

– MAY 19TH

1983: On this day, a major investigation was launched after workers uncovered a fifteenth- or sixteenth-century building beneath modern shop fronts in Lichfield's Sandford Street. The discovery was made after builders had been brought in to do a £300 repair to plaster work at Farmers butcher's shop. As the workmen chipped away the plaster they found extremely old wooden beams that had been covered up. Experts were brought in and they ascertained that the first floor of the building contained ancient timbers and original horse-hair and dung plasterwork. They believed that the building could even be older than Bore Street's Tudor cafe. Local historian Howard Clayton started his own investigation and turned up a drawing of the building which dated back to 1817. Clayton also found evidence that the house belonged to the vicar's choral in 1750 when the building was leased to a butcher called John Startin. It was hoped that following an inspection by Staffordshire County Council the site would become a Grade II listed building and grants would become available for restoration. (*Lichfield Mercury*, May 20th 1983)

- MAY 20TH

1940: On this day, the annual Greenhill Bower, held in Lichfield for 800 years, was abandoned at the last minute due to the worsening international situation. Germany had invaded the Netherlands and Belgium, leading to the decision to cancel the Whit Monday public holiday by the government as the war situation became more serious. However, the ancient court of Arraye, which first began in 1285, did go ahead in the Guildhall, albeit in a rather subdued manner. The council had planned to hold 'a modified Bower Day', with a number of traditional activities such as 'Punch and Judy' shows and a baby show to take place, but abandoned its plans as the developments in Europe seemed to bring German air raids closer. The council called on more Lichfield people to take in evacuated children from Birmingham and residents were warned about the possibility of invasion from the air, as more Local Defence Force volunteers were requested to help guard against the prospect of enemy parachutists landing and causing damage to roads, railways, bridges and communications. (*Lichfield Mercury*, May 24th 1940)

~ May 21st ~

1941: On this day, mother of five Anna Kate Gould, aged 30, was shot and killed at a house in Gresley Row, Lichfield, in the early hours of the morning. Her husband, Lieutenant Albert Edward Gould of the South Wales Borderers Regiment, was arrested and charged with her murder. The couple had been married for thirteen years and had five children aged between 5 and 12. Mrs Gould was at the home of her mother when she was shot four times in the chest. She was taken to the Victoria Hospital but died soon afterwards. Lieutenant Gould, who had served in Norway and Ireland, was on leave when the shooting took place and had discovered a letter which seemed to suggest that his wife was having an affair with another man. Gould later saw his wife with the man, Archibald Keddie, in the Robin Hood pub together. When he was arrested Gould told the police 'I did it' and 'all I want to do is swing'. At his trial, held in July, Gould was acquitted of murder but found guilty of manslaughter and sentenced to eighteen months' hard labour. (*Lichfield Mercury*, May 23rd 1941)

~ MAY 22ND ~

1966: On this day, a memorial service took place at the Methodist church in Tamworth Street for Lichfield's mayor, Frank Halfpenny, who died with two months of his office left to serve. He had first been elected to Lichfield Council in 1937, had served as sheriff and was the first Labour mayor of the city. Born in Stoke-on-Trent, Halfpenny saw service in the First World War with the Staffordshire Yeomanry and, following the war, settled in Lichfield where he started his own business. A Methodist preacher, he also became a Justice of the Peace in 1945 and was the first Chairman of Governors at Netherstowe School. He presented the hall in George Lane, now called the Frank Halfpenny Hall, to the local Labour Party to use as its headquarters. Halfpenny's funeral took place at St Mary's, as the Methodist church was not considered large enough for all those who wanted to attend and pay their respects. The funeral was conducted by Rev. Turner, who had been appointed as the mayor's chaplain and who reminded everyone of the service Frank Halfpenny had given to the city, concluding by saying, 'Thank God for Frank Halfpenny.' (*Lichfield Mercury*, May 27th 1966)

~ MAY 23RD ~

1617: On this day, Elias Ashmole, the famous antiquarian and scientist, was born in Breadmarket Street. He spent the first sixteen years of his life in Lichfield, where he attended the grammar school and was also a chorister at the cathedral. He moved to London in 1633 to train as a solicitor, but remained a benefactor to the city of his birth. The Oxford museum which bears his name was founded in 1682 and was the first public museum in Britain, and arguably in Europe, its original curator being Dr Robert Plot. The Ashmolean's collection was mainly drawn from a bequest made by Ashmole's friend John Tradescant, although, as a great acquisitor, he added to the collection throughout the rest of his life. Although Ashmole gave silver plates, bowls and other gifts to the Lichfield City Corporation he was also not averse to stealing some of the items that took his fancy while conducting his researches in the cathedral, a number of manuscripts making their way into his study and later into the Ashmolean. A founder member of the Royal Society, Ashmole died in 1692, bequeathing his collection to the Ashmolean. (Upton, Chris, *A History of Lichfield*, Phillimore, 2001)

~ MAY 24TH ~

1932: On this day, the foundation stone of Lichfield's new hospital was laid by Colonel Swinfen-Broun. On a fine and sunny day a large crowd turned out to watch the laying of the stone at the site of the new Victoria Hospital on the Friary Road estate. A canopy and platform adorned with floral decorations was set up for the VIP guests and the Lichfield City Band, which had marched to the site, provided a musical accompaniment to the stone-laying ceremony. Mrs Swinfen-Broun should have performed the laying of the foundation stone but was prevented in doing so due to illness. The stone bore the coats of arms of the City of Lichfield and the Swinfen-Broun family, who were great benefactors to the city. The inscription on the stone read: 'This foundation stone was laid by Mrs Swinfen-Broun of Swinfen Hall, Lichfield, on Empire Day, 1932.' The new hospital eventually cost £23,000 to build – a fund had been set up to pay for it as long ago as 1920. By 1932 only £14,500 had been raised and so a bank loan for the rest was arranged by the council. (*Lichfield Mercury*, May 27th 1932)

1882: On this day, two Lichfield people were given 'heavy fines' for having in their possession diseased meat which they had tried to sell for human consumption. Sarah Farmer, a widow of Bakers Lane, and Thomas Farmer, her nephew, were found guilty of having 575lb of beef, 56lb of mutton and 65lb of veal on their premises, all of which was declared unfit for human food under the conditions set out in the Public Health Act of 1865. The two had kept a slaughterhouse at the rear of their house and were accused by expert witnesses of killing the animals 'cruelly and inhumanely'. The carcasses, which were hanging up, were found to be in bad condition and smelling badly. The two were each fined £14 4s 6d (£14.23) or, if not being in a position to pay the fines, they would receive two months' hard labour. The meat was seized and destroyed. The chief magistrate, Mr Gordon, said that he had gone to see the condemned meat himself, describing it as 'a more disgusting sight I never saw in my life'. (*Lichfield Mercury*, May 26th 1882)

– MAY 26TH –

1771: By this day, Benjamin Franklin – scientist, writer and politician – had paid a visit to Lichfield. Franklin was friends with Erasmus Darwin, a like-minded man and fellow scientist, who he had first met in 1758. The two men had subsequently exchanged many letters and Franklin's experiments with electricity and lightning greatly influenced Darwin and the other members of The Lunar Society, a loose group of writers, scientists and industrialists. Franklin stayed with Darwin at his Lichfield house for two days and the two discussed various theories of phonetics, mechanical methods of producing sounds and the possibility of building a machine that could talk, something that Darwin later attempted. Franklin was also introduced to Lichfield eccentric Thomas Day of Stowe House, a man who, he later wrote, he held 'in much esteem'. Franklin was born in Boston, Massachusetts, in 1706 and eventually became one of the chief architects of the United States of America and was actively involved in the drawing up of the American Declaration of Independence in 1776. (Uglow, Jenny, *The Lunar Men*, Faber and Faber, 2002)

~ MAY 27TH ~

1898: On this day, the *Lichfield Mercury* carried an advert for Mr J. Gray's dental surgery, which was based at Dr Johnson's birthplace in the Market Square. Mr Gray, a dental surgeon, 'late of St Bartholomew's Hospital', advertised a number of services including 'extractions, repairs and stoppings' at the premises, which was open every Monday and Friday. Specialties were 'American dentistry' as well as 'artificial teeth, painlessly fitted by atmospheric suction'. A complete set of false teeth could be had for 1 guinea (£1.05) and a single artificial tooth cost 2s 6d (13p). The advert carried a recommendation from a Dr Taylor, stating, 'His reasonable charges should attract to him all classes'. The house, where Samuel Johnson was born in 1709, had been used for a number of businesses over the years. Originally his father's bookshop, where Johnson had spent the first twenty-seven years of his life, the building was bought for the city by John Gilbert in 1900 and opened the following year as a museum. Today it is a Grade I listed building and houses the Johnson Birthplace Museum and Bookshop. (*Lichfield Mercury*)

~ MAY 28TH ~

1770: By this day, Thomas Day, the writer, poet and member of The Lunar Society, was living in Stowe House in Lichfield. Day was a follower of the philosopher Rousseau and believed that with the correct sort of education anyone could be raised to perfection. Day conceived an experiment to attempt to 'create' the perfect wife. He adopted two girls, one 12 and the other 13, from orphanages in Shrewsbury and London and took them to Avignon in France where, he believed, they would be safe from the influence of others. Unfortunately the two girls, Sabrina and Lucretia, first caught smallpox and then took to squabbling between themselves. Returning to Britain he gave up on Lucretia, who he considered was either 'stubborn or stupid', apprenticing her to a milliner in London. In Lichfield, Day decided that Sabrina needed to develop a more stoical attitude to life and tried to accomplish this by firing pistols (without bullets) at her and dropping hot wax on her neck – he was disappointed when she screamed. Eventually he decided to drop the experiment and sent Sabrina off to boarding school. She later married John Bicknell, one of Day's friends. (Uglow, Jenny, *The Lunar Men*, Faber and Faber, 2002)

— MAY 29TH —

1884: On this day, a special service, with the Archbishop of Canterbury in attendance, was held to mark the completion of a whole-scale restoration of Lichfield Cathedral. The restoration work, which started in 1856, was supervised by Sir Gilbert Scott, one of the chief exponents of the High Gothic revival movement in the nineteenth century. A poor restoration had previously been carried out in 1788, when much of the great west frontage of the cathedral had been covered with stucco cement, an act which caused John Ruskin, Britain's foremost art critic in the nineteenth century, to rail against the damage that had been done. Scott got rid of the cement rendering and restored the statues that time and the Civil War in the 1640s had so badly damaged. New reproductions, as faithful to the originals as possible, were made primarily by Robert Bridgemen and his firm of Lichfield craftsmen. The total cost of the restoration, completed between 1856 and 1884, was £82,000. (Clayton, Howard, *Cathedral City*, Abbotsford Publishing, 1981)

- MAY 30TH -

1757: On this day, Erasmus Darwin married Mary Howard in St Mary's church in Lichfield and the newly wed couple moved into a house on Beacon Street (now the Darwin House Museum). Darwin, who first came to Lichfield in 1756, was born in 1731. A doctor of medicine as well as a scientist, botanist, anthropologist, poet and slave-trade abolitionist, his book *Zoonomia* came close to formulating the idea of evolution, a theory that his grandson Charles would later refine. Tall, pock-marked, overweight and genial, Darwin soon made his mark in Lichfield society, which had become, by the eighteenth century, a centre of the arts, sciences and intellectual thought. Darwin famously gave lectures on human anatomy, where he would dissect the bodies of recently executed criminals brought directly to him from the Lichfield gallows. Darwin and a number of friends, such as Matthew Boulton and Josiah Wedgewood, started The Lunar Society, a group of individuals who met once a month at the full moon and which was an 'intellectual driving force' behind Britain's Industrial Revolution. Darwin married twice (Mary died in 1770) and had a total of fourteen children. He died in 1802. (Uglow, Jenny, *The Lunar Men: The Friends Who Made the Future*, Faber and Faber, 2002)

~ MAY 31ST ~

1744: On this day, writer and inventor Richard Lovell Edgeworth was born. Edgeworth, who designed an early form of the bicycle and experimented with telegraphic communications, was a friend of Erasmus Darwin and fellow member of The Lunar Society. He moved to Lichfield in 1771 where he lived, for a time, in Stowe House with his friend Thomas Day, and later with his own wife and daughters, one of whom, Maria Edgeworth, became a writer of some renown. Edgeworth took over the lease of Stowe House from Day and soon fitted in with the 'coterie of bright and exciting people' for which Lichfield was known in the eighteenth century. One of these was Anna Seward, a poet nicknamed 'the Swan of Lichfield', and Edgeworth soon fell in love with one of her friends, Honora Sneyd. However, rather than cause a scandal by pursuing an adulterous affair he left Lichfield and moved to France. In 1773 Edgeworth's wife died and so he returned to Lichfield wooing and marrying Honora. In 1780 Honora herself died and Edgeworth proceeded to marry her sister Elizabeth. Edgeworth died in 1817, after being thrown by his horse. (Clarke, Desmond, *The Ingenious Mr Edgeworth*, Oldbourne, 1965)

⁓ June 1st ⁓

1810: On this day, hundreds of local people watched the execution of three men who had been convicted of forgery. The men, who were hanged on a scaffold erected at the crossroads of St John Street, London Road and Tamworth Road, were 25-year-old John Neve, 26-year-old William Weightman and 39-year-old James Jackson. Neve was a draper from Birmingham whose business had failed and had gone to work for Weightman, who owned a drapery store in Birmingham. Both men had previous unblemished records but went on to use their positions to pass forged notes to unsuspecting customers. Jackson came from Cheshire and was a miner for many years, but fell in with others who drew up forged bills of exchange with the intent of defrauding tradesmen. The trial had been a long one and the sentence of death, passed by the judge on April 18th, came as a shock to the men's friends and families who had hoped for a reprieve. The authorities confirmed the ruling a few days before the executions were carried out; all three men were buried in a single grave in St Michael's churchyard. At some point in the past someone removed the words 'hanged at' from the headstone. (Clayton, Howard and Simmons, Kathleen, *Lichfield in Old Photographs*, Sutton Publishing, 1994)

~ JUNE 2ND ~

1953: On this day, the people of Lichfield celebrated the coronation of Queen Elizabeth II. Many different activities were arranged for the day and street party committees had planned for months, some raising a great deal of money for the festivities. (In some cases so much money had been collected that groups were urged to send any excess funds to the British Empire Cancer Campaign.) Among the items planned for the great day were: a torchlight procession through the city; the band of the 16th Lancers playing in the recreation grounds; a choir singing from a pontoon on Minster Pool; dancing in the Guildhall until 2 a.m.; a celebrity cricket match involving professional footballers; and a firework display in Beacon Park. For the first time people could watch the events from Westminster Abbey on televisions, which were set up in many schools for the benefit of the majority of those who did not have a television of their own. As it turned out, the day was unseasonably cold and wet and many events like the choir and fireworks had to be cancelled. Most street parties went ahead, however, in spite of the weather. (*Lichfield Mercury*, June 5th 1953)

– June 3rd –

1816: On this day, the annual Greenhill Bower celebrations took place in Lichfield, with 'the usual demonstration of joy and enlivened by a good Band of Music and a variety of public amusements'. People at the time were evidently concerned about the cost of the Bower but they were assured by a notice in the *Lichfield Mercury*, which stated that all costs had been 'defrayed by subscriptions', to which local MPs and civic dignitaries had 'liberally contributed'. The Bower turned out to be very successful and 'far exceeded the efforts of many proceeding anniversaries of the custom', with the 'Maurice Dancers' described as being 'as fine as ever'. In the same week the Bower festivities took place, Messrs Gillman and Atkins' Grand Menagerie – 'the largest collection in the kingdom' – was also being exhibited in the city. The menagerie comprised of five lions, a 'beautiful' zebra, a 'stupendous' elephant from 'Hindoostan', a Bengal tiger, a porcupine, hyena and panthers. Admittance to the menagerie was 1*s* (5p) and admittance during feeding time at 9.30 a.m. was 2*s* (10p). (*Lichfield Mercury*, June 7th 1816)

– JUNE 4TH –

1793: On this day, Richard Greene, the founder of the city's first museum, died in Lichfield – the place where he had been born and lived his entire life. Greene was an apothecary, surgeon and printer (he owned the first printing press in the city) and opened his museum at his house in Market Street. He allowed the public in to see his collection and in 1773 had even printed a catalogue, the museum soon becoming one of the principal attractions for visitors to the city. Samuel Johnson and his biographer James Boswell visited the museum in 1776 and Boswell called it a 'wonderful collection', with neat labels printed on Greene's own press. Greene began acquiring objects of interest in 1748 and his collection included armour, local archaeological finds, coins, specimens of natural history and items from the South Seas given to him by David Samwell, the surgeon on Captain Cook's ship *Discovery*. After Greene's death his grandson, Richard Wright, inherited some of the collection and displayed it at the former diocesan registry in the Close before it was eventually broken up and dispersed. (Upton, Chris, *A History of Lichfield*, Phillimore, 2001)

— June 5th —

1894: On this day, the marriage of Mr Herbert Pike Pease and Miss Alice Mortimer Luckock took place at Lichfield Cathedral. The wedding was attended by a number of the 'great and good' including the Bishop of Ely, the Swinfen-Brouns and the Bishop of Lichfield, who performed the ceremony. There was 'a large assemblage' at the cathedral for the wedding, which took place at 2 p.m. A large crowd also gathered outside to watch the arrival of the bride, her 'bevy' of bridesmaids and the 'two little train-bearers'. The bride, accompanied by her father, wore a dress of antique ivory decorated with Brussels lace, pearls and orange blossom', as well as a 'tulle veil, a diamond necklace and a diamond bracelet'. The bridesmaids were dressed in 'white muslin, trimmed with white lace and diamond pins'. Afterwards the wedding party went to the deanery where an 'At Home' took place, attended by a 'large number' of guests. Later, the happy couple left for their honeymoon in Scotland. The wedding presents, which numbered nearly 350, were 'very costly' and included a great deal of silver, an inlaid writing desk, china vases and a Louis Quinze table. (*Lichfield Mercury*, June 8th 1894)

⁓ June 6th ⁓

1956: On this day, the Constitution Inn on Stafford Road shut its doors for the final time. Licensee Gertrude Wood invited a number of her friends and regulars to join her in a final celebration. According to Miss Wood, the Constitution Inn was one of the 'oldest and quaintest in the city'. She could remember a time when the pub had stables which were used by customers who came on horseback. Her brother, John Wood, said, 'The atmosphere in the Inn is more like a club; we never have any drunks and the customers are all very friendly.' Seventy-nine-year-old Frank Horton, who lived in the cottage next door, had used the inn for seventy-six years and related the story of how, as a 3-year-old, he had been sitting on the steps of the inn when the licensee, Mrs Clay, came out and gave him a pint of beer. He added, 'There was no other public house to compare with the Constitution.' The pub was a popular venue, despite its isolated position. It closed down when the western bypass and the traffic island at Featherbed Lane were constructed. (*Lichfield Mercury*, June 8th 1956; Shaw, John, *The Old Pubs of Lichfield*, George Lane Publishing, 2001)

~ JUNE 7TH ~

1946: On this day, the *Lichfield Mercury* published details of how Lichfield residents could obtain their new ration books. Although the Second World War had ended the previous year, many commodities were still very scarce and rationing continued, with readers being asked to cut out the *Mercury*'s information and keep it as a guide to what to do. People were informed that they should take their old ration book, as well as their identity card, to the local distribution centre – which for most people in Lichfield was situated in the Guildhall – and collect their new ration book. Throughout the war the government had tried to help people cope by issuing 'Food Facts', which were published by local newspapers like the *Mercury*. These articles carried on into the post-war years and continued to give 'housewives' tips and instructions on how to prepare dishes from the limited amount of food available and how to make scarce food go further. Rationing of some foodstuffs continued into the 1950s, with sugar and sweets rationed until 1953, finally ending when meat was taken off rationing in 1954. (*Lichfield Mercury*)

~ JUNE 8TH ~

1980: This day saw Queen Elizabeth II visit Lichfield. Her progress around Staffordshire was described by the *Lichfield Mercury* as the 'biggest royal spectacle the county had seen for years'. The queen arrived in the city to be greeted by schoolchildren waving banners and flags and lining the route as she progressed down Stafford Road, Beacon Street, Bird Street and St John Street. The royal party then went to Saxon Hill School, which she officially opened. At the school, which caters for physically disabled children, the queen was presented with some flowers by 9-year-old Claire Thompson, a spina bifida sufferer. The school was determined to run as normally as possible on this day in order to show the royal visitor the sorts of activities that happen there on a day-to-day basis. The queen's tour of the school included the speech therapy rooms, the hydrotherapy pool, physiotherapy room, library, pottery and home economic lessons. She also unveiled a plaque and planted a commemorative tree. The headmaster of the school, David Butcher, said that the visit had gone well, with the children 'speaking when spoken to and answering (the queen's) questions'. (*Lichfield Mercury*, June 13th 1980)

– JUNE 9TH –

1919: On this day, for the first time in four years, Lichfield's historic Bower Day took place. Abandoned in 1916 because of the First World War, the Greenhill Bower celebrations had its origins in the medieval fairs that took place on Lichfield's Greenhill, and dated back to the twelfth century. In 1919 the theme of the Bower Day procession, which wound its way through the streets of the city, was that of victory. The sun shone brightly down on the crowds of locals and visitors who flocked into the city and 'thronged the principle thoroughfares' of Lichfield and who cheered the floats, decorated to represent the various Allied countries that had gained the victory in the previous year – America, France, Belgium and, of course, the British Empire. Accompanying the floats was the City Band, a march-past of demobilised soldiers and a 33mm German field gun, captured at the Battle of Cambrai by the South Staffordshire Regiment. Later on, Morris dancing, cycle races and boxing took place in the recreation grounds where refreshment tents were also set up. (*Lichfield Mercury*, June 13th 1919)

– June 10th –

1977: On this day, the *Lichfield Mercury*'s headline read 'It's drip, drip hooray for the Silver Jubilee', as it reported on the city's celebration of the queen's twenty-five years on the throne. 'Wind and rain failed to dampen the spirits of young and old alike', wrote the *Mercury*, as it reflected on how hundreds of street parties had been held in Lichfield District. The mayor, who visited over forty such parties throughout the day, said, 'I have never seen anything like it in the City before. When the showers came the parties simply moved into garages and people carried on singing and dancing.' Streets everywhere were hung with bunting and, in some places, there were red, white and blue cakes, jellies and trifles. One Chase Terrace woman, Mrs Mary Cox, took on a part-time job as a school cleaner in order to raise money to provide a Jubilee party for fifty youngsters. Burntwood also provided the District's most decorated street as sightseers from 'far and wide', as well as television cameras, descended on Morley Road, where every house in the street was decorated. Over 3,000 watched the mayor light a bonfire and start a firework display in the evening. (*Lichfield Mercury*)

— JUNE 11TH —

1948: On this day, the *Lichfield Mercury* announced the death of Lieutenant Colonel Michael Swinfen-Broun, one of the most generous benefactors of the city, who died at the age of 90 on June 8th. In the past, Swinfen-Broun had paid most of the cost of building Lichfield's Victoria Hospital and had donated Beacon Place to the city, along with 12 acres of land, which became Beacon Park. Born in 1858, he had served in the army from 1876 and had been the commander of the South Staffordshire Regiment, which had served with distinction during the Boer War. He became High Sheriff of Staffordshire in 1907 and was made the Freeman of the city in 1936. His home, Swinfen Hall, just outside Lichfield, dates from 1755 and was extended and improved in the early twentieth century. At Swinfen-Broun's death the hall and its estate was bequeathed to Lichfield and most of the land was sold off. The hall stood empty for a number of years before being converted into a hotel in the 1980s. Swinfen-Broun was buried in the village church of St Mary's in Weeford. (*Lichfield Mercury*)

– JUNE 12TH –

1975: On this day, Margaret Thatcher, leader of the Conservative Party, visited Lichfield. She was greeted by the chairman of Lichfield District Council and by hundreds of people in Bore Street hoping to catch a glimpse of the Tory leader, who was wearing a yellow summer coat and was accompanied by her husband, Denis. Thatcher spoke in the Guildhall to an invited audience of 250. In her speech she commented on the result of the referendum held the previous day and on whether or not Britain should remain in the European Economic Community. She said she was 'delighted' with the overwhelming 'yes' vote of over 64 per cent, a result which had bettered her 'expectations', and added, 'the Great British public has shown what a tremendous amount of commonsense it has.' Now that the referendum was over, she said, 'the Government will now have to turn its attention to doing something about the economy. The European question will not solve it – it still leaves unresolved the problem of inflation.' Thatcher was Leader of the Opposition for four years before becoming prime minister in 1979. (*Lichfield Mercury*, June 13th 1975)

~ JUNE 13TH ~

1957: On this day, one of the first mentions of 'Teddy Boys' in the city was heard when three young, local youths aged 18, 17 and 16 were brought to trial at Lichfield Magistrates' Court charged with wilfully damaging six milk bottles to the value of 6*s* (30p). All were dressed in 'Teddy Boy' fashion one evening when they first jeered and shouted at Thomas Gilbert of Cherry Orchard and then threw milk bottles at him, none of which hit him. Gilbert gave chase to the youths and later complained to the father of one of them, which led the police to investigate the matter. The investigating officer addressed the young men at the trial, saying 'Is it not a fact that you were looking for trouble? You can dress how you like in this country, but if anyone looks at you, you think they are taking a mickey out of you!' All three youths were found guilty and fined £5 each and also put on good behaviour for twelve months. (*Lichfield Mercury*, June 14th 1957)

— JUNE 14TH —

1817: On this day, Mr Webb, innkeeper of the George Hotel and Lichfield's largest coaching proprietor, lost two of his best horses. The George was one of Lichfield's most important coaching inns where coaches would stop, allowing the team of horses to be changed ready for the next stage of the journey, and also enabling passengers to have a comfort break or meal. Unfortunately, this day saw Webb's horses killed when stones, kicked up by the hooves of the leading horses in the team pulling the coach, hit the horses behind. The horses were killed instantly and Webb lost 100 guineas (£105). This sort of incident was all too common in the days of the stagecoach. Although matters had generally been improved by the Turnpike Acts, which established local Turnpike Trusts whose job it was to look after the roads in their area, the roads were still relatively primitive. Repairs were made simply with stones and it was left to traffic to compress the road to a firm and level surface. Broken wheels were also frequent and, of course, there was always the threat of highwaymen. (Clayton, Howard, *Coaching City*, Dragon Books, 1970)

~ JUNE 15TH ~

1884: This day witnessed a 'great disturbance' caused by men of the Staffordshire Yeomanry, who assembled in Lichfield for their training week each June. At the end of a performance of Gilbert and Sullivan's comic opera *Princess Ida*, held in St James's Hall in Bore Street and performed by the D'Oyly Carte Company, some of the officers present attempted to rush the stage in order to get into the actresses' dressing room. Fighting with the stagehands and the theatre manager took place, which spread into the street outside where a number of locals joined in. During the incident the statue of Samuel Johnson in Market Square was daubed with boot blacking. The fighting and vandalism only ended when the commanding officer of the regiment, Lieutenant Colonel Bromley Davenport, while attempting to calm matters, suffered a heart attack and died. St James's Hall, built in 1870, became a cinema in 1912 called the Palladium and later the Lido, and later still the Adelphi. In the 1950s the building became a theatre again. Wilkinson's store now stands where the demolished theatre once did. (*Lichfield Mercury*, June 20th 1884)

~ JUNE 16TH ~

1943: On this day, Shenstone's 'grand old lady' celebrated her 101st birthday. Born in 1842, Mrs Lucy Sutton of Ivy Cottage received many cards, letters and telegrams on her special day. With the exception of her failing eyesight, Mrs Sutton had retained 'all her faculties' and 'does all her own housework daily'. She was also a keen gardener and 'still weeds her own garden', which is situated across the road from her home. Mrs Sutton never learned to read or write and had no 'wireless' and, as a consequence, knew very little about the 'dreadful war', but she did remember the Great War 'very well indeed'. She was born in Walsall and moved to Shenstone 'at a very early age'. As a girl she worked on a farm cutting mangolds and spreading manure on the fields. Her husband, who had worked for the Lichfield benefactor, Sir Richard Cooper, for many years, had died thirty years before. She had two sons, two daughters and 'more grandchildren and great-grandchildren than she can count'. Asked what the secret was to her longevity, Mrs Sutton replied, 'I am sure God helps me … and I have to live until he calls me.' (*Lichfield Mercury*, June 18th 1943)

⁓ June 17th ⁓

1719: This day saw the death of the noted essayist, poet, playwright and politician Joseph Addison, who moved to the city at the age of 3 when his father, Lancelot Addison, became the Dean of Lichfield. Born in 1672, Addison attended Lichfield Grammar School where he gained a reputation after planning an operation called 'barring out', where he and others locked teachers out of the building while waving defiance from the windows. After this incident he was sent to Charterhouse School and from there went to Oxford University. His first book, on the lives of English poets, was published in 1694 and his most famous work of fiction, *Cato: a Tragedy*, was written in 1712. With his friend Richard Steele he founded *The Spectator* magazine, for which he contributed hundreds of essays about subjects as diverse as peace treaties, bowling greens and puppet shows. His essays were noted for their clarity and humour, while his Latin poems were highly praised by Samuel Johnson. Addison became an MP in 1708. His appealing manners and conversation made him one of the most popular men of his day. (Stephen, L. and Lee, S. (eds), *Dictionary of National Biography*, Oxford University Press, 1917)

~ JUNE 18TH ~

1886: On this day, the 'Ladies Column' in the *Lichfield Mercury* suggested the sorts of clothes its more well-heeled readers would be wearing in the coming summer months. Women 'this year', it suggested, might want to consider wearing white or grey frocks, particularly those made with 'Madiera embroidery'. Yellow was also going to be a fashionable colour for women in the summer of 1886, according to the writer of the column, who reported that 'one of the coolest looking gowns' on sale was made with 'pale yellow silk covered with fine black lace'. According to the column, black sunshades were also in vogue, especially those 'lined with yellow and trimmed with yellow silk ribbons', as were bonnets, particularly if they were 'black and very small in dimensions'. The latest hats were 'thatched ones which have a quaint look, with their straw-rope edging and trimming of field flowers'. The writer was also critical of 'this year's dresses' saying that they seemed to 'hang very badly with many skirts longer on one side than they are on the other'. Ladies were advised that the most fashionable materials of the summer would be 'serge and tweed'. (*Lichfield Mercury*)

– JUNE 19TH –

1962: On this day, the Bishop of Lichfield opened the £60,000 extension to Nearfield House, eleven years after opening the old people's home on Stafford Road. The new building, which stands next to the original one, increases the available accommodation for males and females by forty-eight to bring the overall total to sixty-four. The home is provided by Staffordshire County Council and a number of representatives from the County Welfare Services Department were present at the opening ceremony, as well as civic dignitaries from the city. Bishop Reeve said in his address that although the welfare state had recently had certain criticisms levelled against it, he had always felt it was something which had conferred great benefits on the community and the new home was an excellent example of the 'blessings that were conferred on old people by the Welfare State'. He also made a plea to the relatives and friends of the residents at the home to visit them as often as possible, saying: 'There are some institutions that I know very well where some of the elderly people have been left, and apparently abandoned by their relatives and I think it is disgraceful when that happens.' (*Lichfield Mercury*, June 22nd 1962)

– JUNE 20TH –

1944: On this day, a 'memorable ceremony' took place at Lichfield's Trent Valley station when the mayor of Lichfield (Councillor Miss A.M. Thompson) named the latest London Midland and Scottish locomotive (number 6250) the *City of Lichfield*. Also present at the naming ceremony was the Chairman of the LMS Railway Company, Lord Royden. The mayor was presented with a bouquet of flowers by Miss Patricia Williams, the 11-year-old daughter of signalman Williams, an LMS employee. The recently built railway engine, one of the Coronation Class locomotives, was under the control of driver W. Clough, a veteran of the Great War who had been decorated for bravery in 1917. Coronation Class engines, first built in 1937, were the largest LMS locomotives at 74ft in length and weighing 161 tons, and had been built for the high-speed journey from London to Glasgow. *City of Lichfield*'s sister engine, the *Coronation Scot*, had a top speed of 114mph and did the journey in six-and-a-half hours. (*Lichfield Mercury*, June 23rd 1944)

~ June 21st ~

1856: On this day, the *Staffordshire Advertiser* reported the hanging of William Palmer, the notorious Rugeley Poisoner. Special trains ran from Lichfield and all over the country to take people to Stafford for the public execution. Dr Palmer had been convicted of poisoning his friend and gambling companion John Parsons Cook in a trial that lasted twelve days and caused a sensation throughout Britain. 'An enormous influx of spectators' entered the town, most of whom 'had tramped many weary miles to reach Stafford'. Throughout the night trains arrived full of those anxious to see the end of the infamous murderer. Roads into the town were thronged with crowds and barriers were erected so that the crush could be controlled, with women being refused entry. Pubs remained open all day, although the crowd of 30,000 who were there to witness Palmer's hanging was described by the newspaper as 'sober'. Palmer walked to the scaffold with 'a jaunty air and a smile on his face'. The execution was over quickly, but most stayed to watch Palmer's body dangle from the rope for the statutory hour before it was cut down and buried in the grounds of Stafford gaol. (*Staffordshire Advertiser*)

— June 22nd —

1897: On this day, the people of Lichfield celebrated the Diamond Jubilee of Queen Victoria. The day began at 6 a.m. with the ringing of church and cathedral bells throughout the city. The National Anthem was played at various locations in the city before a grand possession left the Guildhall, led by the band of the Queen's Own Staffordshire Yeomanry. The procession arrived at the cathedral where a special service took place. At noon in Market Square an 'assemblage of citizens' watched a pageant entitled 'The Queen's Fables', presented by various children's organisations, after which 'about 2,000' children sang 'God Bless Victoria'. The Guildhall was specially decorated for the occasion with flags, bunting and a large banner bearing the queen's portrait and the words 'Revered and Beloved'. (*Lichfield Mercury*, June 25th 1897; Clayton, Howard and Simmons, Kathleen, *Lichfield in Old Photographs*, Sutton Publishing, 1994)

1984: On this day, Ken Livingstone, the controversial former leader of the Great London Council (GLC), spoke to an audience of 300 at Lichfield's Netherstowe School. Nicknamed 'Red Ken', he described the recent abolition of the GLC as 'an attack on democracy'. (*Lichfield Mercury*, July 6th 1984)

— JUNE 23RD —

1905: On this day, the *Lichfield Mercury* reported on the opening of the new Post Office in Bird Street next to Minster Pool. The building, which had been criticised by some residents for being 'too out of the way', took a year to build and replaced the old Post Office in Bore Street. The Post Office was designed by Sir Henry Tanner and 'is a commodious building well-suited to the needs of the city'. The various departments of the Post Office were indicated by nameplates attached to wire screens which were fixed to a counter, 'a wise precaution considering the large amounts of money that changes hands'. A telephone was situated conveniently near the counter and on either side of the entrance to the Post Office were compartments where members of the public could write their telegrams, which were sent by equipment contained in Minster Pool House that had been specially converted for the purpose. Incoming telegrams were delivered by messenger lads – a rack of cycles was kept nearby for their use. A large, well-lit sorting office to the rear of the public office was 'filled with all the modern accessories'. (The site is now occupied by the Ego restaurant.) (*Lichfield Mercury*)

– JUNE 24TH –

1887: On this day, the *Lichfield Mercury* reported on the celebrations for the Golden Jubilee of Queen Victoria. A sum of £750 had been raised by public donations to pay for the festivities. Tradesmen and citizens 'both high and low' vied with each other to decorate their homes or premises, and the streets all over the city presented a scene the 'like of which has probably never been witnessed in Lichfield'; illuminations turned night-time Lichfield into a 'veritable fairyland'. The day began when church bells rang at 6 a.m. and from 9 a.m. a band played in Market Square and a civic procession, accompanied by men of the Queen's Own Volunteer Yeomanry, marched from the Guildhall to the cathedral for a special service. Free public dinners were provided for 2,500 people at various venues throughout the city and 'athletic sports' were held in Bore Street, with running, three-legged races and egg-and-spoon races. Free teas were provided for the children of the city and there were even celebrations in the Lichfield workhouse, where inmates were treated to roast beef and plum pudding. At night bonfires were lit and a Jubilee ball took place at the Swan Hotel. (*Lichfield Mercury*)

~ JUNE 25TH ~

1943: On this day, the first production of the city's amateur dramatic society, the Lichfield Players, was performed. The Players were born out of a desire by Mrs M. Byas to raise money for the RAF Benevolent Fund, who asked members of the newly formed Lichfield Operatic Society to put on a dramatic production called *London Wall* in aid of the charity. The production was put on at the Guildhall where the actors overcame the lack of a proper stage and unsteady scenery to earn an enthusiastic review in the *Lichfield Mercury*. The company decided to stay together and performed at nearby RAF and army bases and in school halls. In 1945 the company won a cup at the Tamworth Drama Festival for its production of *Black Chiffon* by Lesley Storm. From 1970 the Players were able to present their productions at the Lichfield Arts Centre in Bird Street (the old Post Office building). In 1995, however, the Arts Centre building was declared unsafe and so the Players once again mounted their productions at local schools until, in 2003, they were able to perform at the newly opened Lichfield Garrick Theatre, their current base, where they present five productions each year. (www.lichfieldplayers.org)

– JUNE 26TH –

1905: On this day, Lichfield welcomed a group of delegates from the Canadian Manufacturers' Association, who were in Britain for a short visit. The 120 men and women were greeted at Lichfield City station by the town clerk, Mr Herbert Russell, who then took them to the Guildhall through streets 'gay with flags'. At the Guildhall the Canadians were given a hearty welcome by the mayor, Councillor D. Harrison, and expressed their interest in the history of 'the Loyal and Ancient City', being particularly fascinated by the maces which had been presented to the city in 1664 and 1690. The delegates, who were in Great Britain to develop trading links between the two countries, enjoyed the hospitality of the mayor, the gentlemen being provided with wine and cigarettes in the council chambers and the ladies with light refreshments in the Guildhall. Mr Ewart of Ontario, on behalf of the delegates, said that it was a great honour to visit such a historic city and that they looked on Britain as 'the mother country'. The party later attended a service at the cathedral where hymns and the National Anthem were 'sung with great fervour'. (*Lichfield Mercury*, June 30th 1905)

~ June 27th ~

1902: On this day, Lichfield experienced 'riotous behaviour' of the type 'seldom witnessed in the city' when several police officers were 'badly treated' by a crowd 'some hundreds strong'. The riot began when two men started fighting in an area of Greenhill known as 'The Gullet' (now the area around the alleyway leading to the Duke of York pub). The two fighters had 'cleared off' before the police arrived, but when the crowd was instructed to disperse they became 'rather obstinate'. When the police attempted to arrest a man called Russell they were attacked by the man's companions and in the struggle that followed the attending constables were 'knocked about'. As a result of the 'fracas' six persons were arrested, including one woman, and they all appeared before the police court the following morning charged with being drunk and disorderly and assaulting police officers. The magistrates said they were determined to put a stop to such 'rowdyism' and all the prisoners were fined and received prison sentences, in some cases with hard labour. They were transported to Stafford jail by furniture van and train. (*Lichfield Mercury*, July 4th 1902)

~ JUNE 28TH ~

1885: On this day, the shocking death of 16-year-old Walter Frederick Sharp took place. Sharp lived with his grandparents at Hobbs Hole, Wissage (his parents lived in Brixton, London), and was described by the *Lichfield Mercury* as being 'an imbecile since birth'. To prevent him from injuring himself the boy's grandmother was in the habit of fastening Walter to a chair with a skipping rope wrapped around his wrist, with which he would play. It is believed that the skipping rope was thrown into the nearby fire and caught alight and when the boy pulled the rope back again his clothes caught fire. When the grandmother discovered what had happened she sent for the doctor, Elliot Welchmen, who found that Walter had suffered extensive burns to his body, arms and face and his legs were paralysed. The boy had remained alive for several weeks before dying on this day. An inquest, held at the Smithfield Hotel, found the death to have been accidental, with the ultimate cause of death being 'exhaustion from the suffering caused by the burns'. (*Lichfield Mercury*, July 3rd 1885)

~ June 29th ~

1803: On this day, writer and poet Anna Seward wrote one of her many letters in which she commented on the 'heinous crime' of duelling. The letter, addressed to Dr Percival of Manchester, expounds her view in her typically flowery language, proposing that the 'murderous punctilio of Luciferian honour' ought to be stopped by the authorities. Laws were, she said, being 'scorned' by the participants of duels and often 'foiled' by juries who tended to acquit the survivors. In her view, seconds and surgeons helping out at duels should also be liable to prosecution for failing to let the authorities know when and where a duel was about to take place. People who took part in, or who helped out at, a duel ought to be 'stigmatized and shunned', she wrote. Duelling was very popular in the eighteenth and early nineteenth centuries and some very prominent people took part in them. In 1798, HRH The Duke of York took part in a duel and survived, as did Prime Minister William Pitt. The hero of Waterloo and later prime minister, the Duke of Wellington, fought a duel in 1829. (*Letters of Anna Seward*, Volume 6, letter 15, G. Ramsey & Co., 1811)

~ June 30th ~

1933: On this day, the *Lichfield Mercury* reported on the opening of Lichfield's new Victoria Hospital. 'The magnificent new building' situated in the Friary Road estate was opened by Lord Harrowby, the Lord Lieutenant of Staffordshire. Representatives from every walk of life were present for the opening ceremony and witnessed Lord Harrowby open the hospital doors with 'a silver key, presented to him by the architect, Mr T.A. Pole'. The hospital had been built at a time of great financial difficulty and, according to Lord Harrowby, illustrated that the people of Lichfield had 'not forsaken their ancient charity', as much of the money raised for the building had come from public donations. The hospital was described by the *Mercury* as being situated in 'a pleasant position, well out of the town and surrounded by open countryside'. The building contained an administrative block, a theatre block and X-ray and out-patient rooms. There were two twelve-bed wards, two two-bed wards and six one-bed private rooms, making a total of thirty-four beds. The Victoria Hospital, fondly remembered by Lichfield folk, served the community until 2007 when it was demolished and a new housing development took its place. (*Lichfield Mercury*)

~ July 1st ~

1916: On this day, the Battle of the Somme, one of the bloodiest battles of the First World War, began and the *Lichfield Mercury* soon gave its reaction to it. The battle, it said, was 'a splendid offensive movement' and it referred to 'British and French successes', 'considerable advances' and the capturing of 'many villages and positions heretofore held by the enemy'. The paper stated that on the first day of the battle over 3,500 Germans had been taken prisoner as a result of 'the keen fighting'; little mention was made of British losses, the only problem it referred to was that the British advance had been 'hindered' by heavy thunderstorms. The paper was badly shackled by the restrictions placed on the information it was able to report and the reality was very different. In the subsequent weeks, the *Mercury* would contain column after column of reports about the deaths of young men from the Lichfield district killed at the Somme. On the first day of the battle some 60,000 British soldiers were killed or injured and the terrible losses on both sides would mount throughout the rest of the year. (*Lichfield Mercury*, July 7th 1916)

~ JULY 2ND ~

1951: By this day, local celebrations connected to the national Festival of Britain were well underway. Lichfield's Festival of Britain Committee had planned for a two-week 'Lichfield Festival', which contained many activities for residents and visitors to enjoy, during which people were urged to 'give themselves up to the Festival Spirit'. The mayor, Councillor Mrs C.S. Parker, appealed for tidy streets without litter during the festival, as she wanted to show visitors 'Lichfield at its best'. Activities available were many and varied and included performances by the City of Birmingham Symphony Orchestra, who took part in a 'festival of music', and a military tattoo which took place in the recreation grounds, where members of the Army and Royal Navy presented music and PE displays. A presentation of ancient and valuable books and other treasures was on display at the cathedral and the play, *Murder in the Cathedral*, was presented at the Garrick Theatre in Bore Street. A 'Pageant-Fair' was put on by local schools, the theme of which was 'Lichfield through the ages', and the local Chamber of Trade organised a 'Festival Trades Fair'. (*Lichfield Mercury*, July 6th and 27th 1951)

~ July 3rd ~

1869: On this day, the brewing firm belonging to John, Henry and William Gilbert, based in Tamworth Street, merged with the company owned by Beacon Street brewers, John and Arthur Griffith, to form the Lichfield Brewery Company. Brewing had been an important activity in Lichfield since the Middle Ages and by the nineteenth century was the biggest single industry in the city, rivalling nearby neighbours Burton-upon-Trent. In 1873 the company opened a new brewery, designed by George Scammell, beside the railway on the west side of Upper St John Street; a large malthouse was built on the opposite side of the road at about the same time. The company was eventually bought by Burton brewers, James Allsop and Sons, and brewing continued until 1931. The City Brewery Company started in 1874, with premises again built by Scammell on the south side of the railway between Birmingham Road and Chesterfield Road; the company was eventually taken over by the Wolverhampton and Dudley Breweries Ltd. The Trent Valley Brewery opened in 1875 and had a brewery in Streethay, amalgamating with the Lichfield Brewery Company in 1891. (Greenslade, M.W. (ed.), *A History of Lichfield*, Staffordshire Libraries, Arts and Archives, 1994)

~ JULY 4TH ~

1855: On this day, the American writer Nathaniel Hawthorne (1804–64), famous for such books as *The Scarlet Letter* and *The House of the Seven Gables*, visited Lichfield. During his short stay he noted that the people of the city 'have an old-fashioned way with them and stare at a stranger as if the railways had not yet quite accustomed them to the novelty of strange faces moving about their ancient sidewalks'. Hawthorne visited the 'beautiful' cathedral, the Close and Minster Pool, which he described as 'so very pretty and quietly picturesque', and also visited the birthplace of Dr Samuel Johnson in Market Square – 'not so much a square as the mere widening of the street'. At the time, Johnson's birthplace was a mercer's and haberdasher's shop and Hawthorne was less than impressed with the change of usage. He was much more taken with the statue of Johnson in the square, which had been erected in 1838 and which he described as 'colossal, though perhaps not more so than the mountainous Doctor himself'. (Hawthorne, Nathaniel, *Our Old Home: A Series of English Sketches*, Project Gutenberg ebook, 2005)

~ JULY 5TH ~

2009: On this day, the Staffordshire Hoard, a vast collection of Anglo-Saxon artefacts, was discovered in a farmer's field close to Lichfield. The hoard was discovered by local metal-detector enthusiast Terry Herbert and it comprised 3,940 gold and silver items, making it the largest collection of objects from the seventh or eighth centuries ever found. The high level of craftsmanship displayed in the hoard suggested that the various items belonged to an elite group – perhaps even royalty. Some of the items were decorated with precious stones, which might have come from as far away as India or Sri Lanka. The objects in the hoard were mostly military – war gear, such as the fittings from swords – and many appear to have been torn away from objects they were once attached to, almost as though they were trophies taken after a battle. Why the hoard was buried is a mystery; it may have been to conceal it for later retrieval, or it may have been an offering to pagan gods. The hoard was displayed at Lichfield Cathedral, at Birmingham Museum and Art Gallery and in a number of other venues. (www.staffordshirehoard.org.uk)

~ JULY 6TH ~

1893: On this day, people in Lichfield celebrated the royal wedding of the future King George V and Queen Mary – the Duke of York (eldest son of the Prince of Wales) and Princess May. The city was in a 'happy and joyous mood' on a bright and warm day, 'enlivened' even more by the ringing of church and cathedral bells. The streets of Lichfield were highly decorated and 'wore the gayest aspect', with flags and banners 'displayed in great numbers'. Many events took place during the day including a public luncheon at the Guildhall; the firing of a cannon in the Market Square, where a crowd sang the National Anthem; and a half-day holiday for all shops and businesses. A new bandstand was opened in the museum gardens and recreation grounds, where a promenade concert took place. All of the children from the city's elementary and industrial schools and the union workhouse were marched past the Guildhall where they saluted the mayor, before walking to the recreation grounds, where they were treated to a tea. In the evening there was a fireworks display and a public dance in St James's Hall. (*Lichfield Mercury*, July 7th 1893)

– July 7th –

1815: On this day, the first edition of the *Lichfield Mercury* was published. Printed by James Amphlett in Boar Street (now Bore Street), the newspaper cost sixpence halfpenny (3p). The main story in the *Mercury* (on its back page) was a report about the Battle of Waterloo, which had taken place on June 18th in Belgium, and in which an Allied force under the command of the Duke of Wellington defeated Napoleon's French army. In this first edition was a front-page message from Mr Amphlett to his readers, where he spelled out the importance of 'a public journal to a district which had been deprived of any medium of publicity of its own'. Amphlett went on to write that the newspaper would be open to 'free and liberal criticism on all subjects (including) the political and moral opinions of all men'. Some interesting features appeared in the paper including notices of the sale of land and buildings by auction, and the market prices of various commodities such as wheat, barley, oats, tallow and leather – there were no advertisements of the sort we would recognise. A births and marriages column was included, however, as was the latest news from Parliament. (*Lichfield Mercury*)

~ JULY 8TH ~

1548: On this day, Lichfield was granted a Charter by King Edward VI making Lichfield a city that would, in the future, be governed by two bailiffs (chosen annually on July 25th) and twenty-four burgesses. Prior to 1548, Lichfield was governed by the bishop through a Manor Court, although the Guild of St Mary and St John the Baptist, founded in 1387, also had had an increasing voice in the governance of Lichfield. In 1553 a new charter was granted by Mary I that gave Lichfield county status and enabled the city to appoint a sheriff. A further charter of 1623 assured the independence of Cathedral Close, which had been given self-governing status in 1441, and extended the privileges of the dean and chapter. There were further charters in 1664 and 1686, after which the city's government stayed the same until 1835 when the Municipal Corporations Act established a corporation of eighteen councillors under a mayor. In 1974 the city lost its self-governing status and was absorbed into the newly created Lichfield District Council. In 1980 Lichfield City Council was created, with thirty councillors representing six wards. (Greenslade, M.W. (ed.), *A History of Lichfield*, Staffordshire Libraries, Arts and Archives, 1994)

— July 9th —

1735: On this day, Samuel Johnson married Elizabeth Porter at St Werburgh's church in Derby; he was 25, she was 46. Tetty, as Johnson always called her, had been married to Henry Porter, a Birmingham textile dealer who had died the previous year, and her family disapproved of the marriage, assuming that Johnson wanted her money. He did, in fact, use the majority of her 'small fortune' of £600 to open a school at Edial House, near Lichfield, a venture that soon failed. Johnson always insisted that his marriage to Tetty was a 'love match on both sides', but he did abandon her to move to London in 1737. A number of Johnson's friends, including David Garrick, disliked Tetty, believing her to be a 'silly, affected woman; fat, over-painted and full of girlish airs', and accused her of being addicted to alcohol and opium. Johnson, however, always professed his devotion to her and was seemingly devastated when she died in 1752. He always marked the anniversary of her death with 'tears and prayers'. (Hopkins, Mary Alden, *Dr Johnson's Lichfield*, Hastings House, 1952)

~ July 10th ~

1908: On this day the *Lichfield Mercury* excitedly reported that a statue of King Edward VII would be presented to the city by the then Sheriff of Lichfield, Councillor Robert Bridgemen. The statue was carved in Portland stone by George Lowther and depicts the king, referred to by the *Mercury* as 'Edward the Peacemaker', in his coronation robes holding a sceptre. The newspaper was convinced that the statue, which was placed in the museum gardens facing out to Bird Street, would be a 'great draw for visitors to the city'. The unveiling of the statue took place in September 1908 and was attended by a large number of people amid much flag waving. A telegram sent by the king's private secretary stated that 'His Majesty greatly appreciated the good feeling and Loyalty shown on the occasion'. Edward VII, the son of Queen Victoria, ruled from 1901 (when he succeeded his mother at the age of 59) until his death in 1910, giving his name to the Edwardian era. The statue can still be seen in the museum gardens. (*Lichfield Mercury*)

~ July 11th ~

1908: On this day, General Booth, the veteran leader of the Salvation Army, visited Lichfield. While in the city he addressed the inmates of the workhouse, calling on them to be 'thankful for their lot and the food they received'. The *Lichfield Mercury* observed that the women inmates, 'in their striped frocks and plain red shawls', and the men listened to General Booth with 'as much of their attention as they were capable of giving'. After prayers, 'the distinguished evangelist' drove through the streets of Lichfield in a motor car, before leaving the city to go to Walsall. William Booth (1829–1912) was a Methodist preacher who founded the Salvation Army in London in 1865 and the organisation, which became known for its distribution of humanitarian aid, soon spread around the world. He visited a number of countries, including the United States, and in 1904 set out on a 'motorcade' throughout Britain, visiting many towns and cities along the way. (*Lichfield Mercury*, July 17th 1908)

~ July 12th ~

1901: On this day, the results were announced of the national census, which had taken place in March. The census found that in Lichfield City there were 11,448 people living in 2,360 houses and in Lichfield District (including Burntwood, Hammerwich, Edial, Woodhouses, Whittington and Shenstone) there were 27,804 residing in 5,188 homes. Some people were worried that the population of Lichfield had remained static in the ten-year period since the previous census in 1891. The *Lichfield Mercury* worriedly commented on the lack of growth in the area:

> Lichfield cannot be numbered amongst those towns which, aided by manufactures, have greatly increased in population since the last census in 1891. We should hail with delight the introduction of an industry which would assist us on the high road to prosperity.

Nationally, the census found that the population of England and Wales stood at 32 million people living in 6 million houses. (*Lichfield Mercury*)

~ JULY 13TH ~

1923: On this day, Lichfield was counting the cost of a 'terrific storm' that hit the city on the previous evening. 'The biggest storm in living memory with such an accumulation of water in a short time has not been seen before!', read the article. For over an hour Lichfield suffered 'warm thunder-rain' followed by 'large hailstones', while 'lightning flashed incessantly' and thunder was 'almost continuous'. The consequences of the storm 'were extraordinary' – the drains were not able to cope with the amount of water and gratings were soon blocked with debris. On Birmingham Road (between Ivanhoe Road and the tennis club) there was 4ft of water and traffic had to be diverted, while the flooding on Bird Street made it impassable for pedestrians, with nearly all of the shops flooded, along with all of the ground-floor rooms of the Swan Hotel. Wade Street was also badly affected and the residents of Queen Street had to bail water out of their homes. A chimney stack at the Guardians' Institution was struck by lightning and part of the roof of the Pay Office in Beacon Place collapsed, although luckily no one was hurt. (*Lichfield Mercury*)

‒ July 14th ‒

1830: It was on this day that the first documented game of cricket in Lichfield took place. The match was between Lichfield and Tamworth and 'excited great interest in the neighbourhood'. It was played on a large area of open ground called Levett's Field, owned by Mr Webb, landlord of the George Hotel and sponsor of the game. The crowd for the match was a large one, with 'seats provided for the ladies' and a marquee was set up which contained 'refreshments for the combatants'. By modern standards the game was an extremely low scoring one, with the Lichfield team making just forty-eight runs in their first innings, with only one batsman, A. Hitchcock, achieving double figures. Tamworth, in reply, made only forty-four runs before Lichfield went on to score a further forty-nine runs in their second innings. Lichfield then bowled Tamworth out for forty-one runs, making them the victors by twelve runs. The match, completed in one day, finished at 6.30 p.m. and afterwards 'the members of both clubs sat down to a sumptuous dinner' at the George Hotel. (Clayton, Howard, *Cathedral City*, Abbotsford Publishing, 1977)

~ July 15th ~

1887: On this day, the *Lichfield Mercury* reported on the opening of Lichfield's Victoria Swimming Baths. The site of the baths was the Trunkfields site on Walsall Road, where the Conduit Lands Trustees already had a water-pumping station. The swimming pool was 60ft long and 25ft wide and went from 2ft 6in deep at the shallow end to 5ft 6in at the deep end. Built for economy rather that looks, the functional building had little ornamentation, with red and blue bricks being used, along with a corrugated-iron roof. The baths were opened by Mayor A.C. Lomax and the *Mercury* reported that 'a capital little band' played music for the opening ceremony. The watching civic dignitaries were also treated to 'swimming entertainments' provided by the Tamworth Amateur Swimming Club, who took part in swimming races, a water-polo game and diving for plates. Professor Capes 'performed wondrous feats', including 'ornamental' swimming, life saving, imitating a dead body floating in the water and staying submerged below water for one minute and twenty-five seconds. (*Lichfield Mercury*)

— July 16th —

1942: On this day, King George VI and Queen Elizabeth visited Lichfield for the first time. Thousands filled the streets to see the royal couple and to give them 'a right royal reception'. The visit was part of a tour of the Midlands by the king and queen, who had decided to visit the city after receiving an invitation from the Bishop of Lichfield. The large crowd – which included American Army nurses and American and Australian soldiers – cheered the royal couple when they arrived at Cathedral Close. The king, dressed in RAF uniform, and the queen, who 'looked her usual charming self in a dress of duck-egg blue', were shown around the cathedral by the bishop, who pointed out to them the ways in which the war had affected the ancient building, with its stained-glass windows being removed and the statue of the 'Sleeping Children' covered with sandbags to prevent damage from enemy action. After tea at the Bishop's Palace, the king and queen walked through the 'thickly lined' streets to the birthplace of Samuel Johnson, which they toured before leaving on the Royal Train from Trent Valley station. (*Lichfield Mercury*, July 17th 1942)

– JULY 17TH –

1728: On this day, a strange prophecy concerning Sir William Wolseley of Wolseley Hall came tragically true. Sir William was a great traveller and in 1728 was in Egypt where he bought four magnificent Arab horses. He also had his fortune told and was informed that he and his four horses would die by drowning. Worried about the prophecy, he sent the four animals ahead by boat while he travelled overland – no doubt on tenterhooks as he crossed the English Channel. When he reached Lichfield safely he was convinced that the prophecy was mistaken and he had worried unnecessarily, so he had his four new horses hitched to his coach and set off to Wolseley Hall. A fierce thunderstorm took place as his coach crossed a large ford, and just at that moment a nearby millpond dam burst, sending a torrent of water downstream. Sir William and his horses were drowned; only his servant, who had managed to cling to a tree, survived. One hundred years later a plate with the Wolseley coat of arms was found nearby; it was taken to Wolseley Hall and displayed. The hall was demolished in 1966. (Wright, W.G., *Lichfield and Tamworth Life Magazine*, November 1972)

~ July 18th ~

1932: On this day, Lichfield's Regal cinema, situated in Tamworth Street, opened. Designed by Harold Scott of Birmingham and built in the art deco style, adverts proclaimed it to be 'Lichfield's Luxury Cinema', equipped with the latest 'Western Electric Sound System – The Voice of Action'. The first film shown was *The Old Man*, a 'baffling mystery drama interspersed with sparkling comedy', which starred Masie Gay, who was, according to the ads, 'the British Marie Dressler'. The film cost 2*s* (10p) if you sat in the balcony or 1*s* 6*d* (8p) if you sat in the stalls. The balcony held 400 customers and the stalls 1,000, and people could book their tickets by telephone – the cinema's number being Lichfield 274. The cinema also boasted the Regal Cafe, which was situated on the balcony floor and was open from 11 a.m. to 9 p.m. daily – 'make the Regal Cafe your rendezvous', said the publicity. Two shops, one selling sweets and tobacco and the other a hat shop, stood each side of the entrance. The Regal eventually closed in 1974, becoming first a bingo hall and later a supermarket. At the time of writing the imposing building lies derelict. (*Lichfield Mercury*)

− July 19th −

1901: On this day, the *Lichfield Mercury*, in a column written by 'The Major', suggested how men should dress in the hot weather. Silk hats, for example, were considered better protection from the sun than flimsy straw hats. A plain grey worsted coat with trousers to match would look 'much cooler' than a thin morning or frock coat and a pair of thick cashmere trousers. Advice was also provided concerning the wearing of waistcoats in the hot summer weather. It is better for a man to wear a waistcoat, the major concluded, than having to keep his coat buttoned up all of the time and keep the various small articles, which he would normally carry in his waistcoat pocket, such as a watch, in his coat and trouser pockets. Men, who were not over-particular about their appearance, were advised to wear thin, 'kidskin' shoes rather than boots, although in the major's opinion shoes were not as smart-looking as boots. In conclusion the *Mercury*'s advice to men in the summer of 1901 was not to be in a hurry to take things off but, instead, wear the thinnest of clothes and underwear with a light, well-ventilated hat. (*Lichfield Mercury*)

~ July 20th ~

1952: On this day, a memorial altar was unveiled at St Chad's church in Lichfield, dedicated to the parishioners who had died during the Second World War. Above the altar was placed a memorial tablet containing the names of twenty-four local men who had, in the words of the rector of St Chad's, Dr D.K. Robertson, 'made the supreme sacrifice to make victory possible'. The altar was situated in the east end of the south aisle, the oldest part of the church, sections of which were 800 years old. Relatives of the deceased were present at the special evensong service, along with members of the British Legion and the Old Contemptible's Association. The altar was a gift from St Chad's church in Shrewsbury and the memorial plaque was given by Mr and Mrs Taylor in memory of their son, whose name appears on it. The altar furnishings and alterations that were necessary were carried out by the famous Lichfield firm of Bridgeman and Son, the money being raised by 'public subscription'. (*Lichfield Mercury*, July 25th 1952)

— July 21st —

1963: On this day, after a century and a half, 'the merry clang of hammer on anvil and the cheery glow of the red hot fire' were no longer to be seen at the Forge, the blacksmith's in Beacon Street. The business closed down due to the retirement of its owner, Mr Alfred Goodwin, who shod a horse for the last time then shut down his foundry for good. The business, known by farmers over a wide area, was taken-over eighty years before by Mr Goodwin's grandfather, Enoch Goodwin; his son, the present Mr Goodwin's father, carried it on successfully. Alfred entered the blacksmith's business with his father at the age of 14. During the First World War he served as a farrier in the Royal Engineers Signals Service and in the Second World War he joined the Local Defence Volunteers (LDV), holding the rank of platoon sergeant. After coming through both wars unscathed he suffered several nasty injuries when he was kicked by horses, the last one being particularly serious, as he was injured in the leg and head. Mr Goodwin tried hard to obtain apprentices to carry on the business, but all who tried disliked the work. (*Lichfield Mercury*, July 26th 1963)

~ July 22nd ~

1938: On this day, local historian J.W. Jackson, in his regular column in the *Mercury* entitled 'Reminiscences of Victorian Lichfield', recalled some of the city's eccentric characters. 'Pikelet Poll' lived in Lower Sandford Street and was 'an attractive young woman' who sold her pikelets door-to-door throughout the city. She had, according to Jackson, a 'very persuasive manner' and insisted that her pikelets (similar to crumpets) were made with 'the best flour, rich milk and an extra number of eggs'. 'Betty Bombshell' was another character from Victorian Lichfield who, in Jackson's opinion, 'carried her belongings on her back tied up in large bundles' and who earned money by scrubbing floors. Betty was 'a respectable character and very trustworthy', her main worry being boys who followed her about town untying her bundles and strewing her underwear and other belongings onto the street. 'The poor old soul' ended her days in the workhouse on Trent Valley Road. Another personality Jackson wrote about was a man called Walker who, in the 1870s, lived in a small cottage on Stafford Road and made a 'precarious living' by fetching coal for his neighbours. Jackson recalled how this 'quiet, honest and dependable man' would give rides to local children in his donkey cart. (*Lichfield Mercury*)

– JULY 23RD –

1888: On this day, the tragic and mysterious death of a young woman took place in Lichfield. An inquest was held at the Bull's Head Inn into the death of 19-year-old Emma Jane Mills, who lived at the Windsor Castle Inn in Dam Street where she worked as a barmaid. She was found dead, suddenly and unexpectedly, at the home of Henry Russell, lying undressed on Russell's bed. Mr Russell said that Emma had asked to lie down due to feeling unwell after a supper of rabbit, peas and stout. A doctor, who had pronounced her dead at the scene, told the inquest that the body bore no signs of violence. Russell told the inquest that he had seen the young woman have spasms or fits several times in the past. At the inquest there was confusion about two rings, which for some reason had been taken off the dead woman's fingers, and the jury took a long time to reach a verdict, but in the end decided that the deceased had died 'by a visitation from God' and by 'spasms and the failure of the action of the heart'. (*Lichfield Mercury*, July 27th 1888)

~ July 24th ~

1896: On this day, the *Lichfield Mercury* carried a report of an excursion organised by the Lichfield Brewery to the 'popular and attractive seaside resort of Blackpool'. Employees of the brewery were given two tickets each and the general public were also allowed to buy tickets for the trip. Nearly 700 people travelled on the special train which left Lichfield City Station at 5.25 a.m. and arrived in Blackpool, 'the Brighton of the North', at 10.45 a.m. Most of the visitors from Lichfield soon headed for the beach for which, the *Mercury* commented, 'the resort is noted'. The 'pleasure fair', with its 'shows, exhibitions round-a-bouts, swings and donkey rides', was also visited by Lichfeldians. Blackpool Tower, too, proved popular, with people paying 6*d* (3p) for admittance to the aquarium, menagerie and roof garden. For another 6*d* visitors were allowed to go to the very top of the tower, over 500ft tall, via lifts. The return journey started at 9.30p.m., with the train arriving back in Lichfield at 2.30 a.m. the following day. (*Lichfield Mercury*)

– JULY 25TH –

1917: On this day, Lichfield man John J. Salford was discharged from the army after it was discovered that he had only one leg. The 29-year-old builder's clerk had been called up in April and for three months the fact that he had an artificial leg had gone unnoticed. The truth came to light on the parade ground when he found it impossible to do some of the more difficult drills, but was able to salute the sergeant, who had shouted at him, by lifting his fully articulated artificial limb straight up to his chest. He had lost his leg in a shooting accident when, as a teenager, he had been out hunting on a winter's day in a wooded area close to the city called The Dimbles. His friend's gun accidently went off while they were climbing a stile, shooting John in the leg. His friend ran off scared and did not tell anyone what had happened, leaving John lying on the ground covered in snow until found by a farmer the following day. He was taken to hospital in Birmingham by a horse-drawn ambulance, where his leg was amputated. In later years John Salford ran a tobacco and confectionary shop in Tamworth Street. (Salford, J.H., unpublished memoir)

‒ July 26th ‒

1992: On this day, Lichfield's historic Samuel Johnson Birthplace Museum narrowly escaped being burnt down when a fire swept through a neighbouring coffee shop in the early hours of the morning. Relieved curator of the museum, Dr Graham Nicholls, paid tribute to a passer-by who spotted the fire and alerted the fire service, as well as praising the fire brigade, which arrived on the scene quickly and managed to contain the blaze. He revealed how close the Birthplace Museum came to destruction when he described how smoke had entered the building and had set off smoke alarms: 'It could have done untold damage and it would have been very serious had the fire brigade not got here so quickly.' Six fire-fighters, wearing breathing apparatus, had to smash their way into the burning cafe to tackle the fire, which did considerable damage to the Grade II listed building. This was the second occasion in two years that the museum had been threatened by fire; just two years before a computer shop next door caught fire, but was extinguished before any damage was done to Johnson's birthplace. (*Lichfield Mercury*, July 30th 1992)

~ July 27th ~

1575: On this day, Queen Elizabeth I arrived in Lichfield and spent the week in the city. She had travelled from Kenilworth Castle, the home of her close friend Robert Dudley, Earl of Leicester, as she continued her tour, or 'progress', around the country, something she undertook each summer. In earlier times the royal party would have spent their entire time at Cathedral Close, but by now the monarch would expect to see the whole town and so great preparations had been made for her visit. The market place was paved and the market cross was repaired and the Guildhall was refurbished and repainted, while improvements were made to the road leading out of the city to the south. The accounts of the bailiffs of the city show that a sum of £5 was paid to a Mr Cartwright for making an 'oration' and another, rather more mysterious, payment was made to William Hollcraft for 'kepynge madde Richard when her majestie was here'. Payment was also made to the Earl of Warwick's Players, suggesting that the queen was entertained with a play while in the city. (Upton, Chris, *A History of Lichfield*, Phillimore, 2001)

- JULY 28TH -

1997: On this day, plans to build Britain's first toll motorway were given the go-ahead, despite protests from local residents, councillors and Lichfield's MP. The 27-mile-long road, built and financed by Midland Expressway Ltd., would run from the M6 just north of junction 11, follow the route of the A5 and then join the M42 at Coleshill. Objectors to the road had said that there would be a loss of 'Green Belt' land and increased levels of noise, pollution and traffic in the villages around Lichfield, with Lichfield MP Michael Fabricant arguing, 'While business would benefit, the road would affect the unique quality of village life.' However, local businesses, especially those in the Burntwood area, welcomed the £500-million Birmingham Northern Relief Road (eventually called the M6 Toll). Construction of the road was expected to begin in 2000 and be finished by 2004. Managing director of Midland Expressway, Tom Smith, said, 'It will benefit the West Midlands economy and the rest of the country. It will also create more than 1000 jobs during its design and construction and a significant number of long-term jobs once it is in operation.' (*Lichfield Mercury*, July 31st 1997)

~ July 29th ~

1914: On this day, a statue of Commander E.J. Smith was unveiled in Lichfield. Smith had been the captain of the *Titanic*, which sank on its maiden voyage in 1912 after striking an iceberg. The statue was unveiled by his daughter, Mrs Helen Melville Smith, and the ceremony was attended by many dignitaries, including the Bishop of Lichfield, the Mayor of Southampton and representatives from Belfast, Liverpool and New York – all places with *Titanic* connections. Edward Smith was born in Hanley in 1850 and over the years there has been a lot of discussion as to why his statue was not placed in his hometown rather than Lichfield. One reason advanced at the time was the idea that as Lichfield is located halfway between London and Liverpool it would be more accessible to American visitors. Some put forward the view that Lichfield was the cathedral city of the diocese in which Smith was born. It was also rumoured that the potteries town of Hanley had commissioned the statue before the *Titanic* disaster, after which it wanted nothing to do with Smith, who was seen as partly to blame. The statue, which was sculpted by Kathleen Scott, widow of the Antarctic explorer, stands to this day in Lichfield's museum gardens. (*Captain E.J. Smith's Memorial souvenir booklet*, 1914)

– July 30th –

1943: On this day, the *Lichfield Mercury* published details of government plans for the 'reconstruction' of education in Britain once the war had ended. The government hoped that the changes would ensure 'a fuller measure of education and opportunity for young people'. The school-leaving age would be raised from 14 to 15 and elementary schools would be replaced by primary schools, which would cater for all children aged 5 to 11. There were to be three types of secondary school: grammar schools, which would provide 'training for university and for the administrative and clerical professions'; modern schools, 'giving a general education adapted to local needs and employment'; and technical schools, 'preparing pupils for entry into some branch of industry or commerce'. Children would be selected for these schools on the basis of intelligence tests at the age of 11, as well as their school records. The government eventually brought in these changes as part of the 1944 Education Act, with education costs estimated to rise from £90 million per year in 1939 to £190 million per year. (*Lichfield Mercury*)

– JULY 31ST –

1909: On this day, the Lichfield Board of Guardians' Children's Home was opened by Major Wise, the Chairman of the Board. Situated in Wissage, the home could accommodate thirty children in dormitories, with the buildings arranged so that the boys' and girls' sections were kept isolated from each other. Most of the children at the home were sent from Lichfield's workhouse, where they would be kept separate from the influence of older people 'of the undesirable class'. The building was designed by Richard Barnes, a Lichfield architect, at a cost of £5,488 and was equipped with centrally heated radiators and hot water for baths. The Lichfield Board of Guardians saw themselves as a progressive organisation – the children's home was modern and even luxurious by 1909 standards and was described by Major Wise as 'splendid'. The building was renamed The Poplars in 1989 and became a family centre for children in care. (*Lichfield Mercury*, August 6th 1909)

- August 1st -

1940: On this day, Lichfield airfield at Fradley officially came into service. The home of 51 Maintenance Unit, it became the busiest airfield in Staffordshire and a controlling point for virtually all of the aviation traffic that passed through the Birmingham area during the Second World War. With the Battle of Britain underway the main type of aircraft seen at Lichfield was the Hawker Hurricane, which Air Transport Auxiliary pilots collected and then delivered to front-line squadrons – such as 32 Squadron at Biggin Hill, 310 Squadron at Duxford, 56 Squadron at North Weald and 17 Squadron at Tangmere – all of which were in the thick of the battle. Staff at the airfield also offered civilian training courses such as a 'Roof Watching Aircraft Recognition Course', the first of which was attended by 150 people. In April 1941 the airfield was taken over by Bomber Command and Wellingtons from Lichfield took part in the 'Thousand Bomber Raids' that began in May 1942. The airfield closed in 1958 and the Air Ministry sold the site in 1962 for £240,000. Today, the airfield has virtually disappeared, although most of the aircraft hangars still exist and are used for industrial purposes. (Chorlton, Martin, *Staffordshire Airfields in the Second World War*, Countryside Books, 2007)

- August 2nd -

1803: This day saw the death of John Saville, the vicar choral of the cathedral, whose close relationship with Anna Seward had been the centre of a scandal for over thirty years. Seward, the most popular female poet of her day and nicknamed 'the Swan of Lichfield', had known Saville when she was a young girl. He had arrived at the cathedral in 1755 as a 19-year-old and rumours of their affair started in 1771, when Saville's wife banned Seward from her house in Cathedral Close and her parents put her under virtual 'house arrest'. Annoyed, Seward wrote:

> I love John Saville for his virtue. He is entangled in a connection with the vilest of women and the most brutally despicable. He cannot be my husband but no law of earth or heaven forbids that he should be my friend or debars us from the liberty of conversing together.

The scandal reached a climax in 1773 when Saville left his wife and children and moved into the house next door. Saville carried on working at the cathedral for the rest of his life; Seward never married. (Hopkins, Mary Alden, *Dr Johnson's Lichfield*, Hastings House, 1952)

– AUGUST 3RD –

1884: On this day, the future Lady Charnwood was thrown out of her carriage, damaged her knee and as a result spent the next eighteen months recovering in bed. Lady Charnwood, born Dorothea Mary Roby in 1876, was the granddaughter of the Liberal politician A.J. Mundella. During her long recovery, to help pass the time, she started to collect the letters and autographs of famous people and eventually wrote a book which detailed her collection and included extracts from some of the letters. Her oldest letter and signature was that of Henry VIII and was dated December 1496. Other letters in her collection included ones from Jane Austen, Charlotte Brontë, Emma Hamilton, Samuel Johnson, William Pitt, Andrew Marvell and John Dryden. The only postcard in her collection was written and signed by Rupert Brooke, the First World War poet. As a child she met a number of celebrities and was given signed drawings by the artists Burne-Jones and Millais, among others. Dorothea married Godfrey Benson, 1st Baron Charnwood, who became Mayor of Lichfield in 1909. She lived in Stowe House, which had been bought by her mother in 1902. (Lady Charnwood, *Call Back Yesterday*, Eyre & Spottiswoode, 1937)

~ August 4th ~

1948: On this day, the funeral of Miles Jervis, a pioneer of the Midlands cinema industry, took place. A 'riot of colourful wreaths' sent from many cinemas in the area, and even one from the Hollywood's RKO Radio Pictures Ltd., were arrayed around the graveyard at St Anne's church in Chasetown for Jervis' funeral, who had died at his home in Bridge Cross Road, Chase Terrace, aged 70. 'He will be long remembered as the man who brought cinema entertainment to the Chase area', as well as to many other parts of the Midlands region. Originally from Stoke, he opened his first cinema in 1919 after he had travelled around the country with a fair for a number of years, showing 'living picture shows' using a portable projector. By the 1920s he had acquired a number of other 'picture houses' in places such as Dudley, Walsall Wood and Cheshire. Jervis' son, also called Miles, was managing director of Miles Jervis Cinemas Limited and his daughter, Mrs W. Stevens, managed the Chase cinema in Chase Terrace. (*Lichfield Mercury*, August 6th 1948)

~ August 5th ~

1949: On this day, Kenneth Tynan, a producer and director at Lichfield's Garrick Theatre in Bore Street, replied to criticism that 'constant change' in the repertory company created by the management was causing 'well-loved' actors to move elsewhere. Tynan refuted the accusation and wrote that the aim of the theatre company was to form a 'versatile, unselfish company whose flexible personalities and talents the people of the City may come to regard as an essential part of their weekly lives'. The company put on a different play each week including Tynan's own production of George Farquar's *The Beaux Stratagem*, a play set in Lichfield, which was described by one critic as 'original, and to some, puzzling'. A number of actors who later became famous worked in the Garrick's repertory company, for example Lionel Jefferies and Terence Morgan. The flamboyant, Oxford-educated Tynan was born in Birmingham in 1927 and went on to become a nationally known writer and theatre critic. He wrote for the *Observer* and the *New Yorker* and, notoriously, in 1965 became the first person on British television to utter the 'f' word. (*Lichfield Mercury*)

~ August 6th ~

1914: On this day, Lichfield's Territorial Reservists paraded outside the Guildhall before marching off to their headquarters in Burton-on-Trent. The First World War had begun a few days earlier and the mobilisation of troops was in full swing. The Territorials had been quartered at the Guildhall for the previous two nights and Lichfield folk had witnessed the unusual sight of sentries being posted outside the building into which no unauthorised persons were allowed to enter. Throughout the city other signs of preparations for war were starting to be seen: the Colours of the South Staffordshire Regiment were placed in the cathedral for the duration of the war and throughout the district many horses were commandeered by the military authorities for transport purposes. Most of the horses taken were never returned. The Bishop of Lichfield arrived back after a holiday in Austria and a number of schools were requisitioned for the quartering of reservist troops, 'of whom there was a constant stream into Lichfield' since mobilisation had been announced. However, in the summer of 1914, some aspects continued as normal – cricket fixtures went ahead and the Lichfield Floral and Horticultural Show took place. (*Lichfield Mercury*, August 7th 1914)

~ August 7th ~

1883: On this day, the County Agricultural Society held its annual exhibition in Lichfield at the cricket club ground and its adjoining fields. The previous year's show had been postponed due to a 'foot and mouth' outbreak and this was the first such exhibition held in Lichfield since 1867. The first day of the two-day event mainly concentrated on exhibiting farm implements and poultry, as well as many types of horses such as 'cobs, hackneys, ponies and Yeomanry horses'. The second day of the exhibition was focused on cattle, sheep and pigs and parades of the prize-winners. There was also a show jumping event and a horseshoeing competition. Henry Bamford and Sons of Market Street had a stand showing the latest in mowers, reapers and haymakers, as well as horse-rakes, chaff-cutters, seed-drills, ploughs, cheese-presses, curd mills and butter churns. Bamfords won a number of prizes at the show including medals for the best two-horse mower and the best horse-rake. The *Lichfield Mercury* described the city as being 'gaily decorated' for the event, the show receiving a total of 5,586 visitors, despite the weather being poor. (*Lichfield Mercury*, August 10th 1883)

~ August 8th ~

1881: On this day, vandalism and 'a wanton act of sacrilege' took place at St Michael's churchyard in Lichfield. 'Perpetrated by young men of a certain class', the damage was described by the *Lichfield Mercury* as nothing less than the 'desecration of God's Acre'. Marble crosses and monuments were pulled down and broken and 'the damage done in the churchyard was great'. The *Mercury* was unequivocal in what the punishment should be for the perpetrators when they were eventually found – 'they should be flogged naked through every churchyard in England,' it said. The paper went on to say that, 'It makes us almost ashamed of our City that such a thing could be possible.' The *Mercury* made the point that it hoped that the search for the 'scoundrels' would be 'prompt, active and unremitting' and that a reward would be offered by the paper for information leading to the arrest of 'these animals'. Once they had been arrested, the *Mercury* said, 'it is to be hoped that the law knows how to punish offenders of this class'. (*Lichfield Mercury*, August 12th 1881)

~ August 9th ~

1902: On this day, celebrations took place to mark the coronation of King Edward VII. The coronation day, which had been postponed due to the king's ill health, was an excuse for people across the Lichfield District to celebrate and take part in varied events. In Lichfield City church bells rang out early in the morning and the deputy mayor led a procession of local dignitaries from the Guildhall to the cathedral, accompanied by the band of the Staffordshire Yeomanry. A service at the cathedral was followed by a public luncheon in the Guildhall, a concert at the Recreation Ground, a 'display of physical drill by the lads of the Truant School' and sports for all including cycle races, egg and spoon races and an 'old man's race'. In Burntwood the streets were 'bedecked with flags in a manner which never before, in the history of the village, had been attempted', and 600 children were given tea and presented with a coronation mug. In Whittington there were oranges and sweets for the children, as well as various sports, and the 'aged poor' were presented with envelopes containing money. In the evening there was a bonfire and fireworks. (*Lichfield Mercury*, August 15th 1902)

~ August 10th ~

1922: On this day, the *Lichfield Mercury* strongly indicated that road traffic in Lichfield was beginning to become a big problem, as a number of motorists were charged with offences at Lichfield City Police Court. George Arthur Munroe Levett of Packington Hall, for example, was accused of driving in a dangerous manner and with obstructing the police in the execution of their duty. Levett's car was turning at the junction of Bird Street, St John Street and Bore Street – described by the newspaper as 'one of the most dangerous spots in the United Kingdom' – at a speed of 15 to 16mph and ignored the policeman controlling traffic, Constable Lee, almost running into him and another pedestrian in the process. Levett, who had shouted to the policeman to 'come out of the way', was fined the 'large amount' of £8 5*s* (£8.25). At the same court Robert Durkin was charged with being drunk in charge of a car, Richard Dixon fined for driving his lorry 'negligently' and John Billings fined for having no identification plates on his vehicle. (*Lichfield Mercury*, August 11th 1922)

⁓ August 11th ⁓

1955: On this day, the Regal cinema in Lichfield, rather oddly, began to show the film *White Christmas*, starring Bing Crosby, Danny Kaye and George Clooney's aunt, Rosemary Clooney. The 'silly season' it seems was well underway that week, as the *Lichfield Mercury* reported on a number of quirky news stories, such as 90-year-old Harriet Scoffham of 19 The Dimbles, who won the Colonel Swinfen-Broun cup for the best council-house garden in the city. Mrs Scoffham, who first won the trophy in 1938, was a lifetime gardener and said, 'everyone should take an interest in gardening. It worries me to death to see weeds in any garden.' Despite her age, Mrs Scoffham spent three to four hours every day working in her garden and was looking forward to many more years of gardening. It was also reported that the city's town crier was due to take part in the National Town Crier's Championship, which was to be held in Hastings. Mr Malcolm Johnson had been Lichfield's town crier for two years and was reported to say that he did not expect to win the competition. He was correct. The *Mercury* of August 26th informed its readers that he finished sixth out of twenty-two contestants. (*Lichfield Mercury*)

~ August 12th ~

1892: On this day, the *Lichfield Mercury* carried its usual large number of wanted advertisements for servants. For example, a 'highly respectable', middle-aged gentlemen living at 22 Dam Street required a housekeeper with good references, and Mrs Asher of Bore Street wanted a general maid, 'about 16'. Then there was Mrs Sturgess of Wood End, Shenstone, who wanted 'a strong girl' to work in a farmhouse and Mrs Blore, who required 'useful help' in her farmhouse, saying that 'a farmer's daughter aged 16 or 18 would be preferred'. People from all over Staffordshire appeared to advertise for servants in the *Mercury*. Someone in Newcastle-under-Lyme sought a 'good general servant, about 30, who can produce plain cooking' and a 'nurse-housemaid' was wanted by Mrs Crutchley in Tamworth. A number of servant registries advertised in the *Mercury* too, giving us a good idea of the sorts of wages on offer. Cooks, for example, could expect to earn between £14 and £35 per year; housemaids and kitchen maids between £10 and £20; and between-maids could expect to earn £8 to £12 per annum. The army at Whittington Barracks also advertised in the *Mercury* and were keen that males aged 18 to 25 and unemployed should join up. (*Lichfield Mercury*)

~ AUGUST 13TH ~

1920: On this day, it was announced that an electricity supply would soon be brought to Lichfield. The City Council had received a letter from Walsall Corporation Electricity Supply Department, which was planning to lay a cable that would take electricity to Whittington Barracks, proposing that the cable could also go via the City of Lichfield if there was adequate demand for the 'new' power source. The mayor of Lichfield, Councillor H.G. Hall, thought the council ought to set up a small committee to meet with a delegation from Walsall Corporation in order to discuss the matter. Councillor Wigham said that if the proposal meant electricity in Lichfield it ought to be followed up, adding, 'This would undoubtedly be of great use to the City, not only in the way of lighting, but for power purposes and therefore it would be an important factor in the future development of Lichfield.' A number of other councillors agreed that not having an electricity supply in the city was a great handicap when it came to attracting new industries to Lichfield and, as a result, the council agreed that representatives from Walsall should be met and that the scheme should be pursued. (*Lichfield Mercury*, August 13th 1920)

~ AUGUST 14TH ~

2002: On this day, a local secondary school was ravaged by fire following a suspected arson attack. Chase Terrace High School had only recently become a technology college and staff and pupils were already preparing for the new school year. However, people's plans were forced to change as the fire swept through The Bewley Building and destroyed over half of the entire school, which had originally been built in 1932 as separate senior boys and senior girls schools, before becoming a mixed secondary modern school in 1961 and a comprehensive in 1965. The fire broke out at about 9.30 p.m. and at one time ten fire engines fought the massive blaze. Firefighters needed breathing apparatus and the large crowd, which stood in 'stunned silence', had to be moved due to the heat and flying debris. It was remarkable that, only a few weeks later, the school was able to reopen, a 'village' of mobile classrooms having been erected on the school's playing fields. A new building, costing £8.5 million, opened in September 2004. No one was charged with causing the fire. (James, Byron, *The Chronicle of a School Destroyed by Fire*, Chase Terrace Technology School, 2005)

~ AUGUST 15TH ~

1957: On this day, the rebuilt Bald Buck Inn was opened. Situated on Greenhill, the new pub replaced the old inn that had stood on the site since the eighteenth century and which had been demolished to make way for the construction of the Birmingham Road. Built by Messrs J.R. Deacon Ltd of Lichfield, the new Bald Buck was described as 'a first-class, modern public house incorporating the very latest in features and workmanship', equipped with a large bar, a market room for the use of farmers from the nearby cattle market and a gentlemen's smoke room. In addition, the pub had 'a very essential feature of modern buildings of this nature – a large car park'. Present at the opening was Mr C. Dixon, the district representative of the Wolverhampton and Dudley Brewery – the owners of the pub. The licensees, Mr and Mrs Bayliss, welcomed old and new customers, including their oldest patron, Joe Alport of Rotten Row, who had been going to the pub every night for his pint for sixty years and who was presented with a new pipe and tobacco pouch. (*Lichfield Mercury*, August 16th 1957)

‐ AUGUST 16TH ‐

1907: On this day, the *Lichfield Mercury* reported on the discussions which had taken place at Lichfield City Council regarding the introduction of speed limits in the city for motor cars. Motor traffic had been growing in volume for a number of years and the council had become increasingly concerned that road fatalities would soon occur if the speed of cars on city streets was not regulated. According to one councillor, motor cars could be seen every day 'rushing through the streets, especially Frog Lane, Wade Street, Bore Street and Sandford Street'. Another councillor suggested that motorists' attitude towards pedestrians was extremely rude: 'they tended to sound their horns and shout, "mind out of the way", and if they didn't get out of the way they were run over without the slightest compunction.' Yet another councillor reported that he had seen a motor car 'turn into Market Street at the rate of ten miles an hour and the car had run on to the pavement'. The council eventually decided to recommend a speed limit of 10mph in Lichfield, a suggestion that was rejected by the County Council. (*Lichfield Mercury*)

⟶ August 17th ⟵

1945: On this day, the *Lichfield Mercury*, in a large headline, proclaimed 'Final Victory After Six Years of War' and reported on the announcement made by the prime minister Clement Attlee that the Japanese had surrendered. The paper also reported on the celebrations that had followed in Lichfield where, despite the announcement being made in the early hours of the morning, news had quickly spread and 'men, women, youths and children in perambulators' were soon out on the street banging and blowing all sorts of 'musical' instruments. Flags and bunting appeared as people gathered in the Market Square, where 'citizens, British servicemen and American Army' celebrated in a 'good-natured and harmonious manner', making an 'auspicious occasion the most memorable one in the annals of our ancient and loyal city'. The mayor addressing the gathered crowd said, 'The war is over, it had called for called great sacrifices and hard work, unparalleled in history, but winning the peace would be equally hard.' He went on to acknowledge and thank the members of the British Empire for their help, as well as for that of the great Allies: USA, Russia and China. (*Lichfield Mercury*)

— August 18th —

1910: On this day, the Johnson Society was formed at a meeting held at Lichfield's Guildhall. Among those present were Lord and Lady Charnwood, various councillors and Percy Fitzgerald, who had donated the statue of James Boswell to the city. The society was formed in honour of Lichfield's most renowned son, Samuel Johnson, following the recent bicentennial celebrations of his birth in 1709, when the number of visitors to his birthplace increased markedly. It was agreed that each year a distinguished man would be asked to accept the office of President of the Society, the first being Sir Robert White-Thompson, who was a descendent of the eighteenth-century Lichfield poet Anna Seward. The inaugural meeting of the society took place on September 17th in order to coincide with the Johnson birthday celebrations, when a meal takes place each year in the great man's memory. Annual subscriptions for membership of the society were fixed at 5*s* (25p) each year or £1 1*s* (£1.05) for life membership. (*Lichfield Mercury*, August 19th and September 23rd 1910)

– AUGUST 19TH –

1914: On this day, a bus service started which linked Lichfield with Birmingham. The Midland Motor Omnibus Company ran regular buses between the city's Market Square, Sutton Coldfield and Birmingham every one-and-a-half hours. The fare from Lichfield to Birmingham was 1s 2d (6p) each way and between Lichfield and Sutton Coldfield the fare was set at 8d (3p) each way. The single-deck, 40hp petrol-engine buses also stopped at Shenstone, Blake Street, Mere Green and Four Oaks. Lichfield City Council had agreed to grant a licence to the bus company to run the service, as long as the company met the cost of repairing any damage caused to the roads. The red buses run by the Midland Motor Omnibus Company, better known as Midland Red, would become a familiar sight throughout the Midlands region for many years. From 1921 the company also ran coaches to popular seaside resorts like Llandudno and Weston-super-Mare. Midland Red continued until 1981 when it was broken up into smaller companies. (*Lichfield Mercury*, August 21st 1914)

~ AUGUST 20TH ~

1965: On this day, the youth employment officer for the Lichfield area, Mr Peter Bramidge, called upon local firms to make their job openings for youngsters more attractive if they were to overcome their labour shortage, adding that 'youngsters are now more discriminating' when looking for jobs. In the area more jobs were available than there were school leavers, with 550 local 'boys and girls' finishing school at the end of the summer term. Eighty per cent of those looking for jobs had already found suitable employment, with the remainder either not yet 16 or awaiting exam results. Mr Bramidge added that 'youngsters haven't really experienced too much difficulty in finding employment this year' and that there was a definite trend towards 'white-collar' jobs instead of semi-skilled positions, which employers had found difficult to fill – one local firm had brought in 'coloured immigrant workers' to help. At the time, in an expanding economy, there were plenty of jobs in the city and the country at large. (*Lichfield Mercury*, August 20th 1965)

1959: On this day, the *Lichfield Mercury* reported the opening of the new William Lunn's old people's homes in Stowe Street. The bishop of Lichfield opened the six self-contained cottages and handed over the keys to the 'lucky old people who will be able to live in the new houses for the rest of their lives'. The homes were built on the site of the original William Lunn's almshouses, which were granted to the city in Lunn's will in 1667, in which he wrote that the homes were for 'poor, ancient and needy people inhabiting and dwelling in the City of Lichfield'. Lunn's charity later merged with other city charities to form the Municipal Charities of the City and County of Lichfield. The cost of the six new bungalows was £10,600; each had a living room, kitchen, one bedroom and a bathroom, with a low toilet and bath with handrails. A brass plaque on the wall outside the homes read: 'Municipal Charities of the City of Lichfield William Lunn's Homes. Original grant June 1667. Rebuilt 1959.' It was hoped that more homes would be built on the site, along with warden accommodation. (*Lichfield Mercury*)

~ August 22nd ~

1927: On this day, Queen Mary, the wife of King George V, visited Lichfield Cathedral. Although it was scheduled as a 'private visit', details 'had become generally known' and crowds of well-wishers had gathered at various points along the queen's route to catch a glimpse of her, despite heavy rain showers throughout the day. A large crowd in Cathedral Close 'heartily cheered' her arrival and she, along with the Dowager Countess of Bradford and the Marquis and Marchioness of Cambridge, were received at the West Gate by the bishop and then shown around the cathedral. Queen Mary was particularly interested in Chantry's statue of the 'Sleeping Children' and also spent time in the War Memorial Chapel. The visit to the cathedral lasted three-quarters of an hour, but the *Mercury* failed to record whether or not the queen, renowned for picking up 'souvenirs' of her visits, came away with anything. The royal party left the city en-route to Sutton Coldfield, driving slowly through Lichfield's streets where everyone 'was able to have an excellent view of the Queen'. (*Lichfield Mercury*, August 26th 1927)

~ August 23rd ~

1987: On this day, record rainfall turned Lichfield into 'a mini Venice' and brought 'flood chaos' to hundreds of homes, offices and businesses. Streets in the city centre and in the surrounding villages turned into rivers several feet deep and sparked off frantic calls to the emergency services. Fire officers from Cannock, Stone and Tamworth were called in to help Lichfield fire crews deal with the problems caused by the heavy rainfall – the largest amount ever recorded in the city in a twenty-four-hour period. The deluge caused a massive mopping-up operation that lasted for three days, with many examples of community spirit as neighbours helped out those whose homes had been flooded by turning up with buckets and brushes. In the city centre Bore Street, Conduit Street and Dam Street were all under water and McDonald's restaurant had to close after it was inundated by 'a river of floodwater'. All of the shops under the arches of the Corn Exchange were 'completely awash' and the Earl of Lichfield was one of many pubs in the city where cellars were flooded. It was estimated that almost 5in of rain fell in Lichfield during the day. (*Lichfield Mercury*, August 28th 1987)

~ August 24th ~

1962: On this day, work began on the new £250,000 secondary school sited on waste ground to the rear of Ponesfield Road; it was expected that the first phase of the building would be ready in 1964. Once completed, the school would provide places for 750 boys and girls and there was also provision made for evening school facilities. The first phase of the building was planned to include classrooms, a gymnasium and a large assembly hall 'of unusual design'. As well as these general classrooms there would also be specialist rooms for science, arts and crafts, pottery, domestic science and a drawing office, and a library was planned for the middle of the building. Sports provision consisted of tennis courts and a large playing field and a swimming pool was promised for phase two, in the hope that it would be a community facility which would reduce congestion at the city's one, small public bath. Netherstowe School opened in late 1964 and had as its Latin motto *Altiora Peto*, which meant 'Aim Higher'. (*Lichfield Mercury*, August 24th 1962)

– August 25th –

1905: On this day, a fatal accident took place at Lichfield's Trent Valley station. John Alfred Wood, aged 32, a brakesman from Burton employed by the London and North Western Railway Company, was killed when an engine and two coaches ran over him. The deceased man, who had worked for the company for seven years and had no hearing or sight problems, was killed as he crossed the tracks on his way to deal with a shunting engine – he either fell down or was knocked down on the railway lines for some reason that will remain unknown. The driver of the train had not seen Mr Wood as he backed his train into a siding, only discovering the body after he had stopped and when it was clear that the unfortunate man had died instantly as the train had run over his head, 'leaving blood and brain-matter' on one of the coaches. At an inquest held later at the Trent Valley Hotel, the jury returned a verdict of accidental death. (*Lichfield Mercury*, September 1st 1905)

~ August 26th ~

1946: On this day, for the first time in sixty-three years, a county cricket match took place in Lichfield when Staffordshire played Durham in the Minor Counties League at the Birmingham Road ground. When Staffordshire Cricket Club was founded in 1871, Lichfield was its base until 1884 when other venues were used. This week every effort had been made to revive interest in county cricket in the city and on day one of the two-day game almost 1,000 spectators turned up to watch Staffordshire bat first and score 296 runs, with R. Smith making a century opening the batting. Durham then made just thirty-nine in their first innings, with Staffordshire bowler S. Narcop taking six wickets. Durham were then asked to follow-on and bat again and in their second innings they made 136 runs, with S. Crump taking five wickets; Staffordshire won by an innings and 121 runs. In the crowd was the legendary ex-Staffordshire and England bowler Sidney Barnes, often considered one of the greatest test bowlers of all time. After the game he said that he was very impressed with the Lichfield ground, the excellent pitch and the city's 'cordial welcome' to the two teams. (*Lichfield Mercury*, August 30th 1946)

~ August 27th ~

1976: On this date, the *Lichfield Mercury*, under the headline 'Scorched Earth', reported that people were saying, 'give us back our traditional British summer, macs, scattered showers and all.' The drought that had affected the whole of Britain was in its thirty-ninth day and strict new water-saving measures had just been introduced. Cleaning cars, fountains, the filling of swimming pools and the watering of sports fields had all been banned, and even tighter controls were in the offing if the drought continued. Serious fires had raged across the nearby beauty spot of Hopwas Woods and every available fire crew in Staffordshire was fighting the 'inferno', as a great pall of smoke hung over much of the surrounding countryside. Some people were panic-buying frozen food, following a warning about the potential price rises that would almost inevitably follow the summer's poor vegetable crops. 'The endless days of sizzling sunshine' had also affected clothes shopping, with many women buying dresses to wear instead of jeans and many men queuing to buy shorts. Sales of lawnmowers had dropped by 25 per cent on the previous year's figure, as people's lawns turned brown in the relentless sun. (*Lichfield Mercury*)

~ August 28th ~

1889: On this day, two cases were brought before Lichfield's Magistrates' Court, which shows the city was rather more cosmopolitan in 1889 than we might have previously believed. Patrick Mulrain, 'an Irishman of no fixed abode', was charged with being drunk in Tamworth Street and admitted to the court that he had 'taken a little whisky in consequence of having the toothache' and had then drunk some ale which 'got over him'. Mr Mulrain was fined 1s (5p) and costs. Sam Wilson, a 'negro' of no fixed abode who was, by his own account, a freed slave, was found in Wade Street so drunk he could not stand. Mr Wilson told the court that he had been 'treated' in a pub by a gentlemen and being unused to strong ale had become intoxicated. He also told the court that he had been born a slave in one of the southern states of America and now 'obtained a livelihood by playing the banjo'. The magistrates took pity on Mr Wilson and discharged him, so long as he promised to leave Lichfield at once. (*Lichfield Mercury*, August 30th 1889)

~ August 29th ~

1815: On this day, the *Courier*, a London newspaper, reported on the trial held in Lichfield of John Wright of Sandford Street, who was accused of the murder of his infant child, Elizabeth Neville. Wright was seen to take the 9-day-old baby from her mother, also called Elizabeth Neville, and squeeze the child's throat before twisting her neck and battering her about the head. The witness to the incident, Anne Walker – wife of the landlord of the Swan Inn, who had been attending Mrs Neville 'during her confinement' – immediately sent for Dr Greene, who examined the child and found her to be dead, with a dislocated neck, severe bruising around her head and bleeding from the ears. Wright, who professed to know nothing about what had taken place, had been treated for some years by Dr Greene for epilepsy, which had caused him to 'become insane' for short periods of time. As a result of the medical evidence the jury found Wright not guilty of the murder but he was, on the Judge's orders, confined to an 'Insane Asylum' for the rest of his life. Why the *Courier* reported on a Lichfield trial is unclear. (*The Courier*, August 29th 1815, reprinted in the *Lichfield Mercury*, January 9th 1931)

~ August 30th ~

1963: On this day, the *Lichfield Mercury*'s headline was 'Toward a Safer Lichfield', as the paper reported on the commencement of a ban on heavy traffic through the city. The ban was 'one more step towards bringing Lichfield in line with modern traffic conditions and making the main streets safer for pedestrians as well as for the private motorists', informed the paper. The ban related to all lorries, buses and coaches which could no longer travel down Tamworth Street, Bore Street, Bird Street and Beacon Street. Signs were put up to that effect and police officers on motorcycles and foot patrols were on hand to bring the existence of the new rules to any drivers of vehicles exceeding 3 tons. Also announced on this day were improvements to the Friary Junction and the reconstruction of Market Square, which included the planting of lime trees and the repainting of metal seats. (*Lichfield Mercury*)

~ August 31st ~

1175: By this day, King Henry II had presided over a trial in Lichfield, which found the murderers of a royal forester guilty. The men were hanged in what is the first documented execution of criminals in Lichfield. A permanent gallows was probably situated on the west side of the London Road near the junction with Shortbutts Lane, used for the last time in 1810 when three forgers were hanged. A pillory stood on the west side of Market Square, near to where the statue of Samuel Johnson now stands, a set of whipping stocks were located in Market Square and Cathedral Close, and in 1701 a branding iron was owned by the city. A cuckstool (ducking stool) was mentioned in 1485 and was used at the Bird Street side of Minster Pool for the punishment of prostitutes and hen-pecking wives, and in the eighteenth century such a stool was retrieved from Stowe Pool. Criminals and debtors were consigned to Lichfield gaol, which was located behind the Guildhall and which was fully equipped with fetters, shackles and neck collars. The gaol, which could hold up to fifty prisoners, closed in 1866. (Greenslade, M.W. (ed.), *A History of Lichfield*, Staffordshire Libraries, Arts and Archives, 1994)

— September 1st —

1314: From this day, the Bishop of Lichfield Walter de Langton (1243–1321) started to make his ambitious plans for vast improvements to the cathedral and the town of Lichfield. De Langton ensured that the whole of Cathedral Close was walled, a ditch was built around the walls and great gates were added on the west and south sides. He erected a bridge over Minster Pool – a plaque on the side of the present bridge makes reference to de Langton's bridge – and paved the streets of the town. He also erected a new Bishop's Palace – the Great Hall – which is said to have measured 100ft in length and 56ft wide. He built houses for the dean and other clergy, as well as improving their salaries. In the cathedral itself he constructed a costly shrine to St Chad (it cost £2,000, an immense amount of money in the fourteenth century) and commenced the building of the Lady Chapel. Walter de Langton was one of Lichfield's great benefactors and it was said of him that 'he found the Cathedral mean and left it magnificent'. (Parker, Alfred D.A., *Sentimental Journey in and About the Ancient and Loyal City of Lichfield*, The Johnson's Head, 1925)

~ September 2nd ~

1538: By this day, the dissolution of Lichfield Friary had taken place. The 'Minor Brethren of Lichfield', otherwise known as Franciscan monks or 'Greyfriars', had originally arrived in the city in 1227 or 1228 when they had been granted permission by the Bishop of Lichfield to build their friary; they were well known for working with the poorest in society, including lepers. In 1291 their wooden friary was destroyed by fire, as was most of the city, but rebuilding started almost at once; however, the Black Death of the 1340s killed two-thirds of the friars and the establishment never recovered. The dissolution took place in the reign of Henry VIII, after the Church of England broke away from Rome and the sale of land provided Henry with much-needed money. The Bishop of Dover was commissioned to close down the friary and the site was sold to a Richard Crumbilhome, a land-speculator, who immediately sold it on to Gregory and Alice Stonyng. Today the site lies near to the friary traffic lights and an information board can be found opposite the library. (Upton, Chris, *A History of Lichfield*, Phillimore, 2001)

~ September 3rd ~

1939: On this day, the declaration of war on Germany was greeted in Lichfield with a mixture of trepidation and determination. The city's cinemas were immediately closed until further notice and the *Mercury* published details of air-raid precautions, with incendiary bomb control and locations of public shelters high on the list. A headline on page four announced, in no uncertain terms, that the coming war would be a case of 'Civilisation Versus Hitler', and the paper published details of government plans to call up all male citizens aged between 18 and 40. Prime Minister Chamberlain's radio broadcast in the morning had been listened to all over the city, as was the king's statement in the evening, in which he spoke about Britain being 'forced into a conflict' by Germany. Lichfield soon became a place of 'unparalleled activity' as mobilising troops and military transport flooded the streets and Air Raid Precaution posts were set up throughout the city. All civic functions were cancelled and the city's sheriff, Frank Halfpenny, ended his message to Lichfield people with the words, 'even during the blackout God proves that he has not forgotten us, for one only has to look skywards to see the stars shining forth in their serenity.' (*Lichfield Mercury*, September 8th 1939)

‒ September 4th ‒

1911: On this day, the body of Lichfield man Herbert Freeman was found outside Hanch Hall. Freeman, of Craddock's Yard, Tamworth Street, was discovered with his throat cut and nearby lay his wife Maud, alive but with 'shocking gashes in her throat'. The Freemans, who had only recently been married, had spent the day at Cannock Chase and ended up at the Roe Buck Inn at Wolseley Bridge (they had a history of having loud arguments ‒ on their wedding day they had caused a disturbance at the Castle Inn in Lichfield). At the Roe Buck they persuaded Alfred Black, a drayman from Wade Street, to give them a lift back to Lichfield. When the wagon reached the village of Handsacre, however, the couple started to argue and Freeman threatened his wife and the driver with a knife. They left the wagon at Hanch Hall where Freeman attacked his wife before cutting his own throat. They were found by local police officers, Broadfield and Haynes, who sent for a doctor. Mrs Freeman subsequently spent a number of weeks in hospital before being discharged. (*Lichfield Mercury*, October 6th 1911)

~ SEPTEMBER 5TH ~

1989: On this day, archaeologists working on the Lichfield friary site unearthed two skeletons believed to be those of a man and a woman dating from the mid-fourteenth century. An examination of the bones showed that the woman was elderly and was severely arthritic; the man was probably in his mid-30s and was quite healthy when he died. Both bodies had been buried in an east–west position – a sign that they were Christian burials – and they were found under the cloister of the friary. Both skeletons were reburied. The archaeological team had been at the site for two months, with the aim of establishing what lay beneath the area that was last excavated in the 1930s. They discovered that before it was demolished in the sixteenth century, the paths which marked where the friary walls once stood were accurate. The find was announced on the same day as plans to turn the friary site into a major tourist attraction were revealed, with Lichfield City Council planning to erect information boards on the site for tourists. (*Lichfield Mercury*, September 8th 1989)

~ September 6th ~

1956: On this day, the funeral of Master Baker Fred Garratt, one of Lichfield's most respected tradesmen, took place at St Michael's church. The service was attended by a large congregation, with 'every seat in the church being occupied', and it was conducted by the vicar of St Mary's, H.S. Cresswell. Mr Garratt died at the age of 83 at his home in Trent Valley Road. For forty years he was a member of the City Council and was associated with many of the improvements that took place in the city during that time. He was sheriff in 1920–21, mayor in 1925 and elected alderman in 1935 and had only recently retired from the council due to 'advanced age'. The son of a farmer, his family came to Lichfield when he was very young. He was apprenticed to the owner of a well-established grocery business, of which he later became manager. In 1908 he went into business on his own when he acquired an old bakery in Market Street, quickly making it into a success. Very soon the name Garratt's Bakery became a household phrase in Lichfield, as it evolved into the largest business of its kind in the Midlands. (*Lichfield Mercury*, September 7th 1956)

— September 7th —

1965: By this day, 'quietly and with a minimum of fuss,' Chase Terrace Secondary School had become a comprehensive school. According to the headmaster, Mr Walter Wright, this 'no tears' changeover would have important and far-reaching implications for individual pupils. 'Recently publicity,' Mr Wright said, 'has given the name comprehensive school an ominous ring,' but in his opinion the switchover to comprehensive education was 'a good thing'. He saw the establishment of a comprehensive school in the area as a 'logical and desirable development' and added that his school had never recognised the expression 'Eleven Plus failure'. He had had many pupils at the school who had failed the test but had gone on to find success at training colleges or universities and who were now 'highly qualified professional men and women'. In the past, many of these 'late developers' would have found the 'dice loaded against them' but, according to Mr Wright, these 'border-liners' would follow a common course with those of a comparable ability for two or three years, by which time 'their true capabilities will be apparent beyond question'. (*Lichfield Mercury*, September 17th 1965)

~ September 8th ~

1882: On this day, the *Lichfield Mercury* reported on an outbreak of typhus in the city. The first victim was a man named Wright who was taken ill on August 22nd in a lodging house in George Lane. He was seen by a doctor, who immediately sent him to the Union Workhouse to be isolated and treated. Later, the lodging housekeeper, Mrs Selby, was taken ill and subsequently died; both cases were diagnosed as typhus, an extremely contagious and, at the time, often fatal disease. Readers of the *Mercury* were urged to keep their houses well ventilated and ensure their 'personal cleanliness', as well as to guard against overcrowding in their homes in order to 'check the ravages of the disease'. The *Mercury* was also concerned that an outbreak of smallpox in the Black Country, where hundreds had contracted the disease, might make an appearance in Lichfield. The paper warned that tramps passing through the area might pass on diseases and that overcrowding in the homes of the poor, where often nine or ten people might share two tiny rooms, could contribute to the spread of such diseases. The conditions of the sewers in the city were also a cause for concern, according to the *Mercury*. (*Lichfield Mercury*)

~ September 9th ~

1831: On this day, the *Lichfield Mercury* reported on how the city had celebrated the coronation of King William IV. Council leaders were criticised for not taking a leading part in the celebrations, but local people soon displayed flags and garlands on their houses and in the street and most festivities seemed to involve plenty of eating and drinking. The bailiffs and most of the aldermen of the city dined at 'Mr Cato's establishment', The Three Crowns in Breadmarket Street, where they were presented with a 'profusion of delicacies'. Another party of gentlemen dined at the Old Crown in Bore Street and 'its reputation for good dinners was, we hear, more than sustained'. A Ball in the Guildhall was well attended, but the paper noted that 'the attractions of its feminine ornaments' were an 'inducement' to the gentlemen to turn up. On Sandford Street, 'the most decorated street in the City', residents roasted a whole sheep and 'boiled plum puddings on the same fire', while in Stowe Street 'two capacious booths' were erected and 120 people sat down to dine – 'the day's pleasure was ended by a dance'. Tamworth Street, Dam Street, Greenhill, Market Street, Beacon Street and 'Gay Lane' all held parties. (*Lichfield Mercury*)

~ September 10th ~

1983: On this day, Lichfield's mayor, Derrick Duval, presented a 'tongue in cheek' bill for £125,000 to Flying Officer John Gorton (retired) for the loss in 1943 of a Spitfire fighter plane, serial number BI 812. This particular plane had been purchased in the Second World War with money raised by the people of Lichfield as part of the War effort and had been flown by Gorton, who was serving in the Royal Canadian Air Force. In February 1943 he was involved in a dog fight with a German plane over France when the Spitfire's engine was hit and he was forced to bale out. The last he saw of the Spitfire was it bursting into flames and crash into the earth, as he floated down on his parachute only to be captured by a German patrol. He later met the German pilot who had shot him down – a 25-year-old like himself. After the war Gorton took a medical degree and became a doctor. The mayor's fake 'bill' concluded by saying that in view of the fact that the ex-pilot did not remember where he had 'mislaid' the Spitfire the City Fathers were prepared to 'write-off' the debt. (*Lichfield Mercury*, September 16th 1983)

– September 11th –

1936: On this day, the *Lichfield Mercury* published an article by F.W. Long, a Lichfield tradesman who had just returned from a walking holiday in Germany where he gave his impressions of the country that was dominated by Hitler's Nazi Party. He had been impressed with the countryside and the friendliness of the people, although the general standard of living seemed to be lower than that in Britain – there were 'fewer wirelesses' and no cinemas as elaborate as Lichfield's Regal, apparently. 'The Germans are a proud people and they have every reason to be,' he wrote. He 'could understand' why German remilitarisation had taken place and was sympathetic to Germany's 'fearfulness' about Russia. Mr Long was keen to stress in the article that 'Germany was a factor to be reckoned with in Europe – a country and people to be admired', and also posed the question: 'should we be safer and happier in an alliance with this virile race, which appears to resemble our own national characteristics?' German industry appeared to be very healthy, according to Mr Long, 'vagrants and loafers are unknown and no one is allowed to be idle'. (*Lichfield Mercury*)

‒ September 12th ‒

1933: On this day, for the first time, the Sheriff's Ride was completed with the Sheriff of Lichfield in a car rather than sat atop a horse. The car, which was driven around the boundaries of the city, also carried the sheriff's wife and the mayor and mayoress. It was the last ride around the old boundaries of the city because in the following April they were due to change, with the five parishes of Lichfield becoming four and Trent Valley station being included for the first time within Lichfield's official boundaries. It was, indeed, a momentous day for the sheriff, Councillor F.M. Tayler, as earlier in the day he had been presented with a grandson who had, in commemoration of the day, been named John Sheriff Tayler. The Sheriff's Ride dates back to the 1553 charter, which made Lichfield into a separate county with the right to appoint its own sheriff, as well as commanding the sheriff to 'perambulate' the city boundaries each year on the 'Feast of the Blessed Virgin Mary'. (*Lichfield Mercury*, September 15th 1933)

‒ September 13th ‒

1894: On this day, an assortment of cases were tried at Lichfield Police Court by the mayor, Major Gilbert, and Councillor J. Fowler. Thomas Cartmail of Flowers' Row, Sandford Street, was summoned for failing to send his son William to school regularly. Cartmail told the court that the boy was 'beyond his control' and that he should like him to be sent to truant school. Mr Woodman, school attendance officer for Lichfield, told the court that Cartmail had been summoned on a number of other occasions in respect of his son and, on the last occasion, an attendance order was put in place. Cartmail got his wish and the court ordered the boy should be sent to truant school. Also before the court were two 'women pugilists' who had been found fighting in the street. Lily Wood and Sarah Thacker, 'well known characters in the City', had gathered a large crowd around them in Greenhill when their fight was broken up by the police. They were both fined 2*s* 6*d* (13p). John Wright, aged 13, was charged with stealing pears from the garden of William Robinson in Frog Lane and was fined 5*s* 6*d* (28p). (*Lichfield Mercury*, September 14th 1894)

~ September 14th ~

1984: On this day, the *Lichfield Mercury* highlighted the plight of the city landmark that was under attack from vandals and wood-rot. Lichfield's clock tower, which was crumbling through age and the ravages of deathwatch beetles, was also suffering from the actions of people who had smashed the clock dial with repeated air-gun attacks. The City Council had estimated the cost to restore the stone structure of the clock tower and to repair the clock face to be almost £30,000. The chairman of the City Council's Leisure and Amenity Committee, Councillor Howard Clayton, considered the situation so desperate that he ordered some of the emergency work to be carried out even before the situation was discussed by his committee. The clock tower, built in 1863, originally stood at the end of Bore Street and was moved when Friary Road was constructed in 1926. Councillor Clayton, who was also a local historian, said, 'Lichfield's clock tower is more than a piece of street furniture or a public utility because it has very strong historical connections.' (*Lichfield Mercury*)

— SEPTEMBER 15TH —

1847: On this day, Lichfield's Trent Valley railway station opened. The city's first railway station, it was originally called 'Lichfield' and was built 1 mile north of the city centre at the village of Streethay. Lichfield had been bypassed by the railway network for the previous decade but the new Trent Valley line, run by the London and North Western Railway (LNWR) and which linked Rugby and Stafford, gave access to London in the south and Carlisle in the north. The station building was designed by John Livock in the Tudor–Gothic style, with particularly fine and ornate chimneys. Another station, called Lichfield Trent Valley Junction, opened in 1849 on the line linking Burton with Dudley, a spur line descending to the original station to enable people to transfer to the LNWR main line. In 1871 both stations were closed by the LNWR and they were replaced with a single station called Lichfield Trent Valley, which was built in its present location with high- and low-level platforms. The high-level platform was closed in 1965 when the service from Lichfield to Burton ceased, but reopened again in 1988 with the extension of the Birmingham to Lichfield route. (Hitches, Mike, *The Trent Valley Railway*, Sutton Publishing, 2003)

~ September 16th ~

1939: On this day, the annual Samuel Johnson birthday celebrations were cancelled and the population of Lichfield prepared themselves for the hardships of the war that had been declared on September 3rd. The City Council published wartime regulations which proclaimed that the public baths, Johnson's birthplace and the museum in Beacon Street would all close, although the library would remain open with shortened hours. The council announced that there would be demonstrations each day to show the public how to deal with incendiary bombs and fight fires, and public air-raid shelters were set up at various places around the city. Adverts and posters appeared, advising people how to cope during the blackout and from where they should obtain sandbags. People were also reminded to carry their gasmasks with them at all times. Evacuated children would soon arrive in the city from West Bromwich and an appeal was made in the local press for spare blankets. As it turned out, very little happened for the rest of 1939, in the period that became known as the 'Phoney War', but it did give local people time to get used to the new conditions. (Ashley, Les and James, Ralph, *Lichfield in the Second World War*, The Lichfield Press, 2003)

‒ September 17th ‒

1931: On this day, a meeting of the Lichfield Teachers' Association expressed 'considerable dissatisfaction' with what was described as a 'vindictive cut in their salaries'. The meeting, attended by a large number of teachers from the area, took place at a time of national crisis, with a financial collapse (blamed by many on bankers) gripping the country. The new National government, formed in August 1931, had decided to cut teachers' wages by 20 per cent as one of the methods to reduce the overall national debt. A speaker at the meeting said that teachers 'were not unpatriotic' and were prepared to pay their share towards balancing the budget, but this salary cut was 'vindictive, unfair and harmful to teachers, and to education generally'. The point was also made that before the war all sections of the press agreed that teachers were underpaid and after the war the Burnham Committee had fixed new salary scales promising that these would be operative until 1932. In cutting salaries, the meeting agreed, the government had gone back on its promise and was setting a 'bad example' to all school pupils who had been taught about the 'sanctity of agreements'. (*Lichfield Mercury*, September 18th 1931)

~ September 18th ~

1709: It was on this day that Lichfield's most famous son was born: the writer, lexicographer and literary critic Samuel Johnson. A sickly baby, who was 'more dead than alive', he suffered from scrofula (a tubercular infection of the lymph glands) as well as being blind in one eye and deaf in one ear. However, he survived to become one of the most famous writers in Britain and the eighteenth century's most feted celebrity. He moved to London at the age of 27 and in 1755 published his dictionary – one of the most influential books in the English language – and although it was not the first dictionary written, it was certainly the most authoritative up to that date. He met James Boswell in 1763, a man who would become his main chronicler and biographer. It is because of Boswell that we know so much about Johnson's 'trenchant, shrewd and entertaining conversation'. Lichfield remained close to Johnson's heart throughout his life, writing, 'I lately took my friend Boswell and showed him genuine civilised life in an English provincial town. I turned him loose in Lichfield.' Johnson died in 1784 and is buried in Westminster Abbey. (Martin, Peter, *Samuel Johnson: A Biography*, Weidenfeld and Nicolson, 2008)

— September 19th —

1908: On this day, the unveiling of the statue of James Boswell took place in Lichfield, honouring the man who was born in Edinburgh in 1740 and who became the first biographer and constant companion of Samuel Johnson. The statue, which had been sculpted and donated by Percy Fitzgerald for the citizens of Lichfield, was situated in Market Square, close to the birthplace of his great friend Johnson. It was unveiled by Rev. Robertson Nicoll to coincide with the 199th anniversary of Johnson's birth. The day of the unveiling was one of great excitement in the city, as a 'great influx' of people arrived in Lichfield and many of the businesses around Market Square were decked out with flags. A procession left the Guildhall at 3 p.m., 'headed by a posse of policemen' and comprised of the mayor, the sheriff, the sword and mace bearers, and other local dignitaries. The unveiling ceremony was performed from a specially erected platform and witnessed by a large crowd who had gathered for the occasion. (*Lichfield Mercury*, September 25th 1908)

~ SEPTEMBER 20TH ~

1929: On this day, it was announced that the Midland Red Bus Company was running special, cheap day-return journeys to the seaside resort of Blackpool for the illuminations that took place from September 21st to October 21st. Coaches left the Market Square every Monday, Thursday and Saturday at 10 a.m. and arrived in Blackpool at 2 p.m., giving travellers eight hours in the resort before returning at 10 p.m. A special arrangement had been made with a 'night cafe' on the way back to Lichfield so refreshments could be obtained. The fare for the day excursion was 12*s* 6*d* (63p); Midland Red also offered period returns for 17*s* 6*d* (88p), where the return journey could be made one week later. Four- and five-day holidays in Blackpool were also provided by the company, with a boarding-house room and an excursion to the Lake District included for £3 4*s* (£3.20) and £3 12*s* 6*d* (£3.63) respectively. People could book their tickets at Meacham's at 36 Market Street. Blackpool's illuminations began in 1879 and by the 1920s and '30s had become very popular with visitors from all over Britain. (*Lichfield Mercury*)

~ September 21st ~

1972: On this day, Father Barry O'Hagan, priest at St Joseph's church in Chasetown, said farewell to his parishioners at a social evening before setting off for his new post in Fiji. Father O'Hagan was famous in the area earlier in the year for organising a holiday break for children from 'battle-torn' Belfast. From Northern Ireland himself, he persuaded many local families in the Burntwood area to give temporary homes to over forty children aged from 8 to 11. The children – some from the Catholic Falls Road area of Belfast and some from Protestant areas of the city – were treated to various day trips. Father O'Hagan said, 'All of the children are suffering from the hatred and bitterness and we want to take them out of that atmosphere and show them how normal families live.' The scheme cost over £200, all of which was raised by donations from local people. At his leaving party he said goodbye to over 200 of his parishioners and was presented with many gifts, including a large going-away cake. (*Lichfield Mercury*, September 22nd 1972)

— September 22nd —

1944: On this day, a group of wounded soldiers were entertained by the staff of the Regal cinema in Lichfield. Fifty soldiers, injured in France, left their hospital in Burntwood for the Regal, where they were the honoured guests of the management and staff. During the afternoon they were treated to a film – *Madame Curie*, starring Greer Garson and Walter Pidgeon – and were then served with a 'very appetising' tea of ham, tongue and salad, followed by a variety of cakes and 'cigarettes galore', all provided and served by the staff of the cinema. The guests were 'heartily welcomed' by the manager, Mr S. Tonkinson, the assistant manager, Mr G. Crawford, and the manageress of the Regal Cafe, Mrs Painter. Thanks were given by Regimental Sergeant Major H. Smith, who said he 'could assure the members of staff that their thoughtfulness and kindness had been sincerely appreciated by them all'. All present then gave the staff three cheers. After the meal, the *Lichfield Mercury* reporter noted that 'a deep pall of cigarette smoke' hung over the long table where the men sat. (*Lichfield Mercury*, September 29th 1944)

— September 23rd —

1980: On this day, Lichfield's Bower Queen, Jane Dayus, took the unusual step of complaining to the organisers of the Bower Queen competition that she was not being given enough work to do to justify her title. Crowned in March 1980, prior to the annual Greenhill Bower day celebrations (where the Bower Queen always takes pride of place in the Bower procession around the streets of the city), Dayus wrote to the Bower organisers to see if they could arrange for her to do more official duties. As a result, she was invited to present cheques to various city organisations on behalf of the Bower Committee, who regularly made grants to worthy local causes. Miss Dayus presented cheques to fifty charitable groups and establishments such as Dr Milley's hospital, the Red Cross, St John's Ambulance and the Lichfield Scouts. Dayus later married John Hinch, drummer with the rock band Judas Priest, and later still became one of Britain's top wedding planners and star of Canadian television series *Wedding S.O.S.*, where she solves problems people have with the planning of their weddings. (*Lichfield Mercury*, September 26th 1980)

~ September 24th ~

1973: On this day, Lichfield's new employment exchange opened for business. Named the Job Centre and situated at Guardian House in Birmingham Road, the centre was one of 800 to be established across the whole country. According to its manager, Mr Joseph Needham, the Job Centre offered a different approach to finding jobs. With 'modern furniture and fitted carpets', the new establishment was 'in striking contrast' to the pre-war Employment Exchange in Beacon Street. Describing the Job Centre, Needham said, 'The main feature of the ground-floor site is the self-service section. Here hundreds of vacancies will be on display and job-seekers can browse at leisure. When they see a vacancy that interests them they note the reference number and ask a receptionist to arrange an interview for them. This is done on the spot – there are no forms to fill in and no fuss.' The slogan of the new centre was 'the new way to find a better job' and an advertisement for it revealed that there would be job vacancies from all over the country on offer and customers could also receive advice on training opportunities from employment officers. (*Lichfield Mercury*, September 28th 1973)

~ SEPTEMBER 25TH ~

1959: On this day, the *Lichfield Mercury* reported on the various celebrations in honour of the 250th anniversary of the birth of Samuel Johnson. A special and well-attended service took place at the cathedral, led by the Dean of St Paul's, W.R. Matthews. The annual wreath-laying ceremony took place in the Market Square, with the mayor laying the wreath at the statue of the famous doctor. The mayor also attended the planting of a new 'Johnson's willow' by the side of Stowe Pool – the fourth tree in succession to bear the accolade. The traditional Johnson Supper took place at the Guildhall, where the guest of honour was Sir William Haley, editor of *The Times* and former director general of the BBC. Two hundred people ate the usual dinner of clear soup; turbot and sauce; steak, kidney and mushroom pudding; apple pie and cream; toasted cheese; and ale – all things that Johnson reputedly enjoyed. The meal was rounded off with the smoking of traditional churchwarden pipes. At Friary School a pageant entitled *Samuel Johnson: This is Your life* was presented in a week when messages of goodwill from all round the world were received by the mayor. (*Lichfield Mercury*)

— SEPTEMBER 26TH —

1916: On this day, one of the first fatal road accidents in the Lichfield area took place at the busy crossroads of Muckley Corner. A Ford car, driven by John Preece of Shrewsbury – which also contained his father, Richard Preece, and his brother-in-law, Percy Hall – collided with a taxi driven by Alfred Bufton, who was taking a party of people from Lichfield to Walsall. As a result of the collision 58-year-old Richard Preece was thrown through the windscreen, over a hedge and into a field, suffering injuries to his neck; he died several minutes later. Hall sustained severe injuries to his head and was taken to Lichfield Nursing Home. None of the other occupants of either car were seriously hurt. Another motorist, Thomas Mitchell, who was driving from Shire Oak to Lichfield, narrowly escaped colliding with the taxi, which had spun around in the road. At the inquest it was found that the death of the man was an accident and that the crash had been partly caused by warning signs being too small and too close to the crossroads, which was described as 'one of the most dangerous in the country'. (*Lichfield Mercury*, October 1st 1916)

— September 27th —

1889: On this day, the local newspaper, the *Lichfield Mercury*, expressed the view that the three football clubs in the city should amalgamate to ensure 'there would be a team in the City worthy of taking its stand amongst the leading junior clubs in the country'. The three clubs – Lichfield Leomansley, Fradley and St Chad's – showed, according to the paper, that there was 'without doubt plenty of talent in the neighbourhood, but being distributed among the different clubs, its full force is not felt'. The Leomansley club had high ambitions and had entered three cup competitions, as well as arranging friendly matches against Burton Swifts and Aston Villa, the latter being a founder member of the recently formed Football League and who would finish second only to Preston North End (called 'the Invincibles' in the early years of the League). The St Chad's club had some 'excellent fixtures', the next one being against Rugeley Albion Swifts, and Fradley had arranged some 'high class' matches against such teams as Birmingham Wycliffe, Cannock, Ashbourne and Stafford Rangers. (*Lichfield Mercury*)

— September 28th —

1932: On this day, the official opening of Chase Terrace senior boys and senior girls schools took place. Built on a site on Bridge Cross Road, the schools served the mining villages of Chase Terrace and Chasetown. The two schools, adjoining but separate, could cater for a total of 640 pupils (320 boys and 320 girls) and each one had six classrooms and three specialist rooms for the teaching of science, cookery and housewifery for the girls and science, handcraft and metalwork for the boys. The building had cost £30,000 and was a one-storey, pavilion-style building which would emphasise light and space and was surrounded by lawns and trees – already it had been dubbed 'the university of the Chase'. The first pupils – 260 girls and 260 boys – were admitted on October 5th, summoned to school by the bell in the smart blue and white bell tower; the headmaster of the boys' school was Mr George Dennis and the headmistress of the girls' school was Miss M.E. Alsop. The school building had many name changes over the years and would eventually become a co-educational, comprehensive school in the 1960s. (*Lichfield Mercury*, September 30th 1932)

— September 29th —

1910: On this day, excited residents of Lichfield were able to witness the rare sight of aeroplanes flying around the city's cathedral. The Burton Aviation Society organised a race from Burton to Lichfield and back again, with the cathedral as the halfway marker. Four planes were hoping to make the journey, although in the end only two achieved the feat. Crowds gathered in Lichfield to watch the planes approach from Burton, flying at about 150ft and piloted by two Frenchmen: Mamet and de Lesseps, both flying in Bleriot monoplanes. Mamet returned to Burton and won the race, but de Lesseps' plane was forced to land in a field adjoining Wheel Lane and was slightly damaged in the landing. Paul de Lesseps spent the night at the George Hotel while his aeroplane was repaired and was cheered on his way the following morning by a large group of well-wishers after saying that he would definitely visit Lichfield again. (*Lichfield Mercury*, September 30th 1910)

– September 30th –

1899: On this day, a ceremony took place at Messrs Jones & Co.'s Emporium where some of the first electric lights in Lichfield were switched on by the mayor. The ceremony occurred at the 'very large and commodious' store at 7 p.m. in the presence of a large number of guests. Once switched on, the lights provided illumination that was, according to the *Mercury*'s reporter, 'exceedingly clear and brilliant'. The lights were powered by a generator running on petroleum and connected to a dynamo and accumulator. Two large lamps had been placed over the front of the shop in Bird Street and over the Bore Street entrance and about 120 small lights were distributed throughout the shop and house, including a light in each bedroom. The electricity system, which cost over £1,000, also provided power for sewing machines, a boot cleaner, an oven and a knife cleaner. After the ceremony a large party assembled at the George Hotel for a celebratory dinner. Jones & Co., on the corner of Bird Street and Bore Street, sold a wide range of goods such as furniture, lamps, baby carriages, linoleum and 'every household requisite'. (*Lichfield Mercury*, October 5th 1899)

~ OCTOBER 1ST ~

1857: On this day, the first students (just four of them) were admitted to the Lichfield Theological College. Situated in Cathedral Close and backing on to Minster Pool, the college's aim was to train future clergymen – eleven students were on role for the following year – and they were lodged at various locations around the city. Students were expected to attend cathedral services each Sunday and a daily service at 8 a.m. at St Mary's. Lectures were held between 10 a.m. and 1 p.m. in the principal's house and each student was assigned to a particular district under the supervision of one of the parochial clergy. All had to share in night-school teaching and, in place of sport, students were encouraged to take part in long walks led by the principal, who would keep the students entertained and interested with a 'fund of amusing tales'. The college closed down in 1972, with some of the buildings being demolished and the remainder turned into a social centre in 1980. (Inman, C.E., *History of Lichfield Theological College*, Johnson's Head, 1928)

— OCTOBER 2ND —

1780: On this day, John André of the British Army was hanged as a spy. André had fallen in love with Honora Sneyd, the ward of Canon Seward who lived in the Bishop's Palace in Lichfield. André had met Sneyd while on holiday in Buxton and thereafter often visited her at the Sewards' home. Eventually André asked for Sneyd's hand in marriage but was refused, as his prospects as a clerk were not considered good enough. Disappointed, André joined the army and soon rose to the rank of major, serving in North America during the American War of Independence and always carrying with him a miniature portrait of Sneyd. While on an undercover mission he was captured by the Americans, accused of spying and sentenced to be hanged. Despite his request that he should suffer a soldier's death by firing squad, the hanging went ahead. On the news of his death the whole British Army went into mourning and Anna Seward, friend of Sneyd, wrote a poem in honour of the dead hero. Such was Seward's fame that, when the war had finished, George Washington sent one of his officers to Lichfield to meet her. (Clayton, Howard, *Lichfield and Tamworth Life*, October 1971)

~ OCTOBER 3RD ~

1857: On this day, Lichfield's new Free Library and Museum was inaugurated. Mr John P. Dyott, chairman of the library committee, presented a silver trowel to Chancellor Thomas Law, requesting him to lay the foundation stone of the building. Law then addressed the crowd and a band played the 'Grand Chorus' from *The Creation* by Haydn. After prayers the party then returned to the Guildhall for a luncheon. Lichfield's library and museum was only the second one to be built under the provisions of the 1856 Museums Act (the first being in Manchester) and was designed by Messrs Bidlake and Lovatt of Wolverhampton and built by Messrs Lilly of the same town. The building, which stands at the entrance to the museum gardens, ceased being a library in 1989 and is now the home of Lichfield's Registry Office. On the side of the building is an interesting statue of a sailor which was originally meant to be part of a Boer War memorial in York but was rejected as being unsuitable. The sculptor, Robert Bridgeman, gave the statue to Lichfield in 1905. Lichfield Public Library and Local Records Office is now housed in the Friary. (Rubery, Annette, *Lichfield Then and Now*, The History Press, 2012)

~ OCTOBER 4TH ~

1948: On this day, an inquest was held at the Paul Pry Hotel in Alrewas into the death of two airmen at Fradley aerodrome during a Battle of Britain commemoration. The dead men were 24-year-old Flight Lieutenant Hedley of Main Street, Alrewas, who was piloting the plane, and 40-year-old Squadron Leader Frederick Everard Shaw from London. The men had been killed during a display held on September 18th which consisted of a Spitfire and two Mosquito aircraft flying over Lichfield and then returning to do low-level flying and aerobatics over the airfield for thirty minutes. The Spitfire and one of the Mosquitos had landed but the other Mosquito had remained airborne 'to help keep the audience entertained'. The plane did three flick rolls at a height of between 50 and 100ft before its engines stalled and it hit the ground, exploding on impact. The inquest heard that the flick rolls, not easy to do in a Mosquito, were not in the display programme and a verdict of accidental death was returned. (*Lichfield Mercury*, October 8th 1948)

~ October 5th ~

1888: This day saw *the Lichfield Mercury* reporting on an incident that provides us with a snapshot of crime and punishment in Victorian Lichfield. The report concerns 'an impudent assault' on two women by a man called Arthur Fox. He was charged with assaulting 17-year-old Laura Thompson, the daughter of the landlady of the Kings Arms Inn in Tamworth Street, and Elizabeth Lakin, a servant at the Rose and Crown Inn on Bird Street. The first woman was grabbed and kissed by Fox; the second was flung down on the ground while crossing the Bowling Green Fields and was held there for fifteen minutes and struck as she screamed for help. Fox was arrested soon afterwards and at his trial received a two-month prison sentence and ordered to pay £2 14*s* (£2.70) costs. The same edition of the newspaper published a report of the Whitechapel killings in London (later universally known as the Jack the Ripper murders), the horror of which had gripped the interest of people all over the country. The two victims mentioned in the report, Elizabeth Stride and Annie Chapman, were both described as belonging to 'the unfortunate class' – a nineteenth-century euphemism for prostitute. (*Lichfield Mercury*)

~ OCTOBER 6TH ~

1974: On this Sunday, security in Lichfield was tight as Prime Minister Harold Wilson spoke at Lichfield's Netherstowe school in support of the Labour candidate Bruce Grocott in the forthcoming General Election. The election, which was held on the following Thursday, was the second of the year in what was a time of political upheaval and uncertainty in Britain. The first, held in February, had been called by Edward Heath, largely on the question of 'Who governs Britain?' The electorate decided that the answer to the question was not Edward Heath and his Conservative Party and, instead, narrowly elected the Labour Party. Wilson, however, did not have an overall majority in Parliament and so called another election for October in the hope that Labour would obtain a working majority – a tactic that was to prove successful. In the Lichfield and Tamworth constituency, Grocott went on to defeat Conservative Jack Goldsmid by just 331 votes, with Liberal Philip Rule in third place. He would remain a Member of Parliament until he was defeated in the 1979 election. Bruce Grocott later became MP for the Wrekin and Telford; he now sits in the House of Lords as Baron Grocott of Telford. (*Lichfield Mercury*, October 10th 1974)

⁓ OCTOBER 7TH ⁓

1910: On this day, the *Lichfield Mercury* reported on the opening of Lichfield's new Christchurch school. Opened by the High Sheriff of Staffordshire, the new school building would accommodate 192 children and was built at a cost of £2,190 by Messrs Thorneloe and Sons of Lichfield in just five months. There was some criticism of the school's location in Christchurch Lane, with some people expressing the view that the school should have been built in a more central position. The vicar of Christchurch, the Rev. Keble, said that the main objective in education was that a child 'should be educated so that he will be able to make the best of his life when deprived of the shelter of home and parents'. Much of the finance for the new school came from the Hinckley Trustees and the new building, which replaced the previous Christchurch school that dated from 1847 and which had also been financed, along with the nearby church, by the Hinckley family. (*Lichfield Mercury*)

~ October 8th ~

1915: On this day, the *Lichfield Mercury* reported how army recruitment rallies had taken place throughout Lichfield District in order to replace the mounting casualties of the First World War. The city's rally took place in Market Square and was held to 'bring home to young men the urgent need the country has of their services to enable the war to be brought to a speedy and successful conclusion'. Despite heavy rain (it had been hoped that an aeroplane would drop recruitment leaflets on Lichfield prior to the rally, but the weather made this impossible) a good crowd was present to hear Colonel Greer address the meeting. In his speech he said that more recruits were needed to 'make good the wastage of war'. He also stated that any man who did not volunteer would be considered 'a coward and was leaving the duty to others', adding that parents should do all they could to induce their sons to join up in this 'hour of need'. At the end of the rally ten recruits were signed up. In 1916 the government's Military Service Act introduced conscription and all men aged 18 to 40 years old were forced to enlist. (*Lichfield Mercury*)

- October 9th -

1651: On this day, George Fox (1624–91), the founder of The Society of Friends, or Quakers, began to walk from Derby to Lichfield. Fox, who had been travelling the country preaching, had often fallen foul of local authorities, which persecuted him for his religious views. In Derby he had been arrested for blasphemy – at his trial a judge had mocked his exhortation to 'tremble at the word of the lord' and called him and his followers 'Quakers'. After several months in prison Fox was released and resumed his travels. On seeing the distant spires of Lichfield Cathedral, Fox experienced a vision in which he saw Lichfield surrounded by a pool of blood. He proceeded to take off his shoes, leaving them with shepherds, and continued into Lichfield barefoot. Once there he walked about the streets and Market Square, 'guided by the lord', crying, 'woe to the bloody city of Lichfield'. He was apparently referring to the story that during the time of the Roman Emperor, Diocletian Christians had been slaughtered in the area. Unmolested by the authorities, Fox left Lichfield and returned to the shepherds where he retrieved his shoes. (Van Etten, Henry, *George Fox and the Quakers*, Longmans, 1959)

~ OCTOBER 10TH ~

1774: On this day, the election of Lichfield's two Members of Parliament, George Anson and Thomas Gilbert, was confirmed. Elections at that time were turbulent and corrupt affairs, with those few electors often bribed to vote in a certain way. In this particular election various sums of money were spent in order to persuade men to vote, including the running-up of a large drinks bill – over £140 (a considerable sum at the time) was spent in various inns in the city to bribe voters. Costs were also incurred in providing music, Morris dancers and bell ringing in the churches. In fact, the total cost of getting the two men elected in 1774 was £312 – the equivalent of many thousands of pounds today. Elections in the past could also be violent. In 1826 the George Inn, the headquarters of the Whig party in Lichfield, had all its windows broken by an angry mob, which had to be dealt with by a military force dispatched from Birmingham. The establishment of secret ballots after 1872 saw the end to much of the corrupt election practices in Britain. (Parker, Alfred D., *A Sentimental Journey in and About the Ancient and Loyal City of Lichfield*, The Johnson's Head, 1925)

~ OCTOBER IITH ~

1929: On this day, the *Lichfield Mercury* reported the death of Noel George who, until the previous year, had been the goalkeeper for Wolverhampton Wanderers football club. Aged only 31, the paper revealed that he had died at his Stafford Road home following a long and painful illness. Lichfield-born George had served in France and Salonica during the First World War and had returned to play for Lichfield City United and later Hednesford, playing thirty matches for them before being invited to sign for Wolves in the 1919–20 season. He had played in goal in the final of the FA Cup in 1921 and 'gave a wonderful display', despite Wolves losing to Tottenham by 1 goal to 0. His funeral took place at St Chad's church and a large crowd was present, including some of the Wolverhampton Wanderers team and directors of the club. There were nearly fifty wreaths accompanying the coffin, including one from Coventry City Football Club and another in the gold and black colours of Wolves. The coffin was carried by some of the Wolverhampton players. (*Lichfield Mercury*)

~ October 12th ~

1995: On this day, the *Lichfield Mercury* reported on the 'twinning' celebrations held in the city. Civic leaders from Lichfield, Limburg in Germany and Sainte Foy les Lyons in France paid tribute to the bonds that had been formed between the three cities and spoke of their hopes for the future and the unity of Europe. Lichfield's mayor, David Bailey, stressed the importance of co-operation and community in a world that had become a 'global village', with the Internet, satellite communications and cheap travel all making the world a smaller place. Michel Chapas, Mayor of Sainte Foy, spoke about the problems that needed to be overcome in Europe and how the 'three great cities' could help build unity in Europe. Heinrich Richard, deputy Mayor of Limburg, warned about the growth of intolerance in Europe and how matters would be improved by the 'integration and participation of young people'. Twinning festivities included a special service at the cathedral, afternoon tea at the Guildhall, a 'friendship evening' at St Mary's and a concert in the Civic Hall with music from all three countries. (*Lichfield Mercury*)

‒ OCTOBER 13TH ‒

1978: On this day, Art School Principal John Sanders' call for more people to come forward to sit as nude models for students was answered by Mrs Judy Healey from Wall. Mrs Healey, who had done nude modelling at the Art School in the past, said that the biggest problem about sitting on a stage without a stitch on was 'falling asleep', but advised anyone thinking of doing nude modeling to 'give it a try', saying, 'It's hard work for the first few weeks; I found I ached all over, but once you get used to it there's no problem at all.' Mr Sanders was still keen to persuade others to step forward, saying that anyone who was interested should contact the school ‒ 'They will pose only for advanced students and if necessary can start out fully clothed and gradually go nude.' He added that nude modelling 'had nothing to do with the permissive society. The nude is, and always has been, a source of inspiration to artists.' At the Art School models were paid at a rate of £1.28p per hour and were expected to model for two-and-a-half hour sessions. (*Lichfield Mercury*, October 13th 1978)

～ OCTOBER 14TH ～

1921: On this day, the official list of the names of the soldiers of the South Staffordshire Regiment killed in the Great War was published for the first time. Altogether the regiment had lost 5,999 men, many of whom had come from Lichfield and its surrounding district. Men of the South Staffs had gone to France in the early days of the First World War and were quickly engaged in fierce fighting at Ypres in October 1914 and later saw action in many of the battles on the Western Front, including the Battle of the Somme in 1916, where they suffered devastating losses. The 7th Battalion of the regiment, which had been raised in Lichfield, took part in the Gallipoli campaign and was the first to land at the notorious Suvla Bay, where they repulsed Turkish troops repeatedly until they were ordered to evacuate the beaches. The final action of the war saw the regiment involved in the battles of Messines and Cambrai in fighting that resulted from the German offensive in March 1918, when the South Staffs commanding officer, Colonel Blackall, was among those killed. (*Lichfield Pioneer*, October 14th 1921)

~ OCTOBER 15TH ~

1877: On this day, a ferocious gale hit Lichfield, the effects of which were, according to the *Lichfield Mercury*, 'somewhat disastrous'. So extensive was the damage throughout the city that it would be 'some time before it could be assessed'. At the deanery a chimney stack was blown down onto the roof, scattering roof-tiles 'here and there', but luckily the supports underneath the tiles were sturdy enough to stop the chimney plunging into the room below where two servants were asleep and who doubtless would have been killed. At Dean's Walk, one of the tall lime trees was blown over and fell into the garden of the archdeacon's residence, and stone from the cathedral's south-west turret blew off and fell through the roof, landing in the nave and making a large indentation in the floor. Further damage occurred when ten poplar trees at the side of Stowe Pool were blown down and the iron gates in the gardens at Stowe Hill were smashed by falling trees. Many houses throughout the district were also damaged by falling trees. (*Lichfield Mercury*, October 19th 1877)

~ OCTOBER 16TH ~

1959: On this day, plans were announced to build a £500,000 development in the centre of Lichfield. The plan was designed to remove 'at one stroke' all of the houses in the Levett's Field and Baker's Lane area of the city and redevelop the area to include shops, a general post office, a motel, supermarket and other premises which, it was hoped, would have a 'tremendous impact' on the city and 'provide a link between the old and the new which would be acceptable to all'. At the time the project was expected to take just two years to complete and it was hoped that the shopping area would be built in a way that was 'architecturally sympathetic' with the older parts of the city. It was envisaged that people would be able to shop without having to worry about vehicles and with roads providing rear delivery facilities to the shops. The proposed 'civic precinct' would ensure, the council hoped, a 'restful, landscaped area' in contrast to the, 'busy commercial developments which will surround it'. (*Lichfield Mercury*, October 16th 1959)

~ October 17th ~

1913: On this day, an open-air meeting of the Women's Social and Political Union – the Suffragettes – took place in Market Square in Lichfield. The meeting was addressed by Miss C. Read of London, who said that having women in the government of the country 'would save a great deal of the trouble which was caused at the present time'. She continued by saying that the struggle for votes for women had been carrying on for fifty years – led by people like Mrs Pankhurst – and that lately a number of women had been given prison sentences for disrupting political meetings in a non-violent way. It was Miss Reid's opinion that if constitutional methods failed many believed that 'only militant tactics would win women the vote'. She also observed that all men who paid taxes and rent had the vote but that women who paid the same did not. The *Mercury* journalist present at the meeting reported that it was well attended, but only two questions were asked. (Women over 30 eventually received the right to vote in 1918; those over 21 were granted it in 1928.) (*Lichfield Mercury*, October 20th 1913)

— October 18th —

1929: On this day, the R101 airship was seen flying over Lichfield. The sighting took place in the course of the airship's second flight as it journeyed from its base in Cardington to Derby. The *Lichfield Mercury* described the airship as 'a beautiful sight', as it flew at a height of 1,500ft and at a speed of 60mph, with hundreds of Lichfield residents able to make out 'every detail of its enormous bulk' as it passed over the city. Schoolchildren were allowed out of their classrooms to see the unique sight and traffic stopped as drivers got out of their vehicles to watch the airship's progress. 'Generally,' the *Mercury* said, 'there was great excitement as Lichfield residents obtained a splendid view of the world's largest airship.' The R101 was one of a pair of giant airships developed by the government in the hope that it would provide a service over long-distance routes throughout the Empire. Its crash in France a year later, when forty-eight of the fifty-four people on board were killed – including Lord Thomson, the Government Air Minister who had initiated the programme – ended the development of airships in Britain. (*Lichfield Mercury*, October 25th 1929)

~ OCTOBER 19TH ~

1769: On this day, John André, a clerk based in London, wrote a love letter to Lichfield woman and object of his affection, Honora Sneyd. The odd aspect to this was that the letter was sent not to Sneyd herself but to her friend Anna Seward, the Lichfield poet who lived with her family in the Bishop's Palace. It was the convention at the time that no 'well-bred' young woman would receive letters directly from a young man or send letters herself in reply unless the couple were actually engaged to be married. The letter was very innocent, with André writing that he imagined Sneyd, along with Anna and 'two or more select friends, encircling your dressing room fire-place' and expressing the wish that he would like to 'enlarge that circle' with his presence. André also refers to his previous visits to Lichfield and how he looked forward to his next one when he would again meet with Sneyd. The story did not turn out well. Sneyd's father would not allow a marriage, due to André's lack of money or prospects, and Sneyd married someone else. Tragically both the young people were dead by 1780. (Hopkins, Mary Alden, *Dr. Johnson's Lichfield*, Hastings House, 1952)

~ October 20th ~

1920: On this day, Lichfield's Garden of Remembrance was inaugurated in a solemn service of dedication. The garden, which was established as a memorial to those Lichfield men who died in the First World War, stands in a picturesque setting between the cathedral and Minster Pool and is regarded as one of the most beautiful in the country. Work began on it in 1919 when Lichfield people were keen to honour those who had died. Three projects were suggested – peace celebrations, a concert hall and a permanent war memorial, the latter being by far the most popular idea – and a public appeal was launched to help raise the necessary funds. The stone lions on the gate piers of the garden came from Moxhull Hall in Warwickshire and the stone balustrade and plinth, which separates the garden from Beacon Street, came from Shenstone Court just outside Lichfield. The memorial itself shows the figure of St George, which is made from Portland stone, below which are listed the names of the many local men who lost their lives in the Great War. Names of those who died in the Second World War were added later. (Information from Lichfield City Council)

– October 21st –

1993: On this day, it was announced that the actor Robbie Coltrane would be playing the part of Lichfield's most famous son, Samuel Johnson, in a new television drama. Coltrane would star alongside John Sessions as Johnson's friend and biographer James Boswell in an irreverent comic account of Johnson and Boswell's tour of the Western Isles in 1773. The programme was written by John Byrne, who wrote the television show *Tutti Frutti* in which Coltrane also starred. Coltrane had played the role of Johnson on two previous occasions: on television he depicted Johnson in an episode of *Blackadder the Third*, which centred on his famous dictionary, and he has also played Johnson on stage in a one-man show called *Obedient Servant*. Dr Graham Nicholls, curator of Lichfield's Johnson Birthplace Museum, said, 'I am looking forward to the programme immensely and I believe the comic style might suit the story very well.' Boswell's account of the pair's journey as they walked and talked their way across the Western Isles of Scotland is one of the reasons we know so much about Johnson. (*Lichfield Mercury*, October 21st 1993)

~ OCTOBER 22ND ~

1916: On this day, the *Lichfield Mercury* reported on the fighting that had been taking place during the year, the bloodiest of the First World War. The paper acknowledged the 'heavy casualties' that had been caused 'somewhere in France' and reported on the local men who had been killed in action. These included Private Hodgkins, aged 19, of Backcester Lane; Private Wright, a carpenter from Deans Croft; Private Neville of Sandford Street, who had worked in an iron foundry before the war; and Private Bott, also of Sandford Street, who was in the process of bandaging a fellow soldier when he was killed. Some locals had been wounded, among whom were: Lieutenant Shaw of Red House in Bore Street; Lieutenant George Paget of Elford Hall; Corporal Abel of Chesterfield Terrace; Private Dawson of St John Street, a carver at Bridgeman's before the war who had been gassed; and Private Roberts of Stowe Street, who received serious wounds to his face. Private Oram of George Lane wrote to his wife saying, 'I am wounded just under my right eye and I was lucky it did not blow my eye out, or it might have killed me.' (*Lichfield Mercury*)

~ OCTOBER 23RD ~

1987: On this day, the *Lichfield Mercury*'s front page announced that there was 'fury' after the Lichfield District Council's objection to the building of a 'giant' Safeway superstore on the site of the Chamberlain and Hill foundry had been overturned by the government. The District Council had strongly opposed the planned £3.5 million supermarket scheme and had sympathised with residents in the area who had also objected to the project. One local woman, Joyce Martin of Fern Croft, described the situation as 'a nightmare which could lower the value of our houses', also complaining that 'the traffic problems are going to be terrible and the place will be open from 8 a.m. until late at night for deliveries. What is the point of having local elections when the decisions do not mean anything?' Lichfield was now in line for two new supermarket developments, with Tesco also planning to build a 'huge' store on the Greenhill cattle-market site. City councillor David Wilkins described the situation as 'crazy', adding that 'we are going to be surrounded by superstores without having the trade to support them'. (*Lichfield Mercury*)

~ OCTOBER 24TH ~

1943: On this day, a choir composed of fifty members of the US Army Engineer Department performed a concert at Lichfield Cathedral. The programme consisted of 'negro spirituals' such as *Swing Low Sweet Chariot* and *Climbing Jacob's Ladder*, the first time that local people had had the opportunity to listen to 'inspiring music of this character'. The dean of the cathedral welcomed the choir and their conductor, Corporal William B. Oliver, and said that the concert was important because not only did the choir represent Britain's great ally in the war, but also it was the first time in its long history that the cathedral had heard music 'which had sprung from the common people whose hearts had been touched by the Christian message'. Speaking after the concert, the choir's leader, Captain William Smith, said, 'the Cathedral was an ideal place for the rendering of songs and the choir were very pleased to have the opportunity of performing.' During the war the US Army was segregated, with African-Americans assigned to black-only units commanded by white officers. (*Lichfield Mercury*, October 29th 1943)

~ OCTOBER 25TH ~

1854: On this day, John Brown of Lichfield blew his trumpet to sound the Charge of the Light Brigade during the Battle of Balaclava. Brown was born in 1814 and enlisted in the 17th Lancers in 1836. He survived the Charge, although he experienced near-misses when a musket ball passed through the heel of his boot and a Russian cossack drove a lance through his coat-tail. He retired to Lichfield and lived with his wife Margaret at 40 Wade Street. In 1896 the Lichfield Amateur Minstrel Troupe performed a benefit concert at St James's Hall in aid of the Crimea veteran and raised £21 8s 3d (£21.42) for Brown, who had fallen on hard times. He died in 1898 and many people lined the streets for his funeral procession, which was led by a military band. Two of those who carried his coffin, Sergeant Major Howe from Birmingham and Private Edden from Tamworth, were also survivors of the Charge and wore their old uniforms as a mark of respect. Brown was buried, with his trumpet, in St Michael's churchyard. Unfortunately the headstone was destroyed in the 1920s when a new path was laid, but in 1977 a plaque was placed close to the Second World War Memorial, near the entrance to the church. (Poole, Christopher J., *Balaclava Heroes,* JWB, 2008)

~ OCTOBER 26TH ~

1832: On this day, 12-year-old Princess Victoria visited Lichfield. Already being described as 'the future Queen of England', she was accompanied by her mother, the Duchess of Kent. The Royal Princess first visited Shugborough Hall, the home of the Earl of Lichfield, where she was greeted by a twenty-one gun salute and a parade of the Staffordshire Regiment of Yeomanry, followed by a reception at the Guildhall in the city centre and a visit to the cathedral. Large crowds greeted the royal party and the *Lichfield Mercury*, reporting on the visit, said that the Duchess of Kent addressed the crowds and 'spoke in a clear and distinct tone of voice, and with less of a foreign accent than might be expected'. Victoria's appearance was commented on by the *Mercury*'s reporter, who described the young Princess as having a 'frank and good-humoured countenance' and 'whose features bear a degree of resemblance to the lamented Princess Charlotte' (the daughter of King George IV who had died in childbirth at the age of twenty-one). Victoria's complexion was said to be 'delicate' and she was described as being 'dressed in an extremely simple style with braided hair formed into a small plaited coronet at the top of her head'. (*Lichfield Mercury*, November 3rd 1832)

~ October 27th ~

1916: On this day, the *Lichfield Mercury* reported on the largest fire to have occurred in Lichfield in living memory when the City Brewery Company building was virtually destroyed, causing £30,000 worth of damage. In addition to the Lichfield City Fire Brigade – under the command of Captain J.H. Salford – firemen from Brownhills, Tamworth, Sutton Coldfield and Burton-on-Trent also attended the blaze. When the flames died down after eight hours, very little of the building was left standing, apart from blackened walls of the brewery and the nearby malt houses. Investigations later suggested that the fire had been caused by an electrical fault and the Lichfield Fire Brigade was subsequently accused by Alderman T. Andrews, the managing director of the Brewery, of not responding rapidly enough to the fire. He suggested that the horses had not been attached to the fire engine quickly enough and that one of the alarm bells at the fire station was not working properly. However, at an independent inquiry held later, the Lichfield Force was completely exonerated. (*Lichfield Mercury*)

～ October 28th ～

1950: On this day, for the first time, it was claimed that a flying saucer was seen over Lichfield. It was apparently observed by Mr Frederick Baker of Walsall Road, who said that he saw the object at 5.45 a.m. It appeared, he said, to be slightly smaller than the moon and flew from east to west at the speed of a jet plane. According to Mr Baker it was shaped 'something like a wheel' and flashed by so quickly that he 'had little time to form any definite conclusion'. The strange object was also seen by 30-year-old Mr Leslie Sawyer, a gardener of Beech Gardens, who had been awakened by his baby and had gone downstairs when he heard a 'low drone' from outside. Looking out of the window he saw a 'flat disc-like object revolving at great speed', which appeared to be illuminated and was 'travelling toward Sutton Coldfield'. The following week in the *Mercury* a reader's letter poured cold water on the idea that the object was flown by extra-terrestrial visitors. Mr Bradley, of Chase Terrace, wrote that it was most likely a 'secret aircraft being flown by the military'. (*Lichfield Mercury*, November 3rd 1950)

~ OCTOBER 29TH ~

1924: On this day, the General Election took place and in the Lichfield constituency the sitting MP, Labour's Frank Hodges, was beaten by his Conservative opponent, Roy Wilson. Wilson's majority was 2,076, the turnout was 80 per cent and both candidates polled more votes than they had in the election held in the previous year. A large crowd greeted the announcement of the result outside the Guildhall and 'cheers and counter-cheers' meant that the speeches of the candidates could not be heard. Hodges was carried 'shoulder-high' to the Co-operative Hall where he addressed his supporters and vowed to stand again in Lichfield. Wilson walked to the George Hotel where he spoke to his supporters from the balcony and thanked them for their support. The election campaign in Lichfield had been controversial, with both Labour and Conservative meetings being the target of organised disruption. In the national election the Conservatives gained a majority of 141 over all other parties, enabling Stanley Baldwin to become prime minister. One interesting aspect of the election was the return of Winston Churchill to Parliament, who won the seat of Epping 'after a long sojourn in the wilderness'. (*Lichfield Mercury*, October 31st 1924)

~ OCTOBER 30TH ~

1735: By this date, Samuel Johnson had opened his private academy school at Edial House, using funds given to him by his new wife, Tetty, whom he had married in the previous July. When the school opened only three pupils were enrolled: Lawrence Offley, David Garrick and his older brother George. The school was a failure, despite advertisements, such as that which appeared in the *Gentleman's Magazine* announcing that 'young gentlemen to be boarded and taught the Latin and Greek languages by Samuel Johnson'. There were several reasons for the school's failure. Johnson was, at the time, unknown and despite his great intelligence was not cut out to be a teacher, even though he had great respect for teachers and teaching; furthermore, Edial House was about 2½ miles from the City of Lichfield and there was no real reason for parents to want to send their children there instead of Lichfield Grammar School, which was situated in the city. Johnson's school lasted just over a year and soon after its closure Johnson, with David Garrick, set out for London where they both hoped to discover fame and fortune. (Martin, Peter, *Samuel Johnson: A Biography*, Phoenix, 2008)

~ OCTOBER 31ST ~

1975: On this day, Councillor Jim Bazeley criticised local clergymen who locked their churches for long periods because of vandalism and thefts; many churches in the city were only open for services or when buildings were supervised. The councillor's criticism came after Father Peter Lees had considered locking Holy Cross RC church in St John Street after candlesticks worth £200 had been stolen, but Father Lees defended his decion by saying, 'Whether we get the candlesticks back or have to replace them we cannot afford to have them stolen again.' However, Councillor Bazeley said that it was traditional for churches to remain open for anyone who wants to pray, adding, 'This is a primary duty of the church and we have reached a sorry state when we weigh the worth of a prayer against the cost of vandalism. People do not reach the heights of elation or the depths of despair only on Sundays.' He suggested that 'churches could replace valuable objects during the week with plastic or wooden replicas.' Father Lees eventually did agree to leave his church doors open, but many other churches in the city remained closed except for services. (*Lichfield Mercury*, October 31st 1975)

1918: On this day, the *Lichfield Mercury* reported on the influenza epidemic that was 'causing acute anxiety' in Lichfield. Worries about the epidemic caused many schools to be closed in the city and the outlying villages; so many cases had been reported that a lack of nursing staff soon became evident. A number of reasons had been put forward to account for the rapid spread of the disease in Lichfield, which included overcrowding in houses, with medical staff soon realising that the disease spread more quickly in such conditions and the rate of mortality was higher. The lack of milk, 'an essential food in all cases of illness', was another problem faced by medical authorities in the city and a number of people suggested the setting up of an invalid kitchen in Lichfield where nourishing foods could be obtained either free or at a nominal cost. The devastating 1918 Spanish flu pandemic infected 500 million people across the world and 10 to 20 per cent of those who contracted the disease died, including previously healthy young adults. (*Lichfield Mercury*)

~ November 2nd ~

1914: On this day, the first British casualties of the First World War arrived at Lichfield City station. Despite heavy rain the ambulance train containing seventy wounded men was greeted by a large crowd of well-wishers, including members of the Lichfield Branch of the British Red Cross, who were there to provide them with refreshments before they were transported to the garrison hospital at Whittington Barracks. Most of the soldiers, who belonged to many different army regiments, were suffering from bullet wounds and some talked about how they had been bombarded by 'Jack Johnsons', their nickname for the heavy shells the Germans used. They also gave accounts of how aeroplanes were being used on the Western Front as a means of spotting and identifying targets. Soon after this event, a large number of Belgian soldiers also arrived at Lichfield and they too were taken to Whittington to be treated at the army hospital. In the coming weeks and months the *Lichfield Mercury* began printing the names of the many military personnel killed, wounded, missing or taken prisoner in the conflict. The war would last for another four years. (*Lichfield Mercury*, November 6th 1914)

– NOVEMBER 3RD –

1495: On this day, Bishop William Smythe founded a free grammar school at St John's Hospital in Lichfield. The statutes of the Hospital School (as it was known) stated that the scholars were to be given instruction 'gratis' and that the 'Master of Grammar' was to be paid annually a sum of £10. The school moved to a building over the other side of St John Street in 1577 and was renamed the King Edward VI school. In 1696 the annual salary paid to the headmaster was increased to £20 and the statute relating to free education was removed and the school began charging 'some reasonable allowance for the teaching of children'. Throughout the eighteenth century the school thrived and produced some notable pupils including Joseph Addison, David Garrick, Elias Ashmole and, of course, Samuel Johnson. In 1849 a new school building was constructed on the St John Street site (now occupied by Lichfield District Council). In 1903 the school moved to its present position on Borrowcop and in 1971 amalgamated with the King's Hill School to form a mixed comprehensive. (Taylor, Julia A., *A History of King Edward VI School*, published by the school in 1995)

~ November 4th ~

1955: On this day, the Mayor of Lichfield opened Minster Hall youth centre. After the ceremony, which included prayers from the Dean of Lichfield, various displays were presented by the groups who would be using the hall in the future. Three youth groups would meet in the hall on a regular basis: the Lichfield Boys' youth club, the Lichfield Co-operative youth club and the Women's Junior Air Corps. The Lichfield Boys' youth club met every Wednesday and was open to males aged 14 to 21. Activities on offer included boxing, athletics and recreational sports, as well as a hobby section for pursuits such as woodwork, model-making and photography. The Co-operative youth club was open to 'boys and girls' between 14 and 21 and met every Tuesday and Thursday. Their activities included public speaking, handicrafts, drama, discussion groups and dancing. The Women's Junior Air Corps was open to 'girls' aged 14 to 21 and alongside various other activities they ran a three-year aviation course with scholarships available for those completing the course and wanting to train for their pilot's licence. The professed aim of all the clubs was to 'create honourable citizens of the future'. (*Lichfield Mercury*, November 4th 1955)

⹂ NOVEMBER 5TH ⹂

1878: On this day, a fatal shooting took place at a Lichfield pub, the Gresley Arms, which stood in Gresley Row on what is now the delivery area for the Argos store. The landlord, George Green, fired a gun inside the pub killing a Walsall man, Samuel Bates, who was drinking with two friends. At the inquest Green stated that, as it was November 5th, he wanted to fire the gun as 'a lark' in order to frighten those who were in the pub. He had collected the gun from a young man, Henry Styche, who lived next door to the pub and who testified that he had loaded the gun with powder and paper. However, when the gun was fired a marble, which had somehow found its way into the gun barrel, entered Mr Bates' head and lodged in his brain, killing him instantly. The coroner, in his summing-up, suggested that Styche might have accidently or deliberately loaded the marble into the gun, but as there was no evidence to prove which was the case the verdict had to be one of accidental death. The Gresley Arms closed in 1931. (Shaw, John, *The Old Pubs of Lichfield*, George Lane Publishing, 2001)

— November 6th —

1815: On this day, the Prince Regent, the future George VI, visited Lichfield on his way to Beaudesert Hall, the home of the Marquis of Angelsey. When 'Prinny', as he was nicknamed, arrived at the George Inn in Bird Street, a new team of horses was attached to his carriage ready for the journey to the hall. There was a nervous moment for all involved soon afterwards, however, when the horses 'thrust the carriage into a ditch at the turn of Featherbed Lane'. The *Lichfield Mercury* was obviously relieved to report that no one was hurt and that the journey 'terminated fortunately'. Arriving at Beaudesert Hall, the Prince Regent was greeted by 'thousands of people (who) rent the air with acclamations'. While at Beaudesert the future king took part in a shoot where he successfully 'bagged from his own gun, fourteen head of game'. In the evening the Prince Regent dined on the 'choicest food and the most delicious wines'. The following day was a busy one for the royal visitor, as he knighted one of the marquis' bailiffs, inspected a new type of hussar saddle, received a loyal address from the people of Lichfield and attended a concert. *(Lichfield Mercury*, November 24th 1815)

~ NOVEMBER 7TH ~

1983: On this day, one of Lichfield's most historic and popular pubs was demolished. The Old Crown, which stood in Bore Street, had been one of the city's famous coaching inns and the archway where coaches had once pulled into the inn was a spot where flower sellers and other traders could ply their wares. The pub had many rooms including a market room in which, in times past, local farmers would carry out their deals. The Old Crown folk club met at the pub for many years and was a popular and friendly venue for many folk acts that later became famous – Jasper Carrot and Jake Thackery performed there regularly, for example. One of the endearing features of the folk club in the 1970s was the weekly raffle of a plate of breakfast food – bacon, sausage, eggs, tomatoes etc. – ready for cooking the following morning. The Old Crown, a Grade II listed building, apparently fell down during redevelopment into retail units, an incident that was not without controversy and which stirred up a lot of interest in the local press. Today, an optician's marks the spot where the Old Crown once stood. (*Lichfield Mercury*, November 11th 1983)

~ November 8th ~

1929: On this day, it was announced that the Lichfield Palladium cinema would be showing its first ever 'talking picture'. The film, *Broadway Melody*, was described by the *Lichfield Mercury* as a 'masterpiece' that had to be 'seen and heard – to be believed' and Lichfield folk were urged in the cinema's regular weekly advert to book their seats quickly 'to avoid disappointment'. The *Mercury*, in its editorial, decided that the 'talkies' were 'here to stay', although it was worried that the loud noises and singing in the film could cause a 'great many shocks to the nervous system'. The *Mercury* also warned cinemagoers not to talk over dialogue in the film, as others might 'object to their chatter'. The paper was very complimentary about the management of the Palladium as, 'although Lichfield seems behind the world in most matters', the cinema always ensured that 'the best productions always come to the city early'. The Palladium's next talkie, shown the following week, was *The Jazz Singer* starring Al Jolson, often regarded as the first talking film produced by Hollywood. (*Lichfield Mercury*)

~ November 9th ~

1995: On this day, the *Lichfield Mercury* reported on the launch of an appeal to save the 'crumbling' St Mary's in Market Square by raising £450,000. The church, which was converted for community use in 1981, had been 'basically untouched for 120 years'. Appeal Chairman John Rackham said, 'The roof and the stonework of the walls, tower and spire are deteriorating rapidly and restoration on a large scale is now urgently needed.' He called for financial help from 'near or far', as it was 'unthinkable that Lichfield could lose such a historic building in the centre of the City'. Over 2,000 requests for finance had been sent by the appeal organisers to a wide range of local and national companies and charities. The roof and parapets of the old church were first in line for restoration, followed by the west elevation and the tower; the whole project was estimated to take five years. The Grade II listed building now houses a senior citizens' day centre; a heritage exhibition; a Muniment Room, which displayed Lichfield's historic charters; a treasury with civic, diocesan and regimental silver; as well as a cafe and gift shop. (*Lichfield Mercury*)

— November 10th —

1883: On this day, Oscar Wilde, the famous poet and playwright, delivered a lecture at St James's Hall in Lichfield entitled 'The House Beautiful'. The lecture began at 8 p.m., reserved seats cost 3s (15p) and tickets could be purchased at Frederic Brown's Mercury Office in Bird Street. Wilde, at the time, was already one of the most famous men in Victorian Britain, known as much for his flamboyant clothes and wit as for his writing. In his Lichfield lecture he illustrated his remarks with descriptions of the houses of celebrated artists of the time such as Whistler, Millais and Alma-Tadema, concentrating on the proper combinations of colour that should be used in the home. Wilde went on to say that 'the days of the antimacassar and the wax flower are past in houses having the slightest pretence to refinement.' He also talked about education, saying that it would be more useful to teach children to use their hands and draw rather than to learn useless facts about 'the latitudes and longitudes of countries they might never visit'. Wilde, who was dressed in a sober dinner suit for the occasion, received hearty applause from the large audience at the end of his talk. (*Lichfield Mercury*, November 16th 1883)

~ November 11th ~

1918: On this day, the end of the First World War was announced in Lichfield by a buzzer attached to a fire engine in Market Square, followed soon after by the ringing of bells at the cathedral and people putting up flags and bunting on their businesses and houses. The news was formally proclaimed by the mayor, who spoke in Market Square and said that the signing of the armistice would 'guarantee for all time the future of our children and of our children's children'. The mayor also declared a holiday for the remainder of the day and all shops and offices were closed, with a service of thanksgiving held later at the cathedral and a great bonfire lit. Red, white and blue lights were strung across Beacon Street and an 'enormous crowd' assembled in the recreation grounds where there were fireworks, the singing of the National Anthem and cheers for the king and 'the gallant lads at the Front', although there were none of 'the wild outbursts of enthusiasm which marked the close of the South African War' a few years before. (*Lichfield Mercury*, November 15th 1918)

— November 12th —

1909: On this day, the *Lichfield Mercury* reported on a fire that had taken place at Beaudesert Hall, the home of the Marquis of Anglesey. The fire alarm had sounded at 7 p.m. on November 5th and shortly afterwards fire brigades from Lichfield, as well as from Rugeley, Hednesford, Brownhills and Cannock, were in attendance. The fire was mainly confined to the west wing of the house where the servants' quarters were situated. The *Mercury* described the fire as creating a spectacle of 'awe-inspiring grandeur as great tongues of flame shot heavenwards'. Nine rooms in the hall were completely gutted by the fire, and water damage and smoke affected several other rooms. As a result of the fire, a large number of workers were employed in removing costly furniture, priceless heirlooms and works of art. The famous tapestry depicting the first Marquis of Anglesey at the Battle of Waterloo was saved, along with many other historic portraits of the Paget family. Due to the marquis' financial situation the Beaudesert estate was eventually sold off in the 1920s, with the hall being partially demolished in 1935. (*Lichfield Mercury*)

~ November 13th ~

1970: On this day, the *Lichfield Mercury* reported how Billy Newman, 78-year-old veteran of the First World War, had received a medal fifty years after the event. The medal was sent through the post from an association in France that specialised in tracing survivors of the Battle of the Somme in 1916 and honouring them with a decoration. It came with a card in French, which Mr Newman, who remembered some of the language from his time in the war, was able to decipher. Newman, who served in the King's Royal Rifles throughout the war, was gassed twice and spent a long time in military hospitals after the war. In the Second World War he served as a firefighter in Birmingham and later worked for Birmingham Corporation as a painter and decorator. He was also, for a time, an attendant at Birmingham's Museum and Art Gallery. He moved to Lichfield with his wife Tabitha in 1959, but before settling in the city the couple had spent a year in Australia where they were 'terribly homesick'. Mr Newman remembered that he thought 'it was marvellous to get back to England again'. (*Lichfield Mercury*)

~ November 14th ~

1966: On this day, Lichfield City Council was warned that its new multi-purpose Civic Hall, which it planned to build at a cost of £120,000, would turn out to be a 'waste of money'. Councillor W.J. Wilson asked the council to 'think again' about the need for such a hall and to consider other uses for 'the land to the rear of the Guild Hall' and advised that, 'It seems that you are quite determined to build another edifice to civic pomp. I am giving a warning that we shall be building a municipal mausoleum.' He went on the say that a Hall which had facilities for banqueting, dancing, dramatic productions and exhibitions was 'not what the City needed', and that the Guildhall was 'second to none in Staffordshire'. Councillor Garratt, Chairman of the Civic Hall Committee, detailed what he saw were the drawbacks of the Guildhall and how 'many larger functions' have to go out to Sutton Coldfield or Tamworth. He said, 'If the City is to grow to 40,000 people then it is essential that it has a Civic Hall on the site we have earmarked for it.' (*Lichfield Mercury*, November 18th 1966)

~ November 15th ~

1904: On this day, a special sitting of Lichfield City magistrates took place at the Guildhall to deal with a number of prosecutions under the 1853 Betting Act. Thomas Bowdler, the licensee of the Mitre Inn in Tamworth Street, was charged for using the smoke room of his public house for the purpose of receiving bets. A number of other Lichfield men were also charged with using the room for betting purposes. These included David Williams, an army pensioner; William Wootten, a butcher's assistant; and Alfred Swain, a butler from Wade Street. Bowdler was found guilty and fined £25, a large sum in 1904, and the others were fined lesser amounts. What the men had done was legal until the 1853 Act but there had been so many betting venues in pubs and other places that the government of the day decided to ban them. Off-course betting remained illegal until 1961 when betting shops were once again legalised. (*Lichfield Mercury*, November 18th 1904)

~ NOVEMBER 16TH ~

1898: On this day, a 'smoking concert' was held at the Assembly Room in the Swan Hotel in Bird Street, Lichfield. As part of the evening, Mr R.H. Fry gave a talk entitled 'Sports and Pastimes' to a very appreciative and large audience. It was, according to the *Lichfield Mercury,* 'one of the most successful gatherings of its kind which had ever taken place in the city'. The talk centred on the way in which Britain, unlike other countries, had taken sports and games, such as football and cricket, to a large number of places around the world, as well as to the British Empire, and these had 'brought out the best qualities of those who had taken part in them'. All of those present agreed with Mr Fry that sports and games 'deserved every encouragement'. As well as Mr Fry's talk there was a great deal of music played during the evening, including the songs 'Norah, the Pride of Kildare', 'The Bay of Biscay' and the comic song 'Shoofly'. Mr Olly Oakley entertained the audience by playing a zither-banjo in a manner which 'brought the house down'. (*Lichfield Mercury*, November 18th 1898)

- November 17th -

1997: On this day, soldier turned author Andy McNab made a visit to James Redshaw's bookshop in Lichfield to promote his latest book, *Remote Control*. The novel had the distinction of being the first to be officially 'called in' by the Ministry of Defence (MOD) and the Intelligence Services, but was eventually given the 'all clear' after a few alterations had been made – 'There were compromises made on both sides,' said Mr McNab. The story is based on the experiences of SAS soldiers involved in the Gibraltar shooting of 1988. A former member of the SAS, Mr McNab 'shot to fame' with his best-selling autobiographical accounts of his time in the Special Forces: *Bravo Two Zero* and *Immediate Action*. Both were controversial and the MOD put an injunction on the latter title, and even brought in a confidentiality contract to prevent ex-service personnel from publicising such books without the permission of senior officers. The main concern of the military authorities was that they believed the books could have revealed secrets of SAS tactics and methods. Mr McNab remained unworried about official scrutiny but kept his real identity 'shrouded in mystery' and rarely made public appearances or allowed himself to be photographed. (*Lichfield Mercury*, November 20th 1997)

– NOVEMBER 18TH –

1968: On this day, Lichfield Councillor Harold Hine spoke at a meeting of the City Council to defend what he saw were the rights of the individual against 'mass medication'. He was opposing a Health Committee recommendation which called for an increase in the fluoride content of the city's water supply, in line with most other areas of the country. Councillor Hine felt that the addition of the chemical, which most experts agreed helped to protect children's teeth from decay, was misguided. As proof, he stated that although he was 'a great chocolate eater' he still had his own teeth even though he was in his 68th year. He added, 'surely it is foreign to our way of life ... let anyone who wants to use it have access to it, the same as if they want some other form of medication.' The mayor, Mrs A.G. Millard, pointed out that it had already been decided that fluoride should be added to the water supply, the question was whether the level should be increased. The council agreed that the city's MP, Julian Snow, should raise the question with the government. (*Lichfield Mercury*, November 22nd 1968)

~ November 19th ~

1962: On this day, John Sanders, the Headmaster at Lichfield's School of Art, asked the question, 'What do males in Lichfield and the surrounding area do in their spare time?' Mr Sanders was speaking at the annual prize-giving evening at the art school and speculated on what local men might be doing in their time off – 'Do they sit in front of the television, prop up a bar, play snooker, doze in front of the fire or play bingo?' The question came about as the art school's headmaster expressed concern about how few men joined classes at the school, suggesting that men ought to 'emulate their wives', many of whom attend classes after being at work in at least part-time jobs. Mr Sanders appealed to the 'male citizens of Lichfield' to 'come to us with their suggestions' and he and his staff would do their best to organise classes in subjects for which there is reasonable demand'. He also expressed worries that there were too few young people signing up for courses, estimating that the average age of students at the art school were 'around the forty mark'. (*Lichfield Mercury*, November 23rd 1962)

~ NOVEMBER 20TH ~

1914: On this day, with the First World War having begun in August, the *Lichfield Mercury* reported on the setting up of the Lichfield Home Defence Force. The Defence Force, the forerunner of the Second World War's 'Dad's Army', was established at a meeting held at the city's Swan Hotel and was open to all men aged over 17. There was some disquiet among the, mainly elderly, city dignitaries, who were concerned that young, local men who *should* volunteer to join the regular army might see the Defence Force as an alternative 'haven of rest'. As a result, it was decided that the Lichfield Home Defence Force would generally be considered as an organisation for men who through age 'or some other disqualification would find themselves unable to join regular forces'. This ruling would apply to those like Lichfield's sheriff who, while being eligible for the regular army, said, 'it gave him great pain and sorrow that for business reasons it was impossible for him to go away to the Front.' At the end of the meeting, the newspaper reported, a large number of those present enrolled for the new organisation. (*Lichfield Mercury*)

~ NOVEMBER 21ST ~

2002: On this day, the *Lichfield Mercury* published an article about the 100-year-old Charles Bridgemen whose 'skilled work and civic service has left a lasting legacy in his home City and ensured that the family name has a special place in its annals'. Charles was the third generation owner of R. Bridgeman and Sons, the famous Lichfield firm of skilled stonemasons and craftsmen. He was born in 1902 and had lived in the city all of his life, brought up in the family home at 8 Dam Street. His grandfather, Robert Bridgeman, founded the company in 1878 and Charles followed his grandfather and father into the family business. During his time in charge he held the position of Surveyor to the Dean and Chapter of the Cathedral and under his supervision R. Bridgeman's and Sons carried out several restoration projects at the cathedral. The family firm was eventually sold to Linfords when Charles retired in 1968. He also followed in the steps of his grandfather and father in another way: all three had been mayor and sheriff of the city and Charles had the honour of reading the proclamation of Elizabeth II's ascension to the throne from the steps of the Guildhall. (*Lichfield Mercury*)

~ NOVEMBER 22ND ~

1963: On this day, Lichfield's representative on Staffordshire County Council announced that the site for the new St Michael's Primary School would be in Cherry Orchard, adjoining Lichfield's School of Art. Not everyone was happy about the decision. A member of the school's management board, Councillor W.J. Wilson, was far from satisfied with the proposed site's location, as it was close to the railway line. Also on this day, advertisements in the *Lichfield Mercury* informed people that a train journey from Lichfield to London would cost 27*s* 6*d* (£1.38) and that a new Hillman Minx Deluxe saloon car could be theirs for £634 18*s* 6*d* (£634.93). As it turned out, the day was marked by the news from the United Stated that President Kennedy had been shot and killed in Dallas, Texas. It was not until the following week's edition that the *Mercury* was able to carry a comment from the Bishop of Lichfield about the incident. The Bishop, Dr A.S. Reeve, spoke about the 'foul act' and said that 'we can only pray that the consequences may not be too disastrous, not just for America, but for the whole world.' (*Lichfield Mercury*, November 22nd and 29th 1963)

~ November 23rd ~

1942: On this day, a fire caused extensive damage to the Lido, one of the two cinemas in Lichfield. The fire, which destroyed the inside of the cinema in Bore Street, was discovered early in the morning by a bakery worker at Garratt's Bakery on the opposite side of the street, who sent a messenger to the fire station 300yd away and soon firemen from there, and also from Burton, Tamworth and Stafford, were dealing with the blaze. The fire was thought to have been caused by the careless dropping of a cigarette on the balcony floor at the end of the previous night's screening and the damage was estimated to represent thousands of pounds. The management of the Lido were quick to reassure the public that the cinema would be reopened as soon as possible and a plan to reconstruct its interior was announced in December 1942. The new 'Lido Super Cinema, Theatre and Cafe' opened in July 1943 and the first film shown was *Random Harvest*, starring Ronald Coleman and Greer Garson. (*Lichfield Mercury*, November 27th 1942)

— November 24th —

1949: On this day, a Lichfield farmer found himself in court charged with assaulting another farmer at Lichfield cattle auctions. Alfred Boston of Brownsfield Farm was accused of assaulting William Peace of Knowle Farm by throwing manure at him before striking him to the ground. It transpired at the trial that the two men had argued on several occasions before the incident took place and that Boston had grown tired of remarks made by the other man about the quality of his cattle, believing that his derogatory comments had led to him getting lower prices for his animals, and he had told Peace several times to 'mind his own business'. Boston said that the 64-year-old Peace was an 'old busybody who liked to attend to other people's business more than his own'. He denied striking the man saying, 'he simply carried him out of the auction ring and dropped him by the public conveniences.' Boston was conditionally discharged by the judge on the payment of £7 9s costs (£7.45), providing he did not commit an offence for two months. (*Lichfield Mercury*, November 25th 1949)

~ November 25th ~

1817: On this day, Pipe Hill and Farewell Association of Farmers issued a list of rewards they would be giving to anyone helping with the apprehension and conviction of anyone who had committed crimes on their land. Spurred on by rising crime levels in the rural area surrounding Lichfield, their list of rewards was extensive. For any public-spirited person supplying information leading to the conviction of burglars, housebreakers or highway robbers, as well as for anyone who had stolen horses, cows, bulls or heifers, a reward of £21 was offered. A reward of 5 guineas (£5.25) was offered for the apprehension of anyone stealing a pig, grain, clover or straw or for wrongfully milking a cow, and a similar reward was offered for information about those who had broken a fence, gate or hedge. The reward for for the discovery of anyone who had illegally pulled up or destroyed potatoes, cabbages, peas or carrots was 2 guineas (£2.10) and 1 guinea (£1.05) was given by the farmers for help locating those who had destroyed or stolen traps set 'for the destruction of moles and other vermin' or had received stolen goods. (*Lichfield Mercury*, November 25th 1817)

~ NOVEMBER 26TH ~

1911: On this day, the twenty-first anniversary of the founding of Lichfield Cycling Club took place. The club, which had started in 1890 at the Goat's Head Pub, held its anniversary celebrations at their usual headquarters, the Old Crown Hotel in Bore Street, the supper being provided by its landlord Mr J. Busby, 'an enthusiastic member'. All those present at the celebration were given a commemorative souvenir postcard, which had on it a photograph of the original founder members. After the meal the chairman proposed a toast to the new king and queen (George V and Queen Mary) who had recently been crowned, and Councillor W.A. Wood proposed a toast to the club, saying that he thought cycling was 'not only a pleasurable sport but also a useful one'. He went on to recall that he could remember the earliest days of cycling when people rode 'boneshakers as they were called' and how these days it would be hard to imagine a world without bicycles, which 'are now regarded as a necessity'. Another member of the club stated that cycling must be very healthy, as most of those in the 1890 photograph were still alive. (*Lichfield Mercury*, December 1st 1911)

~ November 27th ~

1912: On this day, the Lichfield County Ball took place in a 'specially erected ballroom' at the rear of the George Hotel and was 'the most brilliant social function of the year'. Unfortunately the weather 'was by no means ideal; rain falling heavily during the evening and the atmospheric conditions were damp and depressing'; however, inside the hotel 'all was bright and sparkling and the perfect cosiness and comfort was evidenced on all sides'. The whole of the hotel had been 'requisitioned' for the evening and was decorated with green and white throughout. Furniture had been 'so organised as to ensure plenty of alcoves seductively arranged with easy chairs and fancy screens' and electric lights had been especially installed and a 'charming effect was produced by Chinese lanterns and fairy lamps'. The guests numbered 300 and they began to arrive shortly after 9 p.m., their arrival witnessed by a large crowd of spectators in the street outside. Music was provided by the Blue Viennese Band and 'supper was partaken of at small, daintily laid tables'. The menu included consommé, foie gras en aspic, many different meat dishes and Charlotte Russe, with champagne and cognac being the main drinks of choice. (*Lichfield Mercury*, November 29th 1912)

~ November 28th ~

1495: By this day, St John's Hospital in Lichfield had been re-endowed as an almshouse by Bishop Smith. Originally founded by Bishop Roger de Clinton in the twelfth century, St John's Hospital was rebuilt and thirteen almsmen were to be given accommodation for 7*d* (3p) per week and were required to wear distinctive black gowns with a red cross. A school was also started on the same site. By the year 1786 the almsmen received 2*s* 6*d* (13p) per week for maintenance and 10*s* 6*d* (53p) per year for coal. Today, seventeen residents, usually members of the Church of England, live at St John's. In 1981 the trustees opened an almshouse in the Close, on the site of the former theological college, with five flats for married couples and seven for single men. This new residence was called St John's Within the Close, but in 1989, to avoid confusion, the word hospital was dropped and the St John's Street building became known as St John's Without the Barrs. (Greenslade, M.W. (ed.), *A History of Lichfield*, Staffordshire Libraries, Arts and Archives, 1994)

– NOVEMBER 29TH –

1745: On this day, while his army camped outside Lichfield, the Duke of Cumberland and his staff dined at the Swan Hotel in Bird Street. The obese duke and his entourage got through a large amount of food during their overnight stay – meat, bacon, pigs' ears and feet, a calf's head and veal – costing a total of £10 13s (£10.65), a considerable amount of money in the eighteenth century. The next day the duke's army continued their march north in pursuit of the Jacobite army led by Bonnie Prince Charlie, who had invaded England, getting as far south as Derby. The Duke of Cumberland, who was the younger son of King George II, eventually forced the Jacobite rebels back into Scotland. A decisive battle was fought at Culloden in March 1746, resulting in the defeat of Bonnie Prince Charlie, and the '45 Rebellion, as it was called, was over. After the battle, Cumberland's soldiers were encouraged to stab any Jacobite rebel who remained alive, an action that earned the victorious duke the nickname 'Butcher' Cumberland. (Clayton, Howard, *Coaching City*, Dragon Books, 1970)

~ November 30th ~

1771: On this day, the last official slave auction in Britain took place in Lichfield. A young African boy, aged 10 or 11, was sold at the Bakers Arms public house by a Mr Heeley, an auctioneer from Walsall. An advert for the auction appeared in the *Birmingham Gazette* on November 11th, which assured readers that the boy was 'well proportioned, speaks tolerably good English, of a mild disposition, friendly, officious, sound, healthy [and] fond of labour'. It is not known what happened to the boy but it was common at the time for rich families to acquire black servants, particularly young boys, as a sign of their wealth and status. The site where this sale took place still exists today, as part of The Swan public house in Bird Street. It eventually changed its name to The Wheatsheaf around 1818 and later closed down. The slave trade was abolished in the British Empire in 1807. (www.bbc.co.uk/birmingham/content/articles/2007/03/03/did_birmingham_profit_feature.shtml, Shaw, J., *Old Pubs of Lichfield*, George Lane Publishing, 2001)

- DECEMBER 1ST -

1843: On this day, Queen Victoria and her husband Prince Albert visited Lichfield. The royal couple had been staying at Drayton Manor, the home of Prime Minister Robert Peel, where Prince Albert had attended a shoot and killed sixty pheasants, twenty-five hares, eight rabbits and one woodcock. To welcome the queen into the city four imitation stone triumphal arches had been built on her route, which were decorated with evergreens, flags and signs which read 'United for the Good of the People' and 'Welcome Victoria'. People's houses on the route of the 'numerous cavalcade' were also decorated for the day by workmen specially employed by the city. The queen was 'loudly cheered' when she arrived in Lichfield at 3 p.m. in a state coach pulled by four grey horses and accompanied by her husband, Sir Robert Peel and the Duke of Wellington. The royal party spent an hour in the cathedral where they were shown round by the mayor and the cathedral staff before returning to Drayton Manor. (*Illustrated London News,* December 9th 1843)

~ DECEMBER 2ND ~

2011: On this day, a Lichfield walkway was named after a soldier killed by the IRA over twenty years before. Private Robert Davies from Wales was shot by an IRA gunman at Lichfield City station on June 1st 1990. The street-naming ceremony and dedication was attended by Private Davies' parents, Des and Helen Davies, and a lone piper played a lament as army personnel, councillors and clergy were present for the ribbon-cutting ceremony which opened Robert Davies Walk. Commenting on the ceremony, Mr and Mrs Davies said, 'It means a lot to us that Robert has been remembered in this way.' The Rev. Linda Collins of St Michael's church led the service of dedication, which included a prayer read by Jonathan Daniel of the 2nd Battalion The Royal Welsh and the recital of the poem 'Ode of Remembrance' read by the chairman of the Royal British Legion, Tony Robinson. Chairman of Lichfield District Council, Bernard Derrick, who cut the ceremonial ribbon, said, 'It was a moving dedication and I am pleased that Private Robert Davies will not be forgotten by the people of Lichfield.' A plaque commemorating Private Davies is situated at the city railway station. (www.lichfieldlive. co.uk/2011/12/02)

‑ DECEMBER 3RD ‑

1990: On this day, work began on the city's Swan Link road, the long-awaited development for which the District Council had been battling for ten years. In a special ceremony, Councillor John Brooks, Chair of Lichfield's Area Highways Advisory Committee, cut the first sod to start the work. He said that he hoped the project, which would be followed by the pedestrianisation of Bird Street, would mean increased safety for pedestrians and greater protection for Lichfield's 'historic inheritance'. The new Swan Link road would connect Swan Road to the friary and was expected to be completed by April 1991. One sad aspect of the £750,000 project was the enforced demolition of one of Lichfield's historic pubs, which lay in the path of the new road. The Turk's Head dated from the eighteenth century, appearing on a 1781 map of the city. It was originally a coaching inn and was an important staging post for a coach called the *Umpire* which travelled between London and Liverpool. (*Lichfield Mercury*, December 7th 1990 and Shaw, J., *The Old Pubs of Lichfield*, George Lane Publishing, 2001)

~ DECEMBER 4TH ~

1969: On this day, the Chequers pub in Stowe Street was demolished as part of the redevelopment of the area. A few days before, the pub, which dated from the eighteenth century, had held a farewell party for its regulars and glasses were raised for the final time. The licensee, Mrs Edna Lyon, was naturally sad to leave the pub, commenting, 'It's been very nice here, but we were told it would have to come down when we moved here three and a half years ago.' She wouldn't miss one aspect of the pub, however – the building's ghost, 'a hooded figure' reputed to haunt the premises. 'I've only seen it once, but that was enough,' said Mrs Lyon. On the last night, as final orders were called, there were handshakes all round for the pub regulars. The Chequers, which stood where the traffic island at the Stowe Pool end of Stowe Street is now situated, was one of six pubs in Stowe Street. Already demolished by 1969 were the Brittania, the Partridge and the Seven Stars and the remaining two, the Staffordshire Knot and the Cross Keys, would also soon disappear. (*Lichfield Mercury*, December 5th 1969 and Shaw, J., *The Old Pubs of Lichfield*, George Lane Publishing, 2001)

~ DECEMBER 5TH ~

1945: On this day, the *Stars and Stripes*, the newspaper of the United States Army, reported that a number of US Army military prison guards, both officers and men, who had been employed at Lichfield's Whittington Barracks during the war, were facing charges of the 'cruel and inhuman treatment of stockade prisoners'. It was alleged that the men, who had been guarding imprisoned US soldiers, went well beyond the normal disciplinary regimes of military guardhouses. The charges against them included the routine beating of prisoners, making inmates eat cigarettes and forcing black prisoners to crawl and bark like dogs before they were fed. The first person to be brought to trial was Sergeant Judson Smith, who was found guilty of mistreating and assaulting prisoners while acting upon orders that he had been given by his superiors. He received six months and was dishonourably discharged from the army. Smith's court martial led the way to the trials of the others including the commandant of the military prison, Colonel James Killan. He was also found guilty and was issued with a fine, but was allowed to keep his rank and stay in the army. (Gieck, J., *Lichfield: The US Army on Trial*, University of Akron Press, 1997)

~ DECEMBER 6TH ~

1940: By this day, Lichfield's Spitfire Fund, launched in September, was approaching £4,000. Lichfield City Council had been keen to show that the Lichfield public were willing to support the war effort and so committed the city to raise a total of £5,000 to purchase a Spitfire fighter plane. Collections were held around the city and various fund-raising functions took place, including a dance held at the Guildhall with the slogan 'Dance your way to victory'. An auction was also arranged at the old market hall where people could bid for such diverse objects as live chickens and candlesticks. A football match between the army and the RAF, and containing a number of pre-war professional players, was held at the Meadow ground. The amount raised in shops and offices and in door-to-door collections was dutifully printed in the *Lichfield Mercury* each week and by May 1941 a final total of £5,185 was announced. The Spitfire purchased with the money raised in Lichfield proudly bore the city's coat of arms. (*Lichfield Mercury*)

DECEMBER 7TH

1868: On this day, Richard Dyott, Conservative Party representative, was elected as the single Member of Parliament for Lichfield. In previous elections Lichfield had been allowed to send two MPs to Parliament, but the 1867 Electoral Reform Act reduced the number to just one and also increased the number of men who could actually vote in the election. Prior to 1868 Lichfield had often been the scene of considerable division during elections, with the supporters of the Whig Party being based at the George Hotel in Bird Street while the Tory headquarters was the Swan Inn just across the road. From 1885 to 1923 Liberals represented Lichfield but in the General Election of 1923 Frank Hodges, General Secretary of the Miners Federation, won the seat for the Labour Party. In 1924 the Conservatives won and from 1929 the city was represented by a National Labour MP J.A. Lovat-Fraser. Labour won in 1945 and also in 1950 when Julian Snow, who was to represent Lichfield until his retirement in 1970, took the seat. A Conservative, Jack d'Avigdor-Goldsmid, took the seat in 1970 and held until the election of October 1974. (Rallings, Colin and Thrasher, Michael, *British Election Facts*, Ashgate Publishing, 2000)

- DECEMBER 8TH -

1989: On this day, the *Lichfield Mercury* reported on the 'flu bug' which had hit hundreds in the Lichfield and Burntwood district and had pushed health centres to the limit. Local doctors said there was nothing they could do for hundreds of ill people who had shown up at surgeries with headaches, high temperatures and sore throats and the best thing sufferers could do was to go to bed, take paracetamol and drink plenty of water. The health centres themselves had not been immune to the illness, with up to two-thirds of staff failing to turn up to work due to flu symptoms. People were asked not to contact their GP unless they were especially concerned – one spokesmen said, 'we have between 18,000 and 19,000 patients to serve and it only takes a couple of hundred of these to call to put us in big trouble.' The usual flu epidemic normally affected the young and the elderly but the Lichfield bug seemed to be slightly different in that it affected all ages equally. (*Lichfield Mercury*, December 8th 1989)

~ DECEMBER 9TH ~

1980: On this day, the first Lichfield Good Neighbour of the Year Award was presented to Hilda Wright. As part of a contest organised by the 51 Club, Mrs Wright was presented with a trophy and was treated to dinner at a special awards ceremony held at Lichfield's Little Barrow Hotel. The contest was held to find the area's 'unsung heroes' – those people who put themselves out for others without any thought of reward. The 51 Club asked people to nominate the person they thought was 'the best neighbour'. Mrs Wright was nominated by Phyllis Larkins, who said, 'Hilda has always been willing to help anyone who needs helping. I know I speak for everyone she helps when I say that Hilda is the best neighbour anyone could possibly have.' After being awarded the trophy, Mrs Wright remarked, 'It was quite a shock. I wasn't expecting to win. I have never been to anything like this before; I shall remember it for the rest of my life.' The Club 51 Chairman, Harry Spalding, said he hoped the contest would become an annual event. (*Lichfield Mercury*, December 12th 1980)

‒ DECEMBER 10TH ‒

1883: On this day, Molly Bloor, a 20-year-old prostitute from Longton in the Potteries, was brought before magistrates in Lichfield. She was accused of 'feloniously stealing' a silk handkerchief to the value of 2*s* (10p) from Charles Owen, a collier of Lombard Street. Owen had apparently known the young woman for about a month and she had lodged in his house for the previous two weeks; he was therefore able to recognise the handkerchief when it was produced in court. A private in the 80th Regiment stationed at Whittington Barracks, John Hole, said the accused had lent him the handkerchief and he had promptly handed it to the police. Bloor pleaded guilty and the police contacted her parents to see if they would be prepared to pay her fine – they refused. She had had, the court was told, a poor upbringing and her father had spent time in prison for wife-beating. The girl was sentenced to twenty-one days in prison, with the magistrate saying, 'it was a sad thing when such a young girl should turn out so bad,' and urged her to lead a better life when she came out of prison. (*Lichfield Mercury*, December 14th 1883)

– DECEMBER 11TH –

1917: On this day, a lecture was held at the Palladium cinema in Bore Street, the subject of which was work done in the war by the Red Cross. The president of the British Red Cross Society, Mr Frank Hastings, gave a 'vivid description' of the work of the Red Cross on the Western and Italian fronts, with his remarks illustrated by a large number of 'cinematograph films and limelight views' (slides), allowing the people of Lichfield to have 'their best opportunity ever of seeing the most complete set of pictures depicting the arduous work of the troops of Britain and her allies'. Mr Hastings pointed out how much worse the plight of soldiers would be if it were not for the work of the Red Cross and their 'splendidly organised, beneficent and expeditious work'. He also mentioned some of the facts and figures regarding the Red Cross' work, which included '2,500 motor ambulances, cars, cycles, wagons and soup kitchens' which had been sent to the front, as well as £1.6 million raised for surgical dressings and other medical supplies and £1.1 million spent on the cost of running hospital trains to carry the wounded from the battlefields to places of safety. (*Lichfield Mercury*, December 14th 1917)

− December 12th −

1742: On this day, Anna Seward, the Swan of Lichfield, was born in Derbyshire. A writer and poet, she became the centre of literary life in her adopted city, to which she moved at the age of 7. Her father was appointed as canon of the cathedral and so resided with his family in the Bishop's Palace, and Anna was to live in Cathedral Close for sixty years, rarely going into the city itself, which she disliked. She had little time for Lichfield traditions, such as the annual Greenhill Bower, describing it as 'grotesque and vulgar'. In her day she was very popular, being particularly well known for her poem 'Elegy on Captain Cook', as well as her novel *Louisa*. Part of the reason for her fame lay in the fact that she attempted something that few women had done before, actually publishing her writing (literature at the time being deemed a male stronghold). As head of a literary salon she entertained such celebrities as Erasmus Darwin, Walter Scott and the actress Sarah Siddons. A person of great charisma, she had a number of romances, but never married. She died in March 1809. (Clayton, Howard, *Coaching City*, Dragon Books, 1970)

– December 13th

1935: On this day, the *Lichfield Mercury* reflected on the City Council's announcement of the biggest slum-clearance scheme ever seen in the city. On the advice given by the city's medical officer and the sanitary inspector and spurred on by the 1930 Slum Clearance Act, the council had decided to get rid of some of Lichfield's sub-standard housing. The first area tackled included houses fronting Bower Court, Greenhill, Church Street and Rotton Row – the 'famous triangle' at the junction of the Burton and Tamworth roads. Houses in this area were targeted for demolition, with residents being rehoused under the council's Better Housing campaign. It was hoped that once these houses had been cleared the area around the fountain and the drinking trough would become an open space. The council also made plans to demolish houses in Bakers Lane and in all fifty-three slum houses disappeared from the city in 1935. In addition, the council laid down plans for the building of new council houses at sites on Curborough Road and Stychbrook Gardens. (*Lichfield Mercury*)

~ December 14th ~

1923: On this day, the result of the General Election in the Lichfield constituency was announced. For the first time in twenty-seven years the Liberal Party failed to win the seat, which was won by the Labour Party. Frank Hodges, the General Secretary of the Miners Federation, won the election with a majority of 2,019 over his Conservative and Liberal opponents and vowed to keep the seat for the Labour Party in the future. The turnout for the election was 68 per cent and a large crowd had gathered outside the Guildhall waiting for the result to be declared. Mr Hodges' speech was given 'an enthusiastic reception by his supporters', who later carried him on their shoulders to his car in a 'triumphant procession'. The 1923 General Election produced a hung Parliament and the Labour Party, under the new prime minister, Ramsay MacDonald, formed a minority government. The Labour government was short lived, however, for, just ten months later, another General Election was called, which the Conservatives won in a landslide and in which Frank Hodges lost the Lichfield constituency to the Conservative candidate Roy Wilson. (*Lichfield Mercury*)

~ DECEMBER 15TH ~

1648: On this day, the genealogist and statistician Gregory King was born in Lichfield. Described by later writers as 'the first great economic statistician', he became clerk to Sir William Dugdale at the age of 14. Dugdale was an antiquarian and attendant to Charles II and he took King on extensive tours of the entire country. King would later go on to design Soho Gardens in London (previously known as King's Square) and became a teacher of writing and arithmetic. However, it is as a statistician that he is best known. In his book *Natural and Political Observations Upon the State and Condition of England*, published in 1696, he estimated the wealth and population of England and even predicted the future population growth. In his home town of Lichfield he conducted a detailed census of the population, noting the age, gender, marital status and number of children in each family, recording that 2,833 people lived in the town and 205 in Cathedral Close. He later observed that the people of Lichfield were 'addicted to drink'. King died in 1712. (Upton, Chris, *A History of Lichfield*, Phillimore, 2001)

— December 16th —

1965: On this day, the Tesco store became the latest addition to Lichfield's new Bakers Lane shopping precinct. Engineers worked through the night to get the shop ready for its big opening, which was performed by the sales promotion 'girl' of the Green Shield Stamp Company – Miss Shirley Bower. The new store, situated opposite the site for the new General Post Office, was within 'easy reach' of the city's bus station and was one of hundreds in the Tesco chain of stores. A special feature of the new store was a 20ft-long refrigerated display of freshly cut meat and frozen foods. The store manager, Mr Raymond Davis, had worked in a number of Tesco stores throughout the country. From its first store in Middlesex in 1929 the Tesco group had expanded rapidly and by 1965 had 5,000 stores in the South and North. Opening offers in Lichfield included potatoes at 1*s* (5p) per pound; jellies 6*d* (3p) each; Macdougall's flour at 1*s* 6*d* (8p) for 3lb; and Cheddar cheese at 2*s* 6*d* (13p) per pound. (*Lichfield Mercury*, December 17th 1965)

~ DECEMBER 17TH ~

1880: On this day, the festive season was in full swing and Lichfield shops were offering many Christmas related goods and services such as winter fashions and Christmas novelties, which were available at Shakeshaft and Playfer's store in the market place. The Goats Head Inn, also in the market place, was ready to provide breakfast and dinners of chops and steaks to visitors to the city and Egginton and Brown's Fancy Warehouse in Bird Street, opposite the Swan Hotel, offered many items for Christmas presents including satin pocket photo albums, ivory napkin rings, leather collar and cuff boxes, opera glasses, tea caddies and Japanese goods. Adrian Shemmond's shop in Market Street offered an array of wines and spirits for sale, including a bottle of port for 2*s* (10p), sherry for 1*s* 3*d* (6p), claret at 1*s* (5p) and Scotch whisky at 2*s* 3*d* (11p). Christmas meat was displayed in Henry Evans' butcher's shop in Sandford Street and for those citizens of Lichfield anxious to leave Britain, passages aboard ships bound for North America were on offer in the city, with cabins at 10, 12 or 15 guineas (£10.50, £12.60, £15.75) or steerage for 6 guineas (£6.30). (*Lichfield Mercury*)

~ December 18th ~

1557: On this day, Joyce Lewis was burned alive for heresy in Lichfield's Market Square. Lewis was from Mancetter, a village near Atherstone, and was the daughter of Sir Thomas Curzon of Croxall and also a niece of Bishop Hugh Latimer, who himself was burned at the stake. She was a Protestant married to a Catholic and her husband had demanded that she worship at his church. In protest she turned her back on the altar, a dangerous thing to do during the reign of the fervent Catholic queen 'Bloody Mary' Tudor. The Bishop of Lichfield, Ralph Baine, ordered her immediate arrest and she was quickly tried for heresy and sentenced to death. The sheriff of Lichfield refused to carry out the sentence and was dismissed, being replaced by someone who was willing to oversee the execution. Just before she was burnt at the stake at 9 a.m., she was offered comfort by Margaret Biddulph and Joan Lowe, the wives of prominent Lichfield citizens, who gave her some wine to drink. The following year Queen Mary died and the country was returned to Protestantism under Elizabeth I. Bishop Ralph Baine was dismissed from his position and imprisoned. (Greenslade, Michael, *Catholic Staffordshire*, Gracewing, 2006)

~ DECEMBER 19TH ~

1956: On this day, a thick fog descended on the city, causing the local *Lichfield Mercury* to proclaim in its front-page headline that 'Lichfield Suffers One of the Worst Fogs ever'. The fog soon mixed with smoke from businesses and houses to create the dreaded 'smog' that was so dangerous to the young, old and those with respiratory complaints. It is estimated that some 4,000 people died prematurely in the United Kingdom as a result of the smog, most due to conditions such as asthma and bronchitis. Although by today's standards road traffic in the 1950s was sparse, the fog caused 'innumerable accidents' in the Lichfield District, including a fatal one at Freeford on the Lichfield to Tamworth road, which led to the road's closure for many hours; at one point all routes from the city were blocked. Ambulance men and firemen on their way to the many incidents across the area had to walk in front of their vehicles, acting as guides. Christmas deliveries were also hit and around the country burglaries and muggings increased as a result of the fog. A heavy fall of snow soon afterwards added to people's woes. (*Lichfield Mercury*)

~ December 20th ~

2003: By this day, Lichfield's first professional pantomime was delighting young audiences at the City's recently opened Garrick Theatre. The pantomime, *Cinderella*, which ran until January 10th, starred Irish comedian Jimmy Cricket, who brought years of 'panto' experience to his role of Buttons. He said, 'When it was first mooted that it was a new theatre, I was really excited that we would be the first panto.' He added that he was enjoying his stay in Lichfield and although it was his twenty-first year in pantomimes he was enjoying the role as much as ever. He acknowledged that his road to such shows had been long and hard, having, over the years, performed on television in such programmes as *Search for a Star*, *The Night of a Thousand Stars* and his own prime time television show *And There's More*. Also in the pantomime were local stars Charlotte Gibson as Cinderella and Bryn Christopher who played Prince Charming. The *Lichfield Mercury*'s review of the pantomime two weeks before had been somewhat mixed. Jimmy Cricket and the local stars were praised but 'adults expecting a host of witty gags and turns of phrases will be disappointed,' it read. (*Lichfield Mercury*, December 23rd 2003)

— December 21st —

1917: On this day, the *Lichfield Mercury* gave its readers some indication of how difficult the fourth Christmas of the war was liable to be, both for those serving in the trenches of the Western Front and for their families at home. The paper urged people, in spite of all the shortages of basic foods like eggs and sugar, to 'adopt a bright and happy spirit' when writing to their loved ones in the services and save them from worrying about their loved ones back home. It asked Lichfield folk to send the troops cards and gifts, which would be 'duly delivered to them in their dug out or trench'. Those troops in France, the paper assured its readers, would each receive a ration of plum pudding – half a pound for each man on Christmas Day. Advertisements at this time in the *Mercury* seemed to reflect the general mood of the times and although cards, fancy goods and toys were still on offer, the number and jollity of adverts for Christmas related goods was very much less than in previous years. (*Lichfield Mercury*)

~ December 22nd ~

1922: By this day, radios and radio broadcasting were being referred to on a regular basis in the local press. Russell and Rymond, electrical engineers based in Lichfield and Erdington, for example, advertised in the *Lichfield Mercury* radios from the Marconi Company: 'the very best obtainable on the market.' Hoskison's of Fradley, near Lichfield, advised readers to listen to radio broadcasts on a 'Gecophone' – for £5 10*s* (£5.50) a set could be purchased with a reception range of 25 miles. A.P. Sander's of Chasetown urged readers of the *Mercury* to 'listen in tonight' on an 'Ethophone' crystal set costing £3 10*s* (£4.50) on which 'two people could listen at once'. Mr H. Powell-Rees, managing director of H.P.R. Wireless Ltd., speculated in the *Mercury* about programmes people might listen to on the radio in the future, saying that he fully expected there to be a summary of the news each morning, as well as 'soothing music'. Wireless signals, he assured readers, would also one day be used to send written messages over a great distance as well as to fly unmanned aircraft. (*Lichfield Mercury*)

~ December 23rd ~

1912: This day saw the opening of the first cinema in Lichfield: the Palladium on Bore Street, previously St James's Hall. The hall had been renovated and redecorated inside in scarlet and grey, creating what the *Lichfield Mercury* called 'a most pleasing effect on the eye'. A new 'operating room' (presumably a projection room) had been added and a large canopy constructed above the entrance with the word Palladium picked out in gold lettering. The 'whole' of the hall was lit 'by electricity' – a 'powerful gas engine and dynamo having been installed for the purpose' – and new seating had been provided, which had been 'constructed on the most up-to-date principal with tip-up seats and backrests'. Oddly, apart from saying that the cinema would be showing 'the world's best cinema pictures', no indication was given as to what exactly would be shown. There would be two performances each day at 7 p.m. and 9 p.m., with a children's matinee on Saturdays. Seat prices ranged from 3*d* to 9*d* (1p to 4p). (*Lichfield Mercury*, December 30th 1912)

~ December 24th ~

1999: On this day, the *Lichfield Mercury* highlighted local people who would be working during the Christmas holidays. Police Sergeant Peter Grove, based at Lichfield Police Station, was one of many police officers required to be on duty over Christmas, stating that 'it is part and parcel of the job'. Sergeant Grove, who had been in the police for twenty-four years, added, 'All police officers know they will sometimes be called upon to work anti-social hours.' At the cathedral, eighteen choirboys, twelve choirmen, two organists, volunteers and priests would all be hard at work during the Christmas season. Canon Charles Taylor, who had worked in Lichfield for five years, would be in charge of a number of cathedral services and admitted that it was 'quite draining and mentally exhausting'. Martine Colley, who was a staff nurse on the general ward of Lichfield's Victoria Hospital, would be working on Christmas Eve and Christmas Day – 'I have worked as a nurse for twenty years and have only had two Christmases off.' Nurse Colley added that there were would be eight nurses on the general ward on Christmas Day and that she was looking forward to Boxing Day, which she would spend with her family. (*Lichfield Mercury*)

~ DECEMBER 25TH ~

1397: On this day, King Richard II and his wife Queen Anne stayed in Lichfield for the Christmas festivities. The king and his whole royal court spent all twelve days of Christmas in the town, or more precisely in Cathedral Close, where a specially built house was constructed for the royal couple to reside. The royal party dined in a magnificent banqueting hall that had been built by Bishop Walter de Langton some hundred years before, which contained paintings of previous kings of England and was the scene of much royal feasting. It has been estimated that during their stay the king and his guests consumed 2,000 oxen and 200 barrels of wine. However, less than two years later in August 1399 Richard was being kept a prisoner in the same Cathedral Close after being captured during an uprising led by his cousin, Henry Bolingbroke. He was kept in Lichfield while in the process of being moved to the Tower of London. According to some sources, Richard attempted, unsuccessfully, to escape from the north-east tower of the fortified Close by using a rope to clamber down the wall. (*The Times of Lichfield*, The Guild of the St Mary's Centre, 1982)

- December 26th -

1902: On this day, the *Lichfield Mercury* commented on what Christmas shopping had been like in the city. The shops had been crowded with 'eager shoppers' and the goods displayed in the shops had been very popular. Wigham's grocery shop, in addition to its displays of dried fruits and 'provisions of every description', were selling iced cakes, fancy chocolates and Tom Smith's crackers and had also disposed of 200 plum puddings, which had been made on the premises. Henry G. Hall's butcher's shop in Market Square had an 'imposing array of healthy looking joints displayed amid the evergreen with which his premises was decorated'; all of the meat at Hall's, and also at Berry's butcher's in Tamworth Street, was from local farms and the *Mercury* found it comforting that local butchers were selling local produce rather than meat from 'foreign rivals'. Mr Welch's shop in Tamworth Street had been stocked with turkeys, geese and ducks and Stanton's in Conduit Street had a fine show of fancy chocolates and sweets made in their Chasetown factory. Salloway's in Bore Street had 'a very nice collection of clocks, watches, gold rings, silver charms and opera glasses'. (*Lichfield Mercury*)

— December 27th —

1781: By this date, Mr Snape of Wishaw had made a detailed plan of Lichfield showing what the city was like at the time. According to Snape there were 722 houses in the town containing a total of 3,555 people and 43 dwellings in the Close with 216 inhabitants. Names of some streets were spelt differently to what they are today: Beacon Street was known as Bacon Street; Bore Street was Boar Street; Gaia Lane was called Gay Lane; and today's Market Street was known as Sadler Street. A tollgate was placed at the end of Bacon Street, which was on the 'post-road' or coaching route to Chester – there were seven tollgates around the city. Four conduits, where water was brought into the city, were shown on the plan and the 'New Walk' at the north side of Stowe Pool is clearly marked, as is the nearby Parchment House, the site of Michael Johnson's (Samuel's father) parchment factory. Also next to Stowe Pool was a leather tanning yard and a water mill. Snape noted that Lichfield had three annual fairs, two weekly markets and returned two members to Parliament. (*Lichfield Maps*, Staffordshire County Council Education Department, 1970)

~ DECEMBER 28TH ~

1949: On this day, Staff Sergeant George W. Ellis of Offutt Air Force Base in Omaha, Nebraska, USA, wrote a letter to the Mayor of Lichfield asking if he could help find him 'a nice English girl for a wife'. Ellis had been stationed at Whittington Barracks during 1944 and thought that the local people 'were grand' and the Lichfield girls in particular 'were naturally pretty and have always remained in my mind as the most wonderful in the world'. He had apparently been disappointed by the women in America, who seemed, he said, 'to want too much out of life' and would not be happy with just 'a decent home and a good husband'. In his letter, Ellis specified his requirements in detail – he wanted a blond or redhead with blue eyes, no taller than 5ft 5in and with a 'sweet disposition'. He was 5ft 7in, had black hair and brown eyes, liked dancing and movies and 'was very easy to get along with'. He asked whether the letter could be published in the local newspaper and was sure that he would get some replies. (*Lichfield Mercury*, February 3rd 1950)

~ December 29th ~

1922: On this day, at a meeting of the Lichfield Board of Governors, a letter from the Ministry of Health was read out denouncing recent marches of the unemployed and instructing the administrators of Lichfield's workhouse to discourage inmates from participating in any such marches. The ministry described the marches as 'useless and mischievous' and further reminded the Board of Guardians that only the 'really destitute' ought to be given food and lodging in the workhouse. Some doubts were expressed at the meeting as to whether the people on the marches were actually unemployed; one of the board members said he had heard of some of them 'pulling out wads of notes when paying for their fares at railway stations'. Another board member said that he doubted the marchers represented the 'genuine unemployed', but were those 'out to make a name for themselves'. Unemployment marches organised by the National Unemployed Workers Movement were a regular occurrence in the 1920s and '30s in an economy ruined by the First World War and where unemployment reached 2.5 million. The most famous of them was the Jarrow March of 1936. (*Lichfield Mercury*, January 5th 1923)

– December 30th –

1727: By this date, Daniel Defoe, novelist, political writer and journalist, had visited Lichfield and had written about what he had seen in the city. In his three-volume travel book, *A Tour Through the Whole Island of Great Britain*, he described Lichfield as being 'a neat, well built and pretty large city'. It is not known how long the author of *Robinson Crusoe* and *Moll Flanders* spent in Lichfield, but it was obviously long enough to take in most of the sights of the city. He wrote, 'There is a kind of sluggish water which runs or rather glides heavily through it,' describing how the water (obviously Minster Pool) divided the city into two parts – the town and the Close. The town had, he wrote, 'a market place, a fine school and a very handsome hospital dedicated to St. John' and the Close contained 'one of the finest and most beautiful Cathedrals in England'. He went on to describe Cathedral Close as having 'a great number of well-built and well-inhabited houses which make Lichfield a place of good company above all the towns in this, or the neighbouring counties'. (Hopkins, Mary Alden, *Dr. Johnson's Lichfield*, Hastings House, 1952)

– December 31st –

1775: On this day, the first formalised meeting of The Lunar Society took place. Meetings of a dinner club and learned society had been taking place for a number of years, involving scientist and writer Erasmus Darwin and his circle of friends, notably Matthew Boulton, the Birmingham industrialist. However, it was on this day that the men decided to meet once a month during the full moon from 2 p.m. until 8 p.m. – the lighter nights helping them more easily get home – and, officially, give their discussion group its famous name. The meetings, 'warmed by wine and friendship', would discuss and reflect upon various aspects of science, mechanics, invention and philosophy. Meetings of the society usually took place at Darwin's home in Lichfield or Boulton's Soho house in Handsworth, Birmingham. As well as Darwin and Boulton, membership of the group included other eighteenth-century luminaries and 'provincial manufacturers, professional men and gifted amateurs' such as Josiah Wedgewood, James Watt, Joseph Priestley, Richard Edgeworth and Thomas Day. The Lunar Society continued to provide an 'intellectual impetus' to Britain's Industrial Revolution until 1813. (Uglow, Jenny, *The Lunar Men: The Friends Who Made the Future*, Faber & Faber, 2002)